"But the People in Legal Said…"

A Guide to Current Legal Issues in Advertising

"But the People in Legal Said..."

A Guide to Current Legal Issues in Advertising

Dean Keith Fueroghne

DOW JONES-IRWIN
Homewood, Illinois 60430

To my wife, Lynn.
And to my dad—I think he would have been proud.

Acquisitions editor: Susan Glinert Stevens, Ph.D.
Project editor: Suzanne Ivester
Production manager: Bette Ittersagen
Jacket design: Mark Swimmer
Compositor: Weimer Typesetting Company, Inc.
Typeface: 11/13 Century Schoolbook
Printer: Arcata Graphics/Kingsport

LIBRARY OF CONGRESS
Library of Congress Cataloging-in-Publiction Data

Fueroghne, Dean Keith.
  But the people in legal said— : a guide to current legal issues in advertising / Dean Keith Fueroghne.
      p.   cm.
  Bibliography: p.
  Includes index.
  ISBN 1-556-23091-5
  1. Advertising laws—United States—Popular works. I. Title.
KF1614.Z9F84 1989
343.73'082—dc19
[347.30382]   88–14077
                                                                      CIP

Printed in the United States of America

 2 3 4 5 6 7 8 9 0 K 5 4 3 2 1 0 9 8

PREFACE

A number of years ago, I took an advertising law class at UCLA. The class was attended mostly by lawyers and professionals in advertising. The professor began by announcing that there would not be a text for the course because none existed.

That experience—combined with the naivete about the implications of law that I've seen in the advertising business—led to the creation of this book. Although advertising is a creative business, I have seen many agencies create more liability for themselves and their clients than awards for their ads. Most advertisers feel that advertising laws (the few that they are aware of) restrict the power of their message. Nonetheless, they need to understand these laws and their consequences.

The law has built a wall around itself with unfamiliar words and uncommon reasoning—a wall that most cannot break through. Until now there was simply no one source to provide the advertiser with ready access to information about advertising law. This book attempts to provide one source a person can use to learn about such areas of law as agency, contract, copyright, trademark, privacy and publicity rights, FTC regulations, and others.

This book is addressed to all who produce, distribute, and prosper from advertising—the account executive, the art director, the copywriter, the creative director, the advertising manager—whether in the agency business or an in-house advertising department. I have tried to explain the legal principles as clearly as possible, using cases as examples to illustrate each of the points.

Because of the impact of legislation, court decisions, and consumerism on the advertising field, the law should be well understood by anyone who creates and implements advertising. While I have tried to assure that the examples used in this book are current, the case law, statutes, and legislation should not be used as authoritative unless the user researches same at the time of use to determine their validity or the changes or modification since the date of publication. This book is intended to provide insight into the areas of law that affect advertising and to allow the reader to know when to seek specific legal advice. It is not intended to be construed as offering legal advice in any way. As with any legal problem, when in doubt, consult an attorney who specializes in that area.

So many people have added to this book that I must acknowledge their help. I wish to thank my contributing editor, Lee Lefton, for his guidance, help, and encouragement in this project, and for the endless hours he spent editing, refining, and helping me see the trees for the forest.

I also wish to acknowledge the following people who reviewed various portions of this book as it was written and who provided valuable insights and stories: Laurel Federick, attorney for Ogilvy & Mather, L.A.; Dan Katz, associate creative director for Orenstein & Savage Advertising; Erin Foley, advertising manager for the Samuel Goldwyn Company; Don Barshinger, associate creative director for The Good Guise Advertising; and Pete Bleyer, commercial photographer in Los Angeles.

Special thanks to Susan Glinert, senior editor at Dow Jones-Irwin, for her enthusiasm, advice, and help throughout this project. I hope it is justified by the result.

To all the people I've worked with over the years in this business, who have provided the stories—sometimes humorous, sometimes sad—that have helped to illustrate the book, I extend my thanks. Many I have learned from; some I have walked away from shaking my head. But all have contributed to this book—some more than they would have liked.

Finally, my gratitude goes to my wife, Lynn, who read and reread every page, provided invaluable assistance, and put up with the seemingly endless hours that went into the research and writing of this book.

Dean Keith Fueroghne

INTRODUCTION

Here are some interesting trivial tidbits.

Did you know that advertising expenditures in the United States exceeded $109 billion* in 1987? This is more than is spent on all of public education in this country in a year. And it's a third of what the United States spends yearly on national defense. The combined expenditure on advertising for the 10 largest companies in the country is greater than most nations' gross national product!

Did you know that a major national television commercial will be viewed by more people than the total number of people who have seen *Gone with the Wind?* The average American watches about 20,000 television commercials each year. Major manufacturers will spend a quarter of a million dollars to produce a 30-second television commercial that is designed to promote a 30-cent item.

What this trivia illustrates is that advertising is a very expensive, very pervasive, very specialized, and very institutionalized segment of our social and economic environment. But did you ever stop to ask yourself, how does advertising interact with the restrictions of society? This is one of the primary questions this book will explore.

It is generally accepted that advertising is a part of the business process. Advertising goes hand-in-hand with moving products and services from the rawest of materials to the ultimate consumer. Although it is difficult to precisely define

*Source: *The Wall Street Journal,* June 8, 1987, p. 10, col. 1.

advertising, in essence it is the catalyst that keeps a free-enterprise market operating. Countries that don't have a free-enterprise system don't have advertising in the commercial sense because they don't need it. A prime example of this situation is Red China. Before trade was opened up with the West, consumerism was controlled by the government. Afterwards, Western products were introduced into the Chinese culture along with something new—"advertising."

Most textbooks teach that modern advertising began in the early 1900s. Greats like William Benton, George Batton, Albert Lasker, Chester Bowles, Bruce Barton, Ernest Elmo Calkins, Leo Burnett, David Ogilvy, and others whose names you may recognize did not create the process of advertising. What we consider to be advertising in its purest sense has been around for thousands, perhaps millions, of years before the time of these industry giants.

Because it is such a powerful marketing tool, advertising draws more than its share of criticism, despite an ever-increasing awareness and emphasis on social responsibility. Those advertisers who have taken a naive attitude and ignored their responsibilities have learned the pitfalls of viewing the consumer as simply a passive and unquestioning viewer of commercial messages.

The consuming public's skeptical impression of advertising will continue to increase. Because of this, a major challenge for the advertising community is to restore the credibility of its product and to check the public's skepticism lest it turn to cynicism.

The demands of advertising professionals require that they keep current on all aspects of their profession. Law is one of those areas that has a powerful effect on advertising. Therefore, the new policies dictated by regulatory agencies and the interpretations of court decisions must be well understood by advertising professionals.

As our economic system has grown over the years, it has by necessity become more complex. This complexity has forced the legislature and courts to create an equally complex system to maintain the delicate balance that exists between free enterprise and consumer protection.

On one side stand the advertiser and his agency trying to display their product as favorably as possible. On the other side stands the consumer, guarded behind a protective legal barrier in which he can feel a sense of security in making purchasing decisions. The legislature has seen to that. Between these two constants lies a fine line. As you will see throughout the book, it is one beyond which neither side would be prudent to extend.

Throughout history, as promoters of products and advertising services have become more sophisticated and indeed clever, the legal system has had to keep pace. This book was written to discuss the relationship between advertiser and legislator, what brought it about, and its practical applications.

Many years ago, Calvin Coolidge said that "advertising ministers to the spiritual side of trade." While some consumers have expressed a fear of—and others have indicated a hope for—the demise of advertising, it is still integral to our market environment. Advertising provides a valuable service to the seller, the buyer, and the public and indeed serves the spirit of trade only so long as it remains truthful and honest.

As you read this book there are a few things I feel that you should keep in mind. Advertising is affected by many areas of law. In fact, each chapter of this book covers a separate area of law. One point that the reader must remember is that the law tends to be compartmentalized. As a result, one area of law differs from another. And, therefore, the subject of each chapter differs. The regulation of each area of law varies—copyright has no effect on publicity rights, comparative advertising regulation has no effect on products liability.

As you read, you may see inconsistencies in logic from chapter to chapter. What you're actually noticing is the variations in the different areas of law. Always consider the subject of the chapter, and you'll see the law in the proper light. Also, read each chapter carefully and completely—do not skim. The subject matter is far too complex for that. I would strongly recommend reading the book straight through the first time. Many of the topics build on each other, and there is a reason that the chapters are in the order that they are. When questions arise about specific subjects, you can then go back to the appropriate chapter for reference.

Another important point to consider is that you will find many examples of ads that were produced that don't follow the laws illustrated in this book. Citing such examples will not protect you if you are caught in similar violations. The fact that 20 people get away with robbery doesn't make it legal!

Finally, as you read, you will undoubtedly have questions that will be brought up by the book. That's the idea—that's your clue that your question might best be answered by an attorney who specializes in that area. This book cannot answer every question that arises; although it should answer many. What it can do is teach you the basics and give you the wisdom to know when it's time to consult an attorney.

NOTES ON CITES

In this book you will notice that each case has a citation (cite) following the name of the case. For those who have a background in law, these cites are all too familiar. But for those who do not, they represent some unknown code. Here is how to decipher the code.

The citations indicate where the specific court opinions can be found. A typical cite may look like this: *Dawn Donut Co. v. Hart's Food Stores, Inc.*, 267 F.2d 358 (2d Cir. 1959).

The name of the case appears first: *Dawn Donut Co. v. Hart's Food Stores, Inc.* The first number following, indicates the volume of the reporter: 267. The next series indicates the name of the reporter: F.2d (in this instance; Federal Reporter, second series). The next set of numbers shows the page where the case begins: 358. In parentheses is the circuit court where the case was decided and the date it was decided.

The various sources are cited by abbreviations as we saw above. The following is a list of the most common sources used in this book.

U.S.	United States Supreme Court Reports
F.	Federal Reporter (decisions by the Circuit Court of Appeals)
F.2d	Federal Reporter, second series

F. Supp.	Federal Supplement. (decisions of the United States District Courts)
F.C.C.	Federal Communications Commission Reports
F.T.C.	Federal Trade Commission Reports
U.S.L.W.	United States Law Weekly
U.S.P.Q.	United States Patent Quarterly
A.	Atlantic Reporter
A.2d	Atlantic Reporter, second series
N.E.	North Eastern Reporter
N.E.2d	North Eastern Reporter, second series
N.W.	North Western Reporter
N.W.2d	North Western Reporter, second series
P.	Pacific Reporter
P.2d	Pacific Reporter, second series
S.E.	South Eastern Reporter
S.E.2d	South Eastern Reporter, second series
S.W.	South Western Reporter
S.W.2d	South Western Reporter, second series
S.	Southern Reporter
S.2d	Southern Reporter, second series

In addition, each state court system has its own reporters and digests where cases are recorded. While there are far too many to list here, I will give a few examples of the basic California sources. A complete list of abbreviations for all states can be found at any law library.

Cal.	California Reports (series one through three)
Cal.App.	California Appellate Reports (series one through three)
Cal.Dec.	California Decisions
Cal.Rptr.	California Reporter

CONTENTS

CHAPTER 1

THE DEVELOPMENT OF CONTROL OVER ADVERTISING

There's a sucker born every minute.
—*P. T. Barnum*

W. C. Crosby was an astute businessman. He understood all too well the power of advertising. Crosby had a knack for practicing the subtle art of persuasion. He knew how to pique a person's interest by using the right words: how to light a fire in the prospect, how to promote, how to sell—abilities that any great ad man must possess. He lived during the early 1900s, when he eloquently described his profession as "a business, like all business," which "takes rise from the conditions of life about it and adapts itself as does social life. And . . . plays an invariable chord in the human make-up . . . according to the times and circumstances."

His was not a name that would go down in the history books as one of the great advertising giants of the past. He would, however, be remembered as a craftsman of the art of persuasion. W. C. Crosby was a con man, and one of the best. He kept company at the turn-of-the-century with such notables as Willie "The Sleepy Kid" Loftus, Jimmy McViccor, Charley (changed to Henry in the movie *The Sting*) Gondorf, "The Crying Kid," "Hungry Joe" Lewis, George Pole, and Big Joe Turley.

The con man's migration to America was a natural occurrence. One frontier opened itself up to another. Long before the Civil War, the con man could be found in the Gold Rush shanty towns of California, riding the paddle wheelers down the Mississippi to New Orleans, drifting through high society in the East and riding the first rails to the West.

W. C. Crosby and the others brought with them the skills of the great European harbinger Richard Town, who had so incurred the wrath of his victims that on May 23, 1712, in London, he was hanged. His open-air execution was viewed by a cheering throng of spectators. "My friends, this is my birthday," Town stated coolly. "I see you have come to help me honor it. Madam, my compliments, and thank you for coming to my adventure."

THE POSTAL FRAUD LAWS—THE FIRST FORM OF ADVERTISING REGULATION

In 1872 stringent postal fraud laws were passed in order to wage a relentless war against the con man who was perpetrating his grandiose schemes through the mail. While these laws were needed, they did not do away with the con man overnight. Unfortunately, passage of these laws was only a small step toward stemming the tide of mail fraud. Even in the early 1900s, American con men still ran rampant among a gullible public—a public that responded to advertisements for mining rights, real estate, securities, inventions, cure-alls, and medicines of all types.

The bulk of advertising during that time was carried through the newspaper—the only media available to reach the masses. All that was required on the con man's part was the up-front capital to purchase relatively inexpensive newspaper space and postage stamps. Despite teeth-gritting indignation, the victims were virtually helpless against the guile of the con man. In fact, the Post Office estimated that in 1911 alone, con men netted $77 million from duped investors in mail-order schemes.

Peddlers placed advertisements offering nostrums and medicines guaranteed to cure anything. A man named Perkins sold through the mails two shiny rods he called Metallic Tractors. These were to be passed over the ailing victim and redirect his "electrical" current to cure him of any disease. Perkins believed his own swindle so well that when he contracted yellow fever, he refused medical attention believing his Metallic Tractors would heal him. For three days the rods were passed over Perkins; then—as you might expect—he died.

The Essence of Life

A newspaper ad appeared in the *Connecticut Courant* in October 1834:

MOORE'S ESSENCE OF LIFE
A safe and efficient remedy for whooping cough
Sold by appointment at the sign of the
Good Samaritan

The Essence of Life was nothing more than colored water.

Many bogus doctors and pharmacists offered products that would cure almost any ailment known to man. Turlington's Original Balsam, for example, promised to remedy 51 deadly diseases. In another instance, Dr. Spear offered his magic Balsam of Life through newspaper advertisements. It was claimed that the product would cure consumption (tuberculosis) overnight. The con man who offered Brandreth's Pills placed advertisements in newspapers for years which read:

Remember in all cases of disease no matter whether
it be cold or cough, whether it be asthma or
consumption, whether it be rheumatism or pleurisy,
whether it be typhus fever and ague, or bilious fever,
cramp or whooping cough or measles, whether it be
scarlet fever or small pox, Brandreth's Pills will
surely do more than all the medicines of the Drug Stores
for your restoration to health.

A Portrait of the President

When the mail-order fraud reached its peak, the perpetrators seemed to take a perverse pleasure not only in the fraud itself, but in pouring salt into the victims' wounds. They exhibited the sort of "I dare you" attitude that challenged the victims to protest. The following classic nose-thumber appeared in over

200 newspapers in 1882—the year after President Garfield's assassination caused immense national grief:

> I HAVE SECURED the authorized steel engravings of the late President Garfield, executed by the United States Government, approved by the President of the United States, by Congress, and by every member of the President's family as the most faithful of all the portraits of the President. It was executed by the Government's most expert steel engravers, and I will send a copy from the original plate, in full colors approved by the Government, postpaid, for one dollar each.

To each person sending in the required $1, the con man mailed the promised engraving of President Garfield—a 5-cent U.S. postage stamp.

Some 15 years later an offer appeared in newspapers promising a way to eliminate annoying moths:

> **DO THE MOTHS BOTHER YOU?**
> If so send us fifty cents in stamps, and we will furnish a recipe CERTAIN SURE to drive the pests from furs or rugs or any other old things.

A few weeks later the consumer received the foolproof recipe, as advertised. The reply read as follows:

> Dear Madam: Dampen the article in question in kerosene thoroughly (to soak it is even better) and add one lighted match. If the moths do not disappear, your money will be cheerfully refunded. Yours truly, The Buncomb Company

Indeed, it was the era of the con man—of getting wealthy off the gullibility of the consumer. Some got very wealthy. In 1927 (his last year of operation) a con man named Hugh B. Monjar brought in a cool $7,666,631 before being sent to a federal prison for mail fraud.

In the late 1800s and early 1900s the exploits of the con man were the main form of deceptive advertising. This is without a doubt where consumers learned distrust for all advertising—a skepticism many consumers have to this day.

Times, however, have changed. No longer can the advertiser rampantly seek out the weaknesses in consumers and exploit them as did early con men. The consumer now has stiffer advertising controls on his side. These controls have brought heavy restrictions for today's advertiser, who has to deal with the problem of being heard in our overcommunicated society. Yet, he must be very careful about how he gets the consumer's attention.

With the advent of the Federal Trade Commission in 1914, a force of regulation against taking unfair advantage of the consumer began. Over the years since its inception, the consumer has been given substantial protection.

CREATION OF THE FEDERAL TRADE COMMISSION

The FTC was conceived by Congress in 1914 to enforce the country's faltering antitrust laws. Ironically, the first two cases it heard involved false advertising.[1] The only intent of the FTC at that time was to preserve fair competition between businesses by preventing restraint of trade—that is, such acts as creating a monopoly, which reduce or eliminate competition. Although this concerned only how businesses dealt with each other, in essence, the Federal Trade Commission Act protected consumers because it protected sellers against each other. This was an indirect consumer benefit at best.

Since its establishment the FTC's scope has been enlarged with the adoption of the Wheeler-Lea Amendments in 1938. These brought direct protection for the consumer by modifying the authority of the FTC. The commission was originally authorized to regulate "unfair methods of competition in commerce." The Wheeler-Lea Amendments, however, added to this definition the phrase " . . . and unfair or deceptive acts or practices in commerce," thus expanding the act's coverage to con-

---

[1]*FTC* v. *Circle Cilk,* 1 FTC 13 (1916), and *FTC* v. *Abbott,* 1 FTC 16 (1916).

sumers as well as to competitors. The emphasis was now on protecting the consumer against injury.

In 1962, President John F. Kennedy gave a special message to the Congress on protecting the consumer interest.[2] This sparked the modern consumer movement. Since that time, major new legislation and amendments to prior regulation have been enacted. The FTC and the courts have dramatically increased their efforts to protect the consumer and to place him on equal ground with the advertiser. Thus, the pendulum seems to be swinging more in the direction of the consumer.

The Long Arm of The FTC

The FTC, as a federal organization, is assigned the task of policing advertising on a national level under Section 5 of the act. As a result, Section 5 only covers advertising that promotes products involving interstate commerce—transactions between one state and another. The advertiser must realize, however, that he is not safe from the FTC if his products are sold only in his own state. Courts are broadly interpreting the act to bring also intrastate activities within its authority. In essence, if any part or ingredient of the product was manufactured or purchased out of state, the courts consider interstate commerce to be involved; therefore, the product falls within the control of the federal act.

The FTC's influence reaches into state activities in another way. Most states have laws that carry the same implications as the federal act. In fact, many of these state statutes direct the state courts to be guided by FTC decisions. California, for example, controls false and deceptive advertising under Section 17500 of the California Civil Code.

Disclosure of Information

An obvious element in creating advertising is determining what to say in an ad. The advertiser must determine which of

---

[2] 88th Cong., 1st Sess., pt. 1, at 465 (1963).

all the facts and points about a product he should feature in the limited space of an ad. Generally, regulation of advertising addresses the availability of information and how it is presented. Enough information should be made available to the consumer for him to make a valid purchasing decision in which he gets everything he bargained for without surprise or deception.

In recent years, legislation has required accurate information be disclosed in many areas of the marketplace. Such areas include durability of light bulbs,[3] octane ratings for gasoline,[4] mileage per gallon statistics for new automobiles,[5] and care labeling of all textile wearing apparel.[6] The list continues to grow. (See Appendix A.)

The way in which the advertiser provides information and the relevance of that information are areas that must be carefully considered. Because of the competitive nature of our market system, every advertiser tries to show his product in the best possible light. As everyone in advertising knows, a good ad demonstrates the product's strengths while playing down its weaknesses; but when the strengths are distorted or when significant weaknesses are either played down or ignored altogether, a deception is created.

The concept of information disclosure creates certain problems simply by the nature of the marketplace. Well-established manufacturers tend to avoid disclosing too much product information in their advertising for fear of opening opportunities for new competitors to enter or expand their market. An example of this situation is found in the history of the gasoline industry.

Gasoline manufacturers attempted to avoid disclosing gasoline octane formulation because this would have highlighted the fact that ratings of high-priced brands were substantially the same as those of low-priced, unadvertised brands. Since the survival of the small independent manufacturers depended largely on their ability to maintain a cost advantage, they

---

[3]16 C.F.R., section 409.1.
[4]16 C.F.R., section 422.1.
[5]16 C.F.R., sections 259.1 and 259.2.
[6]16 C.F.R., section 423.1.

could not have easily undertaken expensive advertising campaigns to inform consumers about comparative octane ratings.

In other product areas, information disclosure may create an industrywide disadvantage for all sellers. An intensive advertising campaign promoting the smoking of low tar and nicotine cigarettes as a way to reduce health hazards would obviously play up the fact that smoking any cigarette creates health problems. Total cigarette sales would suffer as a result.

Even after scientific evidence was discovered to prove that smoking is harmful, advertisers of both low and high tar cigarettes played down negative comparison claims to avoid negative reactions toward other brands in their product lines. In fact, aggressive marketing of low tar, low nicotine brands has only recently occurred.

In December of 1970, cigarette manufacturers responded to threatened action by the government by voluntarily including the government test results for tar and nicotine contents in their advertisements. Soon after, television advertising of cigarettes was ended. Now there is talk of a legislative ban on all cigarette advertising.

Another problem in gathering and disclosing accurate product information is the extreme expense, especially in certain industries. For example, such technical data as chemical formulas for over-the-counter drugs probably have no meaning to the average consumer. Yet the cost of providing this information could, for many manufacturers, be prohibitive.

COUNTERADVERTISING

Other considerations for the advertiser lie in the area of counteradvertising. One form of this occurs when manufacturers go head to head to challenge each others' claims. Specific counteradvertising of products, if inaccurate, tends to open up the challenger to the possibility of a disparagement suit or FTC intervention based on deceptive advertising practices. The Lanham Trademark Act provides a remedy against comparative advertising as well. These areas will be treated more fully later.

Most advertisers resist this form of advertising since a manufacturer who brings a competitor's claim to the public's attention may be looked upon negatively by the consumer. It tends to become a situation of "people who live in glass houses shouldn't throw stones." The reputation of an overly aggressive advertiser may be diminished in the eyes of the consumer by exposing another company. Thus, most manufacturers tend to spend their advertising budget on the positive features of their own products.

Counteradvertising to Change Public Opinion

In recent years, we have seen another form of counteradvertising take hold. It is a more useful and beneficial form, designed to offset public opinion. A recent example is Tampax's advertising campaign designed to counter the ill effects that it experienced because of the toxic shock syndrome scare. Another was Bristol Myers's advertising campaign to try to offset consumers' fears about product safety after a series of tamperings and resultant poisonings had frightened consumers away from purchasing Tylenol.

In a recent issue of *TV Guide,* the R. J. Reynolds Tobacco Company ran this ad that clearly demonstrates this use of counteradvertising:

Passive Smoking. An Active Controversy.

Periodically the public hears about an individual scientific study which claims to show that "environmental tobacco smoke" (ETS) may be harmful to nonsmokers. These reports usually receive sensational media coverage.

Yet, three times within two years, groups of distinguished experts have gathered to review not just one study but the whole body of evidence on this subject. In all three cases, the scientists came to similar—and far less sensational—conclusions.

Yet the media have remained almost silent.

In March 1983 there was the "Second Workshop on Environmental Tobacco Smoke" in Geneva, Switzerland. In May 1983 there was the "Workshop on Respiratory Effects of Involuntary Smoke Exposure" in Bethesda, Maryland. And, most recently, in

April 1984, leading experts from around the world gathered in Vienna for a symposium entitled "Passive Smoking from a Medical Point of View."

After this symposium was over, the presidents of the two organizing groups issued a press release summarizing their findings.

The summary said, "The connection between ETS and lung cancer has not been scientifically established to date." It also said "there is a high probability that cardiovascular damage due to ETS can be ruled out in healthy people."

And it went on to say, "Should lawmakers wish to take legislative measures with regard to ETS, they will, for the present, not be able to base their efforts on a demonstrated health hazard from ETS."

Perhaps the media would say they cannot be blamed for devoting little attention to what some would consider "non-news." But we at R. J. Reynolds are concerned about the effects such one-sided coverage may be having on the public.

For today, many nonsmokers who once saw cigarette smoke merely as an annoyance now view it as a threat to their health. Their growing alarm is being translated into heightened social strife and unfair antismoker legislation.

We believe these actions are unwarranted by the scientific facts—and that it is rhetoric, more than research, which makes passive smoking an active controversy.

—R. J. Reynolds Tobacco Company

INDUSTRY SELF-REGULATION

Consumer abuse or exploitation from false, misleading, or deceptive advertising doesn't necessarily have to be controlled by the government alone. Deceptive advertising may also be controlled by the advertising industry through self-regulation.

Self-regulation of advertising can be accomplished through a number of avenues. The various trade associations have established codes of conduct or ethics. Such agencies as the American Association of Advertising Agencies, the Printing Industry Association, American Society of Magazine Photographers, American Advertising Federation, Graphic Artists Guild, and American Federation of Television and Radio Artists have specific conduct requirements for their members to follow. Typically, these agencies also have other methods of resolving grievances.

Censorship

The television networks also have rules about what they will and will not accept for commercials. Their clearance departments set standards that commercials must meet in order to be aired. The National Association of Broadcasters is another review board for the advertiser to deal with, for NAB gets involved, as do the networks, in passing judgment on TV commercials.

In his well-known book on the ad agency business, *From Those Wonderful Folks Who Gave You Pearl Harbor,* Jerry Della Femina says this about NAB censorship: "One of the biggest problems that all agencies have is the headache of censorship. There is simply no reason for it. Censorship, any kind of censorship, is pure whim and fancy. It's one guy's idea of what is right for him. It's based on everything arbitrary. There are no rules, no standards, no laws."

In many instances, this censorship can get out of control. One time the Ted Bates agency produced a TV commercial for a toy company. The spot showed a little boy playing with the toy machine gun. The scene was shot on a mound of dirt with the kid blasting away at whomever it was we were blasting away at in the late 60s—Vietcong maybe.

"This commercial is not acceptable," said the censor. The agency was sure that the rejection had something to do with the portrayal of war and violence with children. Not so.

"Well, it's obvious that the mound of dirt is part of the game," said the censor. "The kid will obviously think that it's part of the game since it's on the screen for the entire commercial, and the kid spends his time on the top of the mound of dirt." The censor felt that kids would expect to get a mound of dirt with the toy machine gun. But, he would approve the spot if it were run with a line of copy on the screen telling kids that the mound of dirt was not included.

When the agency tried to explain that a child wouldn't actually believe that the dirt came with the gun, the censor replied, "It's not the five-year-olds we're worried about. It's the one- and two-year-olds who might be swayed." The censor wasn't concerned with the five-year-old who might be deceived, but rather about younger children who couldn't read anyway.

The smaller independent stations also tend to follow the lead of the networks. If the networks won't clear the spot, then the local station probably won't run it.

Even print media has its codes. Some years ago, I produced an ad for vitamins. The ad was to run in a series of health and fitness magazines. One of these rejected the ad because they had limits as to the levels of each ingredient. If one multi-vitamin contained 500 mg. of C, they said the maximum you could claim was 300 mg., even if the product contained a higher level. We had to produce a special ad for that magazine showing lower levels of the vitamins.

While these self-regulation efforts don't have the force of law behind them, they have become an increasingly effective method of checks and balances. And they are gaining in power. It's only when they get overly aggressive and arbitrary that they lose credibility.

DAVID VERSUS GOLIATH—CONSUMER ACTION

It is also possible for consumer interests to be protected directly by the consumers themselves. The consumer can sue an advertiser directly, although this hardly ever occurs. The rare consumer suit against an advertiser typifies a larger pattern in our legal system—one where consumers find themselves powerless to take advantage of their legitimate legal rights. Most people simply cannot afford the often prohibitive expense of a lawsuit, especially when battling the virtually unlimited resources of a major company.

In most cases, the deceptive practice involved a purchase of such small cost that it made no practical sense to consider retaining an attorney to pursue the matter through the courts other than for reasons of principle. Although fighting for a principle can be rewarding, it can also be very expensive.

The extent of consumer injury from a deceptive advertisement is naturally difficult to prove, and the extent of the damage even more so. Unlike the FTC—who doesn't need to show that damage actually occurred, only a tendency to deceive—the individual consumer who sues must prove damages in order to win an award in court. All this adds to the complication and expense in a court battle.

Class-action suits, as an alternative, have become nearly impossible to pursue because federal court decisions do not allow individuals to combine separate claims in order to satisfy the minimum $10,000 damage amount required to file a lawsuit in federal court. While a few states have rejected the federal approach (notably California), opportunities for consumers to pursue class actions in state courts vary. What this all boils down to is that even when consumers are aware that their rights have been violated—and that retribution is available on their behalf—they are often frustrated by the obstacles that lie in their path.

ADVERTISING'S ROLE IN PRODUCTS LIABILITY

There is another area of real concern to advertisers. More and more, consumers are recovering substantial damages in products liability litigation. These are actions to recover damages when a defective product causes injury. For example, a can of beans is intended to be edible. If a consumer buys the product and gets food poisoning, products liability is involved, and the consumer can sue for damages.

Advertising has begun to play a large role in these lawsuits since product advertising can considerably influence liability. The problem occurs when the image created in a product's advertising may not be substantiated by the product's actual performance. Courts assume that a product will perform as claimed. So does the consumer. When it doesn't and damage results, the advertising may be instrumental in showing the advertiser's failure to "live up to" the product's claim.

Products liability is an area where the FTC can become involved under false advertising violations, and the consumer can receive punitive damage awards in private lawsuits. The many areas of law that fall under *products liability* create an arsenal for the consumer who has been damaged from the use of the product. As you can well imagine, cases of this nature can be a tremendous financial burden on an advertiser and its agency. Chapter 4 is devoted exclusively to the subject of products liability.

UNFAIRNESS VIOLATIONS

In contrast to straight deception, the FTC has developed a category of unfairness violations. Unfairness takes into account whether a practice, which is not considered unlawful, offends public policy as established by statute, common law, or otherwise. Also, a practice is considered unfair if it is immoral, unethical, oppressive, or unscrupulous, or causes substantial injury to consumers, competitors, or other businesspeople. This gives the FTC room to maneuver. It allows the commission to pursue activities that it couldn't under principles of straight deception.

As the FTC has expanded on the unfairness concept, it has determined that there are three types of advertisements that could possibly be considered nondeceptive, yet still be unfair. The advertiser should be aware that these are: (1) claims advertised without prior substantiation, (2) claims which tend to exploit such vulnerable groups as children and the elderly, and (3) instances in which the advertiser fails to provide consumers with necessary information about competing products with which to make valid choices.

CRIME AND PUNISHMENT—DECEPTIVE ADVERTISING

The most significant developments in recent federal regulation of advertising involve sanctions for deceptive or unfair claims. Previously, the standard remedy for deceptive advertising was a cease-and-desist order. This consisted of an order to stop the action and not continue with the deceptive practice. Today, however, violation of the commission's cease-and-desist order can be quite expensive.

The original cease-and-desist order proved to be grossly inadequate. Advertisers, as well as their advertising agencies, commonly violated the law and went virtually unpunished, or even more accurately, unnoticed. Advertisers were taking a calculated risk that the chance of being detected and ultimately prosecuted was extremely small, given the limited resources of the Federal Trade Commission and the tremendous amount of advertising that it was required to review.

However, recent efforts by the FTC have concentrated on eliminating the lag in enforcement of deceptive advertising violations. One development involves the use of corrective advertising orders. These direct the guilty advertiser to spend a specific percentage of its future advertising budget to inform the public as to the false claim that was originally made. The reasoning behind corrective advertising was that this provided a way of dissipating the effects of a previously misleading advertisement since the original ad that misled could not be removed or discounted from the minds of the consumer. Yet, it could be counteracted (or at least neutralized) if the original deceiver was required to disclose information to "properly" inform the consumer. It was hoped that this corrective ad would offset the original inaccurate impression.

In 1975 the commission proceeded against Warner-Lambert and the advertising of its product Listerine mouthwash.[7] Listerine's advertising had claimed that the product could prevent colds because it killed germs associated with colds. This was an unsubstantiated claim, which left an inaccurate message with the consumer. The commission, in this case, first imposed the remedy of corrective advertising.

Sanctions

The price advertisers must pay under this sanction can be quite imposing if they are found to have used misleading or deceptive advertising. For example, in 1971 the manufacturer of Ocean Spray Cranberry Juice Cocktail was required to de-

---

[7]*Warner-Lambert Co.*, (1973–1976 Transfer Binder) Trade Reg. Rep. (CCH) & 21, 066 (FTC 1975), appeal docketed, No. 76–1138 (D.C. Cir., filed Feb. 13, 1976).

vote 25 percent of the company's advertising budget for one year to informing the public of a previous deception.[8] The makers of Profile bread were required to expend 25 percent of their advertising budget for one year toward advertisements that stated: "Profile bread will not engender weight loss," contrary to the claims of its previous advertising.[9]

"Enterprise liability" is probably the most powerful area where the FTC can sanction an entire industry. This is a relatively new concept, but one that has given broad power to the conventional cease-and-desist order. When a cease-and-desist order is filed against a particular advertiser to prohibit a deceptive practice, it applies industrywide. All other advertisers and their agencies are bound by the same order. One advertiser cannot sidestep the responsibility for a practice found to be deceptive simply by avoiding to get caught. This is the FTC's version of the shotgun effect. It gives the widest coverage from a single shot.

These sanctions are typical of the nature, extent, and impact of the commission's punitive efforts and of what these efforts bring to bear against deceptive advertising and those who create it. Today, false, misleading, deceptive, or unfair practices carry a much greater deterrent to the would-be lawbreaker.

OTHER AREAS OF LAW AFFECTING ADVERTISING

We have explored, up to this point, how the FTC and the courts have played a major role in the regulation of advertising by prohibiting deception, misrepresentation, and unfairness. While Section 5 of the Federal Trade Commission Act accounts for the majority of legal activity concerning advertising, there are, however, other areas of law that the advertiser must be prepared to deal with.

Comparative advertising is one such area. It stems basically from the Lanham Trademark Act of 1946 (15 USC, Sec-

---

[8]*Ocean Spray Cranberry Inc.,* 80 FTC 975 (1971).
[9]*ITT Continental Baking Co.,* 79 FTC 248 (1971).

tion 1125 a), Section 43(a). This act allows a remedy for people or companies "likely to be damaged" by "false descriptions or representations" regarding comparisons of products or services. In other words, when Company X publishes an advertisement that compares its product to Company Y, and that ad proves to be untrue, Company X can be held liable.

Basically, comparative advertising litigation concerns situations where a company implied a superiority of its own or an inferiority of the competitor's product. A good example of this can be found in *Smith* v. *Chanel, Inc.*, 402 F.2d 562 (9th Cir. 1968). In this case, the perfume manufacturer Smith claimed in its advertisement that its version of Chanel perfume was "equal to the original." That claim was found by the court to be false, and under the Lanham Act, Smith was held liable.

In situations where the comparative ad claim does not fall under the Lanham Act (this is a federal act as is the FTC), there are remedies available under state law as well. False statements of this nature may well be actionable under laws against unfair competition or under tort remedies of disparagement or libel. We will discuss the Lanham Act and its relation to advertising claims more thoroughly in Chapter 8.

The client-agency relationship is another area of concern to the advertiser. A client-agency relationship is basically one where an individual or company makes use of the services of another to accomplish things that could not be accomplished alone. When a client-agency relationship is created—whether intentionally or in the eyes of the law—it involves a well-developed area of law. The law defines the rights and liabilities of the parties, their relation to each other, and their relation to third parties. Therefore, we have seen an increasing number of court actions in which the advertising agency is brought in with the miscreant advertiser and held jointly liable. In most cases, each party is liable for the actions of the other. This subject will be discussed in Chapter 11.

In conclusion, we have spent a good deal of time up to now introducing the FTC and its role in controlling advertising practices. We have also seen how other areas of law apply to the regulation of advertising. Indeed, there are many different areas of law above and beyond those of misleading and deceptive advertising. These include issues of copyright and trademark, laws covering the rights to privacy and publicity of individuals, and specific problems of advertising concerning warranties and guarantees, contests, and the like. All of these areas will be discussed in detail throughout the balance of this book.

It is undeniable that the right to advertise is directly tied to the right to do business, and the law will keep a watchful eye on how one does both. Therefore, it is absolutely critical that the advertiser be aware of and understand the role that the law plays in regulating advertising.

CHAPTER 2

AN OVERVIEW OF THE FEDERAL TRADE COMMISSION'S ROLE IN ADVERTISING REGULATION

Big brother is watching.
—*George Orwell*

In 1946 Frederic Wakeman wrote a novel about the exploits of an advertising agency and an arrogant client named Evan Evans. Since then, *The Hucksters* has become the public's image of the advertising profession. In the movie adaptation, Clark Gable plays the part of the advertising account executive caught in a struggle of right and wrong with the ne'er-do-well soap king played by Sidney Greenstreet. As these two battle, symbols of good conscience and selfish motives dominate the screen. "Advertising," exclaimed the soap tycoon, "is nothing more than pompous ranting," which he relishes when accomplished with the poorest of taste.

George Washington Hill, the real-life Evan Evans and owner of the American Tobacco Company, was well-known for his exaggerated advertising claims. When "creating" his own preference test statistics, Hill said, "I know the great preference for Lucky Strike is a fact, but the public won't believe it. Anyway, two-to-one has a better ring to it."

The Hucksters was written in an era when the advertiser took many liberties in selling his merchandise. For almost forty years moviegoers, however, have overlooked the fact that Wakeman's book was a work of fiction. The book convinced the public that advertising flourished—with the consumer falling victim to the guile of the advertiser—in a sea of broken promises that were never intended to be kept. Unfortunately, this feeling has prevailed. Today, the type of blatant deception demonstrated in *The Hucksters* is rigidly policed, primarily through the efforts of the Federal Trade Commission, which has successfully raised the standard of conduct of the advertising industry.

THE FEDERAL TRADE COMMISSION

As most advertising people already know, the Federal Trade Commission (FTC) has probably the greatest control over advertising and the way it is used. Yet, few understand the extent of the FTC's involvement. The mandate from Congress (under Section 5 of the Federal Trade Commission Act) is a simple and straightforward one: to prevent "unfair or deceptive acts or practices . . . [and] . . . unfair methods of competition."

The commission, as part of its scope, has the task of preserving a variety of marketplace options for consumers. Its efforts against deception help ensure that consumers will not make choices on the basis of misleading information. Also, the ban on unfair practices broadens the FTC's scope by protecting consumers from practices that are "exploitive or inequitable . . . morally objectionable, [or] seriously detrimental to consumers or others."[1]

As we discussed earlier, Section 5, which was once considered only a tool against unfair methods of competition between businesses, was expanded in 1938 to cover unfair and deceptive acts against consumers as well. While the rationale to abolish unfair methods of competition grew from the need to protect competitors from each other, the reasoning against unfair and deceptive acts and practices evolved out of the desire to protect the consumer from the advertiser.

We see in this chapter how the FTC's activities have greatly expanded the definition of *unfair* and *deceptive*. This chapter concentrates on the concepts that the commission and the courts have developed. It also covers the guidelines that the FTC uses to determine if a violation exists. The next chapter will examine specific types of violations under Section 5.

---

[1] 29 Fed. Reg. 8324, 8355 (July 2, 1964).

REGULATION OF ADVERTISING

Because the FTC's goal is to protect the consumer from false claims, deception, and misrepresentation, the level of control that it exerts over advertising has increased in recent years. The commission has gained increased authority and effectiveness for two reasons: first, through the cases that it has heard and decided; and second, through the courts' confirmation of the commission's decisions. In fact, the courts have upheld the majority of the commission's decisions.

An advertiser must understand how the FTC views an ad. Overall, what deceptive qualities does it look for? What qualifies as a deceptive ad? Or an unfair one? How does the advertiser know if the ad he creates will be acceptable in the eyes of the commission? The answers to these questions follow.

As I mentioned, the FTC follows certain guidelines where advertising claims are alleged to be unfair or deceptive. It first examines the advertisement to interpret all of the information contained in it to determine if the ad has a tendency to deceive. It looks at the net impression of the advertisement—the overall impression that the ad projects to the consumer. The commission also views the materiality of all the representations in the advertisement and particularly the claims that are alleged to be false. It also determines if the claims are simply sales exaggerations or puff. Now we'll examine each of these concepts in detail.

The Materiality Requirement

To reach the conclusion that an ad is deceptive, the questionable representation (or omission) must be a material one. A claim is material if it is likely to affect the consumer's choice of product and his conduct in purchasing that product. In other words, it is material if it is important to the consumer in making his purchasing decision. Another way to understand this concept is in terms of injury to the consumer. Finding that a claim is material is finding that injury is likely, and injury exists if the consumer would have chosen differently had there been no deception. The consumer would be injured because he would be purchasing something other than what he thought he was purchasing. Thus, injury and materiality are different sides of the same coin.

Let me give an example of this concept. In most of the cases throughout this chapter and the next, we will see deceptions that are material. The Rapid Shave case, where a television commercial demonstrates that the shave cream can shave sandpaper (when in reality it can not), is a perfect example of a material deception. This ability is central to what the product is purchased for—its ability to shave sandpaper must mean that it is great for a beard. The consumer would probably be swayed to purchase the product after seeing this demonstration. Thus, the demonstration creates a material deception.

On the other hand, when can a deception not be material? I recently produced a television commercial for a resort community in Palm Springs. In the commercial a craftsman was shown carving a silver sign that was the logo of the community. This was done to develop a theme of pride and detail of the craftsmanship that went into the development of the community itself. In reality the craftsman was not carving the actual sign, but only chiseling silver wax from the sign. This was deceptive but not material. Why? Because the consumer would not purchase a home at this resort based on the carving of the sign. It had nothing to do with his decision to buy the product.

The commission feels that certain types of claims are unquestionably material in nature. Such claims include express claims; implied claims as intended by the advertiser; claims relating to health, safety, and other similar areas of concern to the consumer; claims that relate to the main characteristics of the product or service; claims establishing the purpose, efficiency, cost, durability, performance, warranty or quality of a product; and statements regarding findings by a governmental agency concerning the product.

Tendency to Deceive

The FTC and the courts take a very close look at an advertisement if a false representation or omission has the "tendency or capacity" to deceive a significant number of consumers.

Actual deception is not necessary under the FTC Act to constitute a violation. It is generally held that only a tendency to deceive need be present. This is a very important point for the advertiser. Tendency or capacity to deceive, rather than actual deception, has become the standard against which the commission judges an ad to determine if it is deceptive.

One early case that dealt with this concept of tendency to deceive was *FTC* v. *Raladam Co.*, 316 U.S. 149, 62 S. Ct. 966, 86 L. Ed. 1336 (Black, J., 1942). In that case the United States Supreme Court decided the issue of whether a cease-and-desist order by the commission (issued after its hearing in 1935) should stand. The case involved Raladam's product Marmola. Marmola was a preparation for weight-reduction and was advertised as such. The company made claims in its advertisements that were misleading and deceptive. The statements concerned the product's qualities as a remedy for obesity.

Raladam did not argue whether the statements were deceptive (they had been caught before in 1929 as well). Its argument was that no proof was offered to show that injury occurred. However, the court held that no actual injury need be proven, only a tendency to deceive. The court felt that it was impossible to determine whether any injury occurred, or would occur in the future, because of Raladam's false claims. In fact, one of the principles of the act was "to prevent potential injury by stopping unfair methods of competition in their incipiency."

There's an interesting, similar case from the history of the con man's role in early advertising. A man named Edward Hayes, a con man extraordinaire, for years marketed a product called Man Medicine. Hayes claimed his product would bestow the purchaser "once more with gusto, the joyful satisfaction, the pulse and throb of physical pleasure, the keen sense of man sensation." Man Medicine was merely a laxative that Hayes used to bilk millions of dollars from a susceptible male market.

Hayes was caught and brought to trial by the Postmaster General for fraud. He was found guilty in April 1914, fined $5,000, and had to promise never to get involved with such wild schemes again. Only months later, Hayes was back out in the market advertising a new miracle product—a foolproof cure for obesity. The product was called Marmola, the same product which, with its new owner Raladam, was taken to court many years later.

Susceptibility of the Audience. In determining the consumer's interpretation, the guide is the susceptibility of the audience to which the advertisement is directed. The level of susceptibility is flexible and is adjusted to the norm of the audience. It is different for children than for adults. It is also different for the elderly or terminally ill than for the healthy young adult.

In *Doris Savitch,* 50 FTC 828 (1954) affirmed per curiam 218 F.2d 817 (7th Circuit 1955), the commission measured the susceptibility of an audience to which the ad was directed. Personal Drug Co., owned by Doris Savitch and Leo Savitch, manufactured and advertised products under the names *Quick-Kaps* and *D-Lay Capsules.* Quick-Kaps were advertised as medication that would relieve a woman's overdue period. A typical advertisement read as follows:

PERIOD DELAYED?
(Overdue)
Don't Risk Disaster
Don't Worry
At last—it CAN BE SOLD, a new, extra effective, Doctor approved formula—"Quick-Kaps" capsules may relieve you of your biggest worry—when due to minor functional menstrual delay or borderline anemia. Scientifically prepared by registered Pharmacists, "Quick-Kaps" capsules contain only medically recognized drugs, having no harmful after effects—Complete supply—packed in a confidential box only $5.00. Send no money and we will mail COD plus small postal and COD charges or send $5.00 cash and we will rush AIR MAIL.
"Just the thing to have on hand."

The implication here is strong. Relief from delayed menstruation due to pregnancy will be achieved by using Quick-Kaps. The advertisements also represented that its use would provide relief from delayed menstruation due to "minor functional disorders and borderline anemia." The first problem here is with the causes of delayed menstruation. The biggest cause is pregnancy. A more infrequent cause is iron deficiency anemia. Borderline anemia is not a cause of delayed menstruation other than in those rare cases when it is due to iron deficiency anemia.

Some of the phrases used in the advertisement are significant—for example, "Don't Worry"—"Don't Risk Disaster"—"May relieve you of your biggest worry"—"Medically recognized drugs having no harmful after effects"—"At last—it CAN BE SOLD, a new, extra effective, Doctor approved formula." The above-quoted phrase would seem to imply that, either because of a change in the law or recent medical discoveries, a new preparation was now being put on the market. This was not the case.

The commission felt that it was a commonly known fact that selling preparations or devices that would induce an abortion is generally prohibited by law. People looking for such a product would not expect to find it advertised as obviously and openly as products that were not prohibited. This advertisement seems to invite reading between the lines. It is reminiscent of bootlegging days when a knowing wink to a buyer implied that the "cold tea" being sold was in fact illegal liquor.

As you can see, the implication about a product is as important as the literal truth of each sentence or picture. "The ultimate impression upon the mind of the reader (or viewer) arises not only from what is said, but also from what is reasonably implied."[2] We explore more on this area of interpretation of an ad later in this chapter.

The *Doris Savitch* case illustrates quite well the susceptibility of an audience to which an advertisement is directed. It is reasonable to say that a woman would worry about delayed menstruation and could believe that this was caused by pregnancy. If she wanted to alleviate that situation, the advertisement for Quick-Kaps might be interpreted as promising that relief. In any event, the commission stated in its conclusion to the case: " . . . the mental condition of such a person is an element to be considered in arriving at which construction might reasonably be put upon the advertisement."

---

[2]*Aronberg, trading as Positive Products Company* v. *F.T.C.*, 132 F.2d 165.

Ads Directed at a Specific Audience. Let's take another situation. Suppose that an advertisement appeared in a medical journal. The ad was not deceptive to a physician. Yet it fell into the hands of a layman who was actually deceived. Under these circumstances the advertisement would not be deceptive even though the person was actually deceived.

That was the situation in *Belmont Laboratories, Inc.* v. *FTC,* 103 F. 2d 538, (3rd Cir. 1939). Obviously false claims regarding the curing potential of Mazon, a soap and an ointment, had been made. In medical pamphlets addressed to doctors and nurses, Mazon claimed to permanently eliminate specific ailments.

> Mazon—an ethical preparation compounded under the personal supervision of its originator—is the original treatment of its character for:

Eczema	Ring worm
Psoriasis	Athlete's foot
Head scalds	Barber's itch
Ivy poison	Other skin disorders

> The colloidal nature of the base of Mazon and its strong penetrating characteristics, together with its healing and soothing ingredients, afford quick and permanent elimination of Eczema and other skin disorders. No other treatment for permanent cure has ever been discovered. Some of the best-known skin specialists in the city are using it exclusively and praise it highly.

The claims found in the example were medically untrue. A major problem was with the claim that the product "permanently eliminated" certain diseases. The ad tends to convey that by an external application of an ointment, internal disorders can be cured. It fails to recognize the need to apply internal remedies to diseases caused by internal problems. Many of the diseases listed (eczema, psoriasis, etc.) are caused by internal disturbances. The application of an external remedy can do little more than alleviate the exterior symptoms. The ad also creates an impression of newness. One may have a vision of thousands of doctors and druggists working diligently at hundreds of hospitals and laboratories to develop the new medical wonder—Mazon. This was certainly not the case.

These advertisements were found in pamphlets, which were circulated to the medical profession, and in a medical journal. Leaflets were also included inside the packages. The court said:

> that physicians and readers of professional journals are too smart to be deceived and that lay purchasers buy blind because the leaflet is inside the carton containing the ointment. We think that one position is untrue legally and the other factually.

In other words, the advertisements were blatantly untrue. Doctors and nurses would know that, but the consumer would not. The consumer would buy the product blindly because the leaflet was inside the package.

The benchmark of this concept is who is deceived. If a person of low intellect is deceived by an advertisement for a Rolls-Royce, does this demonstrate a tendency to deceive? The test for tendency to deceive is rooted in the market that the advertisement is directed to. However, if the advertisement reaches another market, the perception of that reader or viewer will be considered. Based on that reasoning, Belmont Laboratories lost.

There is a problem though. How do you set a standard that will be used as the picture of the average consumer? The courts have had a problem with this question over the years as well. The standard by which tendency to deceive is judged has been developed by the courts as the "reasonable man."

The Reasonable Man Standard

Although the standard has gone through much change (from the "reasonable man" to the "ignorant man" and back), the FTC has decided, for the time, on the reasonable man. The reasonable man standard was first mentioned in 1837.[3] He is a man of average prudence and ordinary sense, who uses ordinary care and skill.

---

[3]*Vaughan v. Menlove*, 3 Bing. N.C. 468, 132 Eng. Rep. 490 (1837).

To understand why the FTC has changed its stance over the years regarding the reasonable man standard, it is helpful to look at how the standard evolved. Soon after the Wheeler-Lea Amendments to the Federal Trade Commission Act were passed in 1938, the reasonable man standard began to be replaced with a new ideology: the ignorant man standard. This new standard was based largely on a case concerning an encyclopedia company that had used many false statements in a sales campaign. These were not simply innocent misrepresentations, but rather blatant untruths intended to deceive potential buyers. However, some or all of these falsehoods could have been detected by consumers.

The case was *Federal Trade Commission* v. *Standard Education Society,* 302 U.S. 112, 58 S.Ct. 113, 82 L.Ed. 141 (Black, J.). In selling their *Standard Reference Work* and *New Standard Encyclopedia,* the company representative convinced the prospects that they had been selected (because of their prestige and stature in the community) from a small list of well-connected, representative people in various areas. The company was presenting them with an "artcraft deluxe edition" of the encyclopedia free. As the scheme developed the representative would state that "they [were] giving away a set of books . . . free as an advertising plan . . . that the prospect [had] been specially selected, and that the only return desired for the gift [was] permission to use the name of the prospect for advertising purposes."

The prospects were told that they would only have to pay for the loose leaf extension service, which was $69.50. This, the prospects were told, was "a reduced price and that the regular price of the books and the extension service is $150, sometimes even as high as $200." These statements were false and were part of the scheme. In fact, the $69.50 price was the regular price for both the encyclopedia and the loose leaf extension and research privileges. Clearly, it was the practice of Standard Education Society to mislead customers into believing that they were being given a free encyclopedia, and that they only were to pay for the extension service. The record in this case is filled with testimony from people in 10 states that confirms this.

What is interesting here is that the Circuit Court of Appeals for the Second Circuit (the lower court that heard the case before the U.S. Supreme Court) had decided that they could not seriously entertain the notion "that a man who is buying a set of books and a 10 year extension service, will be fatuous enough to be misled by the mere statement that the first are given away, and that he is paying only for the second."[4] Here the court felt that no reasonable man would believe the claim that he was getting one item for free if he paid for the other. The U.S. Supreme Court, however, felt—as did the FTC originally—that the lower court was wrong; an ignorant man could believe the claim.

To illustrate that point, Justice Black in the opinion authored by him in 1937 wrote:

> The fact that a false statement may be obviously false to those who are trained and experienced does not damage its character, nor take away its power to deceive others less experienced. There is no duty resting upon a citizen to suspect the honesty of those with whom he transacts business. Laws are made to protect the trusting as well as the suspicious. The best element of business has long since decided that honesty should govern competitive enterprises, and that the rule of caveat emptor should not be relied upon to reward fraud and deception.

This case could have been interpreted in several ways, and it was by the various appeals courts. However, it was interpreted by the Supreme Court as having abolished the reasonable man standard altogether. In fact, it firmly entrenched the ignorant man standard, which would continue for some time.

The Ignorant Man Standard.   During the decade that followed, the ignorant man standard flourished, as was illustrated in *Gelb* v. *FTC*, 144 F.2d 580, (2d Cir. 1944). The case concerned an advertising claim that, among other things, a shampooing and coloring preparation known as Progressive Clairol and Instant Clairol permanently colored hair. One of

---

[4]*Standard Education Society* v. *FTC*, 86 F.2d 692.

the questions in this case dealt with the standard of perception of the consumer—specifically, whether an order should be upheld that would enjoin Clairol from "representing that the effect produced upon the color of the hair by the use of said preparation is permanent."

Looking at the advertisements for Clairol literally, as the court did, it is obvious that the preparation permanently colors hair to which it is applied. But the commission found that it (and this would seem obvious) has no effect on new hair. Hence the commission concluded that the claim of the preparation *permanently* coloring hair was misleading. It seems absurd that any user of the preparation could be so simple-minded as to suppose that hair not yet grown out would be colored. (One witness was found who, after some prodding, finally testified "that you would think 'permanent' means you would never need to bother having it dyed again," although the witness knew better.) Yet the commission construed the advertisement as representing that it would do just that. Therefore, it ruled that the claim was false and deceptive.

Basically, the court validated the commission's decision. Both the court and the commission reasoned that Section 5 of the act was for the protection of the trusting, as well as the suspicious. The result of this case was that evidence of deception, regardless of how unintended or unreasonable, was sufficient for a finding of deceptive advertising, even if only a single person were deceived, and even if that person were incompetent or a fool. The status quo at the time was that "People have a right to assume that fraudulent advertising traps will not be laid to ensnare them."[5] Yet it appears that the concept was taken to its extreme.

Back to the Reasonable Man Standard.   Beginning in 1963 and continuing until today, the FTC has moved back in the direction of establishing a reasonable man standard of perception. The commission withdrew from the concept that de-

---

[5]*Donaldson* v. *Read Magazine, Inc.*, 333 U.S. 178, 68 S.Ct. 591, 92 L.Ed. 628 (1948).

ception of a single consumer, no matter how foolish or imperceptive, constitutes a deceptive practice.

True, the commission's responsibility is to prevent deception of the gullible and credulous, as well as the cautious and knowledgeable. This principle, however, loses its credibility if it is pushed to an absurd extreme. An advertiser cannot be held liable for every misconception, however outlandish. His representations cannot be subject to interpretation by the foolish or feeble-minded—the *ignorant man*. Some people, because of ignorance or incomprehension, may be misled by even a scrupulously honest claim. Perhaps a few misguided souls believe that all Danish pastry is made in Denmark. Is it deceptive to call a bakery item *Danish pastry* if it is made in California? Of course not! An advertising claim does not become false and deceptive merely because it will be misunderstood by an insignificant and unrepresentative segment of people within the market that the ad is addressed to.

In 1973 the commission presented its opinion *In the matter of Coca-Cola Company,* F.T.C. Docket No. 8839. This opinion illustrates the commission's current stance on the standard of perception issue. In this case the commission dealt with an issue involving the Coca-Cola Company's marketing of a drink called *Hi-C*. It had been advertised as "the sensible drink . . . made with fresh fruit . . . [and] . . . being high in Vitamin C, . . . [and that children] . . . can drink as much . . . as they like." Television commercials and some package labels showed oranges and other fruits, from which the juices are used to make Hi-C. The complaint in this case stated that these advertisements compared Hi-C with natural citrus juices by implication. Therefore it was deceptive.

The commission maintained that Hi-C advertisements implicitly compared Hi-C with natural citrus juices and with orange juice in particular. It was alleged that consumers would be likely to take the advertisement to mean that Hi-C was made from fresh orange juice and was equal to, or better than, actual fresh orange juice in nutritional value.

The situation here was that the advertising representations were "not reasonably likely to have communicated" characteristics of Hi-C which were contrary to fact. It is possible to agree that the statements were "not reasonably likely" to deceive based purely on the facts. However, the statement of Commissioner Jones (dissenting) brings into play the standard of perception model:

> The commission's opinion ignores or perhaps reverses the standard model of the consumer as "the ignorant, the unthinking and the credulous" consumer which the commission has been commanded to use in determining whether a particular act is unfair or deceptive. Instead, without any evidence in the record to support it, the commission implicitly adopts a new consumer model as its standard for interpreting whether a claim is likely to deceive. This standard is actually one portraying the consumer as discriminating, sophisticated, and highly knowledgeable as well as skeptical and unbelieving. This consumer knows that fruit drinks are not the same as citrus juices despite what Hi-C ads said.

In his dissenting opinion, Commissioner Jones hit upon the very issue that has become the standard consumer model used to determine if deception exists—the reasonable man standard.

The Issue of Net Impression

Whether an advertisment is deceptive must not be determined by viewing isolated parts of the advertisement (this has been alluded to earlier), but rather on the net impression of the entire ad. The net impression of the ad is the understanding that the reader walks away with after coming into contact with the advertisement. Keep in mind the *reader* is determined by the reasonable man standard that we have just discussed.

One very well-established case that demonstrated the principle of net impression is *Zenith Radio Corp.* v. *FTC* 143 F.2d 29 (7th Circuit 1944). In this case, the commission alleged two primary issues in a series of advertisements for Zenith radios to determine if they were deceptive. The first involved Zenith's assertion regarding the capacity of its radio to receive foreign broadcasts. The second assertion involved the number of tubes contained in its radio sets.

These claims were found to be deceptive. A typical advertisement read as follows:

> Europe is talking to you every night
> in English. Are you listening?
> With Zenith, the short wave radio that gives
> you Europe direct, you can hear all the leaders,
> all the daily news broadcasts.
> You need not depend on re-broadcasts which bring
> you only a small part.
> Europe, South America, or the Orient every day
> guaranteed or your money back on all short wave Zeniths.
> 1940 Zenith, the guaranteed short wave radio.

In truth, atmospheric conditions existed that made it impossible to receive satisfactory reception of foreign broadcasts. The Zenith radios were incapable of satisfactory reception of foreign broadcasts every day and under all conditions. The commission reasoned that the effect of the claims was to induce consumers to believe that radio reception problems would be completely overcome by using the Zenith radio. This is a good example of how deception was possible due to the consumer's lack of knowledge about the technical limitations of radio reception.

The second issue concerned the number of tubes contained in the radio. The ads stated different models available with the following tubes:

> 6-Tube Superheterodyne Table Model
> 8-Tube Superheterodyne with Wavemagnet Aerial
> 10-Tube Superheterodyne with Rotor Wavemagnet Aerial
> 11-Tube Superheterodyne with Rotor Wavemagnet Aerial

The commission defined tubes as devices that perform "the primary function of detecting, amplifying, or receiving radio signals." However, some of the tubes contained in the Zenith radio and which were included in the advertised tube count had nothing to do with receiving radio signals. They were, in fact, used for tuning and converting alternating current into direct current, and therefore the commission determined that they did not qualify under its definition. The commission, after concluding that a large portion of purchasers believed that a radio was better and more powerful because of the number of tubes it contained, held against Zenith.

The point in the Zenith case was that while the statements about the number of tubes contained in the sets were accurate, viewed as a whole the ad was deceptive. The consumer couldn't determine the relevance of the number of tubes, other than "the more tubes, the better the set." As for the first issue in the case, reception capability, the consumer would believe that reception problems would be overcome with the Zenith set. The net impression created by the ad was therefore a deceptive one.

Distortion of Facts.   Let's take a look at another situation. In *P. Lorillard Co.* v. *FTC,* 186 F.2d 52 (4th Cir. 1950), isolated segments of an article taken from *Reader's Digest* were used in an advertisement for Old Gold cigarettes. Lorillard attempted to use the argument that the ads merely stated what had been stated in that article. By examining the advertisements, however, the meaning of the *Reader's Digest* article had been distorted. In essence, it amounted to the "use of the truth in such a way as to cause the reader to believe the exact opposite of what was intended by the writer of the article."

By comparing the advertisement with the article, we see where the problem lies. The article, referring to results of independent laboratory tests of the leading brands of cigarettes, said:

> The laboratory's general conclusion will be sad news for the advertising copywriters, but good news for the smoker, who need no longer worry as to which cigarette can most effectively nail down his coffin. For one nail is just about as good as another. The differences between brands are, practically speaking, small, and no single brand is so superior to its competitors as to justify its selection on the ground that it is less harmful. How small the variations are may be seen from the data tabulated on page 7.

That table showed the insignificance of the difference in the tar and nicotine content of the various brands. While the tests did show that Old Golds contained less nicotine, tars, and resins than the others, the difference was so small as to be entirely insignificant to the smoker. Yet the company advertised this difference as if it had been awarded a commendation for public health, rather than a slap in the face by *Reader's Digest*. Now that we know this, here's an example of one Old Gold advertisement:

OLD GOLDS FOUND
LOWEST IN NICOTINE
OLD GOLDS FOUND
LOWEST IN THROAT-IRRITATING
TARS AND RESINS
See Impartial Test by *Reader's Digest*
July Issue.
See How Your Brand Compares with Old Gold.
Reader's Digest assigned a scientific testing laboratory to find
out about cigarettes. They tested seven leading cigarettes
and *Reader's Digest* published the results.
The cigarette whose smoke was lowest in nicotine
was Old Gold. The cigarette with the least throat-irritating
tars and resins was Old Gold.
On both these major counts Old Gold was best among
all seven cigarettes tested.
Get July *Reader's Digest*. Turn to page 5.
See what this highly respected magazine reports.
You'll say, "From now on, my cigarette is Old Gold!"
Light one?
Note the mild, interesting flavor. Easier on the throat?
Sure. And more smoking pleasure? Yes. It's the new Old Gold
—finer yet, since "something new has been added."

Almost anyone reading the ad would get an entirely different impression from the actual facts. A person would think that Old Golds were less irritating and less harmful than the other leading brands, all because of *Reader's Digest* research. Few, in fact, would have bothered to look up the article. As we have seen, the truth was exactly the opposite. To this case, the court concluded by saying:

In determining whether or not advertising is false or misleading ... regard must be had, not to fine spun distinctions and arguments that may be made in excuse but to the effect which it might reasonably be expected to have upon the general public. The important criterion is the net impression which the advertisement is likely to make upon the general populace.

The Use of Visual Distortion.   The use of mock-ups (a model built to depict an actual situation) has also been an area of concern, particularly where television is employed.

A problem exists here since television, as well as other media, has certain limitations in the area of reproduction. As we'll see, the deception issue arises when these limitations are overcome in a way that portrays the product as something that it isn't.

In television commercials aired in late 1959, Colgate-Palmolive Company promoted its product Rapid Shave in the following manner.

The spot opens showing a football being kicked and the ball zooming toward the camera. The scene then cuts to a football player whose face is hidden behind a mask of sandpaper.

Voice-over:

"Who is the man behind the sandpaper mask?"
The football player removes the mask revealing a heavy growth of beard. The player rubs his face.

Voice-over:

"It's triple-threat man, Frank Gifford—backfield sensation of the New York Giants . . . a man with a problem just like yours . . ."
Camera cuts to sandpaper mask and a hand brings a can of Rapid Shave into the frame in front of the sandpaper.

Voice-over:

"A beard as tough as sandpaper . . . a beard that needs . . . PALMOLIVE RAPID SHAVE . . . super-moisturized for the fastest, smoothest shaves possible."
Type is superimposed on screen, "Super Moisturized Fastest, Smoothest Shaves."
Hand presses the top of the Rapid Shave can to despense a small amount of the lather into the other hand.

Voice-over:

"To prove RAPID SHAVE's super-moisturizing power, we put it right from the can . . ."
The lather is spread in one continuous motion onto the surface of the sandpaper. The first hand brings a razor into view and shaves a clean path through the lather and the gritty sandpaper.

Voice-over:

"onto this tough, dry sandpaper. It was apply . . . soak . . . and off in a stroke."
The picture then cuts to Frank Gifford lathering his face.

Voice-over:

"And super-moisturizing PALMOLIVE RAPID SHAVE can do the same for you."
In a split-screen, on one side a hand applies Rapid Shave to sandpaper. On the other side a hand applies Rapid Shave to Frank Gifford's face. As Gifford makes a razor stroke down his face, a hand does the same to the sandpaper.

Voice-over:

"In this sandpaper test . . . or on your sandpaper beard, you just apply RAPID SHAVE . . . then . . . take your razor . . . and shave clean with a fast, smooth stroke."
Gifford then strokes his clean-shaven face with a look of satisfaction. Screen cuts to a picture of cans of Rapid Shave surrounded by the words Super-Moisturizing *and* Fastest, Smoothest Shaves.

Voice-over:

"Try RAPID SHAVE . . . or cooling, soothing RAPID SHAVE MENTHOL . . . both super-moisturized . . . for the fastest, smoothest shaves possible. They both outshave the tube . . . outshave the brush."
Musical tune ends spot with the lyrics: "RAPID SHAVE outshaves them all. Use RAPID SHAVE in the morning."

In an attempt to demonstrate the shaving power of its shave cream, the Colgate-Palmolive Company showed the moistening and shaving of a piece of sandpaper, or so the viewer would think. The commercial purported to shave tough, dry sandpaper to demonstrate the moistening power of the cream, and it was blatantly demonstrated that way. However, the sandpaper turned out to be a sheet of plexiglass sprinkled with a layer of sand. The viewers were tricked into believing that they had actually seen the sandpaper test and they had been asked to make their purchasing decisions based on the test they had seen. In the case, *Federal Trade Commission* v. *Colgate-Palmolive Co.,* 380 US 374, (1965), the commission dealt directly with the issue of mock-ups in television. This case addressed a number of important sides to the mock-up issue. The court reasoned that "without this visible proof of Rapid Shave's claimed moisturizing ability, some viewers might not have been persuaded to buy the product."

Initially, it was determined that real sandpaper could be shaved if moistened for a sufficient length of time (in fact a very long time). However, it could not be shaved in the actual length of time used in the commercial, as the demonstration implied. They also found that, through the inadequacies of television, real sandpaper would appear to be only colored paper when photographed by the television camera. The advertiser used this as an excuse to justify the mock-up technique. It didn't work.

In a similar case, *In the Matter of Campbell Soup Co.*, 77 F.T.C. 664 (1970), the commission looked at advertisements that showed a bowl of Campbell's soup. To all appearances, the soup had been prepared according to the directions on the can and was shown in a "ready to eat" situation. By viewing the ad the consumer saw an abundance of carrots, peas, potatoes, onions, and such present in a can of Campbell's soup.

The commission stated quite well the reality of the advertisement:

> In truth and in fact, in many of the . . . advertisements, which purport to demonstrate or offer evidence of the quantity and abundance of solid ingredients in a can of Campbell soup, [the advertiser has] placed, or caused to be placed in the aforesaid bowl . . . a number of clear glass marbles which prevent the solid ingredients from sinking to the bottom, thereby giving the soup the appearance of containing more solid ingredients than it actually contains, which fact is not disclosed. The aforesaid demonstration exaggerates, misrepresents, and is not evidence of, the quantity or abundance of solid ingredients in a can of Campbell soup; therefore, the aforesaid advertisements are false, misleading, and deceptive.

Campbell Soup Co. had placed marbles in the bottom of a bowl of soup that was shown in an advertisement. This caused the solids in the soup to stay at the surface. Here again the respondent claimed that the limitations of the medium necessitated the use of this mock-up to portray the actual viscosity of the product. The commission didn't agree with that reasoning and ordered Campbell to stop using the ads. This case was settled by consent order (Campbell agreed to the commission's determination and consented to abide by it).

As we have seen in the above examples, the reality of an advertisement's net impression must be considered carefully.

THE ISSUE OF PUFFING

Puffing is an area of advertising where the law allows the advertiser to make certain exaggerated statements or opinions about his product. Ivan Preston in his book *The Great American Blow-Up: Puffery in Advertising and Selling,* defined puffing as the use of advertising that praises with "subjective opinions, superlatives, or exaggerations, vaguely and generally, stating no specific facts." Such statements as "Coke is the real thing" and "Sleeping on a Sealy is like sleeping on a cloud" are perfect examples of puff. A certain degree of puffing has always been allowed in advertising. Yet, the tolerance for this practice is limited due to the inherent gray area in its use.

The use of puffing in advertising has generally been acceptable to both the FTC and courts, based on certain rationale. Courts have reasoned that consumers do not rely on expressions of opinion by advertisers about their products. Also, the FTC recognizes that certain statements of general praise are not likely to be relied on by consumers under its "capacity to deceive" standard. Lastly, certain forms of superlative praise are permissible simply because there is no way to establish that they are false.

Legal Interpretation of Puffery

If the puff takes the form of a pure statement of opinion, and if the law prohibits only false factual statements, then it may be impossible for courts to prove that a false representation was made. While exaggerations, superlatives, and unsupported opinions in advertising have been tolerated, it is also clear that the extent of puffing has been reduced over the years. This is because of the increasing desire of the FTC and courts to recognize that false factual representations can arise by implication, as we have discussed. This occurs in the use of some forms of puffing.

The commission investigated a situation of puffing in *The Matter of Better Living, Inc.*, 54 F.T.C. 648, (1957), aff'd 259 F.2d 271 (1958). Better Living, Inc. was in the business of selling and distributing aluminum storm doors, storm windows, and aluminum awnings. They had published advertisements and sales literature that made many blatantly false statements. The company made two claims that relate to puffing. The first was the statement, "WORLD'S LOWEST PRICES." The second was "Better Living, Inc., 'Beauty Prize' storm windows and doors. Acclaimed from Coast to Coast First Prize Winners for Beauty. Choice of Famous Home Stylists."

As to the claim that the products were offered at the world's lowest prices, the company's advertising agent claimed that "for several weeks prior to the publication of the advertisements a check was made of local competitive prices and that the prices [thereafter] advertised were slightly lower than their competitors'." The advertising agent admitted that there was no real factual basis to support the claim and, in fact, stated that the claim was typical puffing.

At this point the commission expressed its definition of puffing to determine whether the statements did fall into this area. The commission said:

> *Puffing* . . . is a term frequently used to denote exaggerations reasonable to be expected of a seller as to the degree of quality of his product, the truth or falsity of which cannot be precisely determined. In contrast, . . . the representation as to "the world's lowest price" is a statement of objective actuality, the truth or falsity of which is not variable and can be ascertained with factual precision. This representation cannot, therefore, properly be termed *puffing*. It is either true, or it is false; and, accordingly, such a determination must be made.

The other statement made by Better Living, Inc. related to the awards it had won in certain beauty contests. Despite the advertising claim, the advertising agent admitted that "these storm windows were never awarded a beauty prize of any kind." To this Better Living added that such a statement was mere subjective puffing, which is acceptable in advertising. The commission disagreed and held that such claims had the capacity and tendency to mislead consumers. The statement was one of fact, which could be proven or—in this case—disproven.

The commission has continued to develop this concept in *The Matter of Dannon Milk Prods., Inc.,* 61 F.T.C. 840. 856 (1962). Here Dannon had made claims about its product Dannon Yogurt. Specifically, Dannon claimed in advertisements, brochures, pamphlets, and radio broadcasts that "Dannon is known as nature's perfect food that science made better." Dannon argued that the perfect food claim was mere puffing. However, the commission reasoned that because of the present day emphasis on dieting, health, and nutrition, to make the claim that a food is perfect far exceeds puffing or exaggeration of qualities. It is a misrepresentation of a material fact.

The Federal Trade Commission is not authorized to foreclose expression of honest opinion. The same opinion, however, may not be utilized to mislead or deceive the public or to harm a competitor. Because the dividing line between permissible puffery and implied deception is vague and because false implications of fact can be easily found, there is an increasing risk of liability from using puffery in advertising. The continued rise in consumerism has affected when puffery will be regarded as appropriate. A claim that was considered as opinion and puffery years ago could now be considered a deception.

Therefore, advertisers must be very careful in using hyperbole in their advertisements. The test is whether the average consumer will recognize or perceive the hyperbole for what it is or be deceived by it. Advertiser be warned; the puffing rule is not a license to lie. Terms like *best, perfect, prime, exceptional, original, comparable in quality, wonderful,* and so on have been dealt with by the commission and the courts and do not qualify as puff. It should be obvious that puffing can cross over into deception very easily.

CHAPTER 3

SPECIFIC AREAS OF CONCERN UNDER SECTION 5 OF THE FEDERAL TRADE COMMISSION ACT

Welcome back my friends to the show that never ends.
—Keith Emerson

In the previous chapter we discussed the scope of the Federal Trade Commission. We analyzed the theory and reasoning the commission uses in its review of advertising. In this chapter we look at specific claims and language usage in advertising that can cause trouble.

We look at the types of advertising claims that the advertiser deals with almost everyday, in almost every ad. We review examples of untruthful ads, and explore problems with the use of the word *free*. Also, we discuss the uses and pitfalls of using qualified language and ads containing claims that a product is unique or will perform in a certain way. Such other problem areas as deception by implication or inference, use of technical language and vagueness, and deceptive truth are presented also. First, let's view the most obvious type of deceptive ad, one that is strictly untrue.

UNTRUTH AND DECEPTION

This may seem to be contradictory, but an untrue claim is not, in and of itself, deceptive. The nature of the untruth must be explored to determine if it is deceptive. In simpler terms, there are claims that are factually untrue, but at the same time are certainly not deceptive.

Fantasy Claims

This type of claim is called fantasy advertising. While the claim, "Coke adds life" is clearly untrue, it is not deceptive because an ordinary consumer would not believe such a blatant claim. As we have seen in Chapter 2, these types of claims are not considered deceptive if we look to the reasonable man standard, that is, the perception of any ordinary, reasonable consumer. While fantasy claims are very similar to puffery, they are more than subjective opinion. They are blatant absurdities.

Claims That Are Considered Untrue

Literal untruths in any other form are almost always deceptive. Samples of some of the most blatant in advertising run the gamut. For example, Alix Cohn, a junk dealer, was sued by the state of Connecticut for advertising his second-hand merchandise as being antique. The merchandise was certainly not "antique" in the true sense of the word.[1] In another case, a product designed to repair aluminum cookware, called So-Luminum, was advertised as being able to withstand a direct flame or 2,000 degrees. The company's claim was absolutely untrue.[2]

Advertisements were created that gave the impression that goods were made of leather when they were not. Duraleather— a material used in cars, suitcases, and upholstery—contained no leather but was painted and embossed with a grain to look like leather.[3] In another example, Sebrone claimed to permanently eliminate dandruff due to new discoveries of scientific research. In fact, the product only temporarily removed dandruff scales.[4]

In one case, Murry Space Shoes circulated reprints of a news article as an advertisement. The article claimed that the

---

[1] *State v. Cohn*, 24 Conn. Supp. 188, 188 A.2d 878 (1962).
[2] *In the Matter of Perfect Mfg. Co.*, 43 F.T.C. 238 (1946).
[3] *Masland Duraleather Co. v. FTC*, 34 F.2d 733, 2 U.S.P.Q. 442 (3d Cir. 1929).
[4] *Sebrone Co. v. FTC*, 135 F.2d 676 (7th Cir. 1943).

manufacturer's shoe would "cure many bodily ailments . . . corrects foot deformities (and cures) . . . corns, fallen arches, and bunions." Murry Space Shoes had no corrective or therapeutic value and could not cure anything.[5]

To further illustrate untrue claims, let's take a more detailed look at two such cases where claims were considered to be plainly untrue. The first, *United States* v. *Hindman,* 179 F.Supp. 926 (1960), involved the manufacturer of military uniforms. Seymour Hindman had been promoting his uniforms as custom-made and custom-tailored. In fact, the uniforms were all mass produced. Hindman argued that the term *custom-tailored* did not mean that the uniform was made individually to fit, but that it was given "particularly fine stitching or other tailoring finish." The court felt that the average consumer would not agree with such a definition, but rather would believe that the uniform was made to order. Therefore, it was untrue that Hindman's uniforms were custom-made.

The second case, *Prima Products* v. *Federal Trade Commission,* 209 F.2d 405 (1954), involved the advertising of certain qualities of a masonry sealer called Aquella. The manufacturer, Prima Products, promoted to the public a waterproofing paint used mainly on brick walls. One of the claims that Aquella made was that it was "easy to apply . . . almost as simple as whitewashing." In fact, the application was somewhat more complex, including numerous washings and repeated applications. The court ruled that Aquella was not "easy to apply" as advertised.

THE USE OF THE WORD *FREE*

Probably the single word that has caused the most anguish for advertisers is *free.* Just plug the word *free* into an ad and you're asking for trouble. It is important for the advertiser to understand how the word *free* can be used and what bargain must be lived up to when it is. Indeed the guidelines in this area are quite clear-cut. The simplest form of free offer is a gift or sam-

---

[5]*Murray Space Shoe Corp.* v. *FTC,* 304 F.2d 270 (2d Cir. 1962).

ple truly given without any strings attached. The operative word here is *any*. The word *free* means the consumer pays nothing and is required to do nothing.

Often an advertisement offers a free sample that will be sent to the consumer for paying a small amount to cover mailing and handling. This is acceptable only if the amount requested is no more than the actual cost to the advertiser of this handling and mailing. But if the consumer must pay more than the actual cost, the offer is improper.

Mark Twain once said, "Few things are harder to put up with than the annoyance of a good example." So here is one. It involves a major furniture retailer by whom I was once employed. The company found out what can happen when the word *free* is used too loosely.

These folks had been running advertisements for appliances. In these ads a simple, direct statement was made: "FREE DELIVERY." Things were going along fine, for many years in fact, until one day we got a call from a distraught older woman. She had not received satisfaction from our local store, so she called our general offices. She had purchased a new refrigerator at a competitor's store and wanted us to pick it up and deliver it to her home. After all, our ad did say "free delivery" and she wanted her refrigerator delivered, free.

The more we argued with her, the worse it got. We finally passed her off as a trouble-maker out to get a free ride—no pun intended. A couple of days later we got a call from the FTC, and they wanted some answers. Unfortunately the ones we gave them weren't the right ones. The statement had to be lived up to—literally—or be changed.

From that day on the ads read: "FREE DELIVERY INCLUDED." You had to buy our merchandise to get us to deliver it free of charge. Granted, the average consumer understands that we will only deliver our own merchandise. But the problem went beyond that because "free delivery" is a deceptive claim. The delivery is not actually *free*. The consumer has to do something—buy the merchandise. In basic contract law this action is called consideration. In this case delivery is not free. It is included in the price of the merchandise—you don't pay extra to receive it. But the point is, you do pay for it because it's built into the price.

A Free Offer Must Contain No Consideration

As we have just seen, *consideration* is the legal term for payment. But payment can be in forms other than the commonly used version, money. Consideration can be any action that induces someone into a contract. It can be a price, or an action, or a motive, or a forbearance (an agreement not to do something). *Black's Law Dictionary* defines consideration as: "Some right, interest, profit, or benefit accruing to one party, or some forbearance, detriment, loss, or responsibility, given, suffered, or undertaken by the other." In other words, an item is not free if it is given with some other consideration.

Along the same lines, *FTC* v. *The Book of the Month Club,* 202 F.2d 486 (C.C.A. 2, 1953) dealt with the use of the word *free.* Here the Book-of-the-Month Club published advertisements that read:

FREE
TO NEW MEMBERS OF THE
BOOK-OF-THE-MONTH CLUB

The "free" was some other book. At the bottom of the ad was a coupon that the consumer filled out and sent in. This constituted a contract with the new member. The coupon stated that the consumer would receive free the designated book, and that that person agreed to purchase at least four books-of-the-month a year from the club. However, in the court's opinion, there was no free book. If the member failed to buy the four other books within the year's time, the club would demand payment for the "free" book. The book was not a gift. It was not free.

In deciding this case the court looked at a definition given by the FTC on January 14, 1948.[6] The definition read as follows:

> The use of the word *free* or words of similar import, in advertising to designate or describe merchandise . . . that is not in truth

---

[6]Federal Register, January 14, 1948, Administrative interpretations with reference to the use of the word *free* and words of similar import under certain conditions to describe merchandise.

and in fact a gift or gratuity or is not given to the recipient thereof without requiring the purchase of other merchandise or requiring the performance of some other service . . . is considered by the commission to be a violation of the Federal Trade Commission Act.

For another example of how not to use the word *free,* let's look at *FTC* v. *Mary Carter Paint Co.,* 382 U.S. 46, 86 S.Ct. 219, 15 L.Ed. 2d 128 (Brennan, J., 1965). Here, Mary Carter Paint had a practice of advertising that for every can of paint purchased the buyer would get a free can of equal quality. However, Mary Carter Paint Co. did not have a history of selling single cans of paint. In fact it only sold two can sets. The company claimed in its advertising that the usual and customary retail price of each single can of paint was $6.98. This was actually the price needed to cover the cost of two cans of paint. What Mary Carter did, in essence, was double the retail price of its paint, sell the cans in twin sets, and then offer one of the cans as "free." Mary Carter's practice was deceptive and violated the FTC Act.

On February 8, 1968, an American Army officer firing on Ben Tre, Vietnam, said, "It became necessary to destroy the town in order to save it." It's not what you call it, it's what it is that counts.

USING QUALIFYING LANGUAGE TO OVERCOME DECEPTION

Another area of concern is when a deceptive statement is made in an advertisement and the advertiser tries to offset the deception by clarifying it elsewhere with other language—the proverbial "small print." The practice of clarifying a deceptive—or possibly deceptive—claim with other language is sound policy for the advertiser. However, if the false statement is more noticeable than the qualification, either intentionally or unintentionally, then the statement will still be considered false.

The idea here is that the qualifying statement must relieve any misrepresentation made by the other statement. If this is effectively accomplished, deception has probably not occurred. But remember, this works only if the qualifying statement is made with the same weight and conspicuousness. But where the qualifying statement is made in an inconspicuous manner (compared to the qualified statement), then it has been held that deception probably exists.

Double Eagle Lubricants manufactured a motor oil that was re-refined from previously used oil. The oil was displayed in the standard one-quart can, the type found in any auto parts store. The trade name of the product was printed on the front of the can. On the side of the can was printed a statement that the oil was re-refined.

The cans were intended for display with the fronts showing, stacked side-by-side on the shelf. The front of the can faced the prospective customer to attract his attention. By placing the clarifying statements on the side of the can, the customer would conceivably pick up the can and purchase it based on the face label. For there to be a clear and conspicuous disclosure, the clarifying statement should have appeared on the front panel of the can.

The court's case, *Double Eagle Lubricants, Inc.* v. *FTC*, 360 F.2d 268 (10th Cir. 1965), discussed this situation and found that the labeling practice was deceptive. True, Double Eagle had made a disclosure about the product, but not with enough weight to avoid a misinformed purchase. What was interesting in this case was that Double Eagle brought in witnesses who testified that the labeling did not deceive them. However, the court reasoned that evidence of deception was not necessary "where the exhibits themselves sufficiently demonstrate their capacity to deceive."

Here, evidence was shown that a product was nondeceptive to certain people. Yet the court, in deciding against Double Eagle, said:

> Evidence of deception is not necessary where the exhibits themselves sufficiently demonstrate their capacity to deceive.

> If the Commission can find deception without evidence that the public was deceived, we believe that it can make the same finding on the basis of its visual examination of exhibits even

though numerous members of the public have testified that they were not deceived.

Visibility of a Qualifying Statement

In *Giant Food, Inc.* v. *FTC,* 322 F.2d 977 (D.C. Circuit 1963) cert. dismissed, 376 U.S. 976 (1964), the qualifying statement was not placed close to the statement that it was supposed to clarify. This case dealt with the small print in an ad. Giant Food, Inc., a large eastern retail chain, advertised its products through the newspapers. Giant Food advertised its sale price along with what it referred to as a regular price. The regular price was derived from a manufacturer's suggested price list and was not indicative of prices that the merchandise was ever actually sold at in the area.

A typical ad, which ran in three Washington, D.C. area newspapers, read as follows:

Proctor Steam & Dry Iron #10010
Regular Price $15.95
Sale Price $8.47

Giant Food used the phrase *Regular Price* in such a way that led the consumer to believe that it had sold the product at that price "in the recent, regular course of its business." That was untrue. Giant Food argued that its advertising was not deceptive because a disclaimer in small print ran at the bottom of the ad. The disclaimer was worded in a rather lengthy and confusing manner. The witnesses who testified at the trial said that they would not normally read the disclaimer, or that they would have been more confused if they had read it. The court said, "That the disclaimer might engender confusion appears to us . . . to be an understatement."

Giant Food also used the phrase *Manufacturer's List,* which represented to the consumer that that was the price at which the product was usually and customarily sold at retail. In fact, the manufacturer's list was substantially in excess of the usual and customary retail price. The way to look at this is if you state a "regular price" in an ad, the product must have actually been offered by you, at that price, within the previous 30 days.

CONSUMER'S KNOWLEDGE OF A FALSE STATEMENT

What happens when the consumer knows that an advertisement is false? Simply because the consumer knows that a claim is false does not relieve its being deceptive.

In *Heavenly Creations, Inc.* v. *FTC*, 339 F.2d 7 (2d Cir. 1964), knowledge of false statements was the issue. Although this case involved dealers, rather than consumers, the practice was still deceptive. Heavenly Creations sold a variety of products to distributors, jobbers, salesmen, and retailers. These products were then resold to consumers. The problem here was with the pricing of the manufacturer's product to the dealers.

Dealers knew that Heavenly Creations had a practice of preticketing goods at inflated prices. Heavenly, as a defense, tried to prove that there was a custom of fictitious pricing within the retail trade. However, the court maintained that "A practice does not cease to be . . . unfair because the falsity of the . . . representation has become so well-known to the trade that dealers . . . are no longer deceived."

CLAIMS OF UNIQUENESS

A claim of uniqueness about a product or service is another area of concern under Section 5 of the FTC Act. It is deceptive to state that a product has extraordinary features or is unique, if it is not. But what is considered to be a claim of uniqueness? Again, it's based on the average consumer of that type of product.

Fedders Corporation manufactured air conditioners and, in the mid-1970s, advertised them as being unique due to their having "reserve cooling power." This was a claim that could not be substantiated. In *Fedders Corp.* v. *FTC*, 529 F.2d 1398 (2d

Cir. 1976), they even admitted that the statement *reserve cooling power* was "intended to imply an unusual ability to produce cold air under extreme conditions of heat and humidity." The false claim that Fedders's air conditioners possessed "reserve cooling power" implied to the consumer that some feature of the cooling, circulation, or dehumidifying systems in the air conditioner allowed them to outperform other brands in extreme temperature situations. In reality, Fedders's air conditioners had no real technical advantage over its competitors' equipment.

The court ordered Fedders to cease and desist from making claims that its air conditioners were unique in any material respect, unless that was a fact which could be proven. In the commission's order, it made a statement to that effect. It would do well to quote from the order, since the reasoning is universal. The order prohibited Fedders from:

> Making, directly or indirectly, any statement or representation in any advertising or sales promotional material as to the air cooling, dehumidification, or circulation characteristics, capacity or capabilities of any air conditioner, unless at the time of such representation [they] have a reasonable basis for such statement or representation, which shall consist of competent scientific, engineering or other similar objective material or industry-wide standards based on such material.

PERFORMANCE CLAIMS

There are specific problems inherent in performance claims. These are claims that a product will do what the ad says it will do. The Fedders case we just looked at was a good example of this. In fact, uniqueness is a claim of performance.

Substantiation of Performance Claims

In *Sears, Roebuck and Co.* v. *FTC,* 676 F.2d 385 (9th Cir. 1982), the claim that "our dishwasher cleans dishes so well that they do not have to be pre-rinsed" was an example of an absolute performance claim. If the claim were made that "our dish-washer cleans better than theirs," it would be considered as a relative or comparative performance claim.

Sears, Roebuck & Co. is the largest retailer of general merchandise in the United States. In the early 1970s Sears devised a program to increase the sales of its "Lady Kenmore" dishwasher. Sears did not reengineer or redesign the product. Instead it attempted to change the image of—or reposition—the product. The objective was expressed by Sears's advertising agency (95 FTC 406) as seeking to:

> transform the consumer image [of the Lady Kenmore] from a price brand to a superior product at a reasonable price. Eventually, the brand should move from market leadership to market dominance as the market share increases.

Sears produced ads claiming that the Lady Kenmore "completely eliminated" the need for prescraping and prerinsing. Sears labeled the machine as the Freedom Maker. In various media over a four-year period, and at a cost of over $8 million, Sears advertising for the Lady Kenmore claimed:

SEARS LADY KENMORE
THE DO-IT-ITSELF DISHWASHER
No scraping. No rinsing. Lady Kenmore has 6 powerful
hot water jets for the bottom rack,
surging hot water with enough force to
scrub every dish, pot and pan really clean.
Even baked-on food comes off.
And the dishes on top get as clean as those on the bottom.

With a Kenmore you'll never have to scrape or rinse again.
Even dishes crusty with leftover food.
Kenmore's 14 powerful hot water jets scour every dish clean
. . . with no scraping or rinsing.

It's great! You'll like the way it makes pre-rinsing
and soaking of heavily soiled dishes, pots and pans
a thing of the past.

Gets even the messiest baking dishes and roasting pans
spotlessly clean . . . without pre-rinsing!

Wouldn't the woman in your life love a Kenmore Dishwasher
for Mother's Day?

> A Kenmore Dishwasher from Sears means no more dishpan hands,
> she'll never have to touch dishwater again!
> Egg, lipstick, peanut butter, jelly, even spaghetti sauce
> come right off with no pre-rinsing.

As a result of the Lady Kenmore campaign, unit sales rose more than 300 percent from 35,029 units in 1971 to 105,570 units in 1973. Sears's total dishwasher sales rose from $73.47 million to $94.5 million during that period.

Now let's look at the reality of the case. Sears's "no scraping, no pre-rinsing" claim was simply not true, and it had no reasonable basis upon which to make the claim. In fact, the instruction manual, which customers received after their purchase, contradicted the claim. The manual specifically instructed the owner to presoak or lightly scour certain dishes.

What the commission ordered Sears to do is worth noting. In addition to a cease-and-desist order, Sears was ordered to maintain written records "in connection with the advertising, offering for sale, sale, or distribution of dishwashers or other major home appliances." The records required included:

1. All materials that were relied upon in making any claim or representation in advertising . . . concerning the performance characteristics of any Sears . . . dishwashers or other major home appliances;
2. All test reports, studies, surveys, or demonstrations . . . that contradict, qualify, or call into question any claim or representation in advertising . . . on behalf of . . . Sears, Roebuck & Co.'s dishwashers or other major home appliances . . . for a period of three years.

Requirements of Substantiation

We've seen that if you make a claim in an ad, you must be able to substantiate it. That brings up a valid question. What type of substantiation is acceptable? The courts have decided that the proof to support a claim must have a reasonable basis. In other words, the proof can't be contrived, out of context, or based on distorted facts or statistics. This was discussed in *F.T.C.* v. *Pharmtech Research, Inc.,* 576 F. Supp. 294, (D.D.C. 1983).

In July 1983, a television commercial aired for a product manufactured by Pharmtech Research called Daily Greens.

The following message concerns a revolutionary new concept in diet and nutrition. According to this report, commissioned by the National Cancer Institute, a combination of cruciferous and carotene rich vegetables, has been proven to help our bodies build certain important biological defenses. Of course, to get the most benefit from any vegetable, you should eat them raw. But that's difficult to do everyday. So I'd like to introduce you to Daily Greens. Daily Greens are not just another vitamin pill. They're natural, fresh, cruciferous and carotene-rich vegetables, dehydrated and compressed, to give you the important nutritional supplements that could be so vital to your future health. So, if you're not getting enough raw vegetables, everyday, rely on Daily Greens—to help your body defend itself.

Advertisements ran in magazines, on the radio, and on television. While each ad varied somewhat, they all claimed that by taking Daily Greens the consumer would reduce the risk of certain cancers. The claim was also made that using Daily Greens would contribute to building certain biological defenses.

The advertisements didn't claim that the use of Daily Greens would prevent cancer. Yet the problem stemmed from the fact that Pharmtech relied solely on a report published by the National Academy of Sciences entitled *Diet, Nutrition, and Cancer.* The report itself states: "These recommendations apply only to foods as sources of nutrients—not to dietary supplements of individual nutrients." The committee also warned "that the removal of water which occurs during dehydration may alter the protective effect of nutrients and other compounds."

Pharmtech's ads represent that the use of Daily Greens is connected to a reduction in the risk of cancer. The Daily Greens ads are deceptive for two reasons. First, they misstate the findings of the report—that the use of supplements reduces the risk of cancer or the building of biological defenses. Second, they fail to disclose some important material facts—that the report's findings did not apply to processed supplements, but only whole foods. In other words, the report was taken and used out of context. The ad substantiation did not have a reasonable basis.

DECEPTION BY IMPLICATION OR INFERENCE

In ads that contain deception by implication or inference there is no specific untruth, yet for various reasons the advertisement's net impression is not one of truthfulness. You may have gathered by now that I am a fan of Mark Twain. In 1884 he wrote *The Adventures of Huckleberry Finn.* In Chapter 1 Huck describes the way Twain had written about him earlier in *The Adventures of Tom Sawyer.* In Huck's honest opinion he said about Twain: " . . . he told the truth, mainly. There was things which he stretched, but mainly he told the truth."

An ad can cause the same effect. Some mainly tell the truth while some are stretched quite a bit. But an ad is not a work of fiction. At least, it's not supposed to be. It's a commercial message that has to create an impression of truthfulness. And it has to live up to that impression. An important point is that an advertiser should not try to hide behind the excuse that there was no intention to deceive. A claim of an *innocent* deception is no defense. The ad speaks for itself.

Innuendo That Creates Deception

Obvious misrepresentations are one thing. But deception through innuendo is much more subtle. The makers of Hollywood brand bread created the impression that its product was a low calorie food. Specifically, the Hollywood bread advertisements claimed that its product was lower in calories than ordinary bread; and, that by using Hollywood in a normal diet, the user would lose weight or prevent a weight gain.

The ads for Hollywood bread showed a picture of a beautiful movie star in a sleek full-length pose. The ads also showed a picture of the product. The copy read:

> When a woman's Panther Slim,
> she's vital as well as slender.

A good figure is more than luck when a lady
watches her weight the famous Hollywood Way.
Hollywood Bread is high in protein, vitamins
and minerals, yet has only 46 calories per 18 gram slice.
Choice of Golden Light or
Nut-like Dark Hollywood.

The court in *National Bakers Serv. Inc.* v. *FTC,* 329 F.2d
365 (7th Cir. 1964), found that the average consumer had no
perception of the average caloric content or gram weight of a
slice of bread. It also felt that the claim "only 46 calories per
18 gram slice" was intended to, and did, convey the impression
that Hollywood bread had fewer calories than other breads.
The claim also implied that by eating the same amount of Hollywood bread as other breads, the consumer could lose weight.

In reality, there is no significant difference in the caloric
content of Hollywood bread and other commercial white
breads. Both contain about 276 calories per 100 grams. However, other breads are sliced into twenty 23-gram slices while
Hollywood is sliced into twenty-five 18-gram slices. The only
reason that Hollywood bread contains fewer calories per slice
is that it is sliced thinner.

The ad was technically true in that there were no incorrect facts. Yet the innuendo created an impression that was not
altogether truthful. Hollywood bread had no fewer calories
than other commercial breads, and, in fact, its only usefulness
in a diet came from the fact that its thinner slices meant the
consumer would consume smaller individual portions and
therefore fewer calories.

Implication That Creates Deception

Another area for concern under Section 5 is deception by inference or implication. Between 1967 and 1968, Firestone Tire
Company ran ads which claimed:

THE SAFE TIRE. FIRESTONE.
When you buy a Firestone tire
—no matter how much or how little you pay—
you get a safe tire.

Firestone tires are custom-built one by one
by skilled craftsmen.
And they're personally inspected for an extra margin of safety.
If these tires don't pass all of the exacting
Firestone inspections, they don't get out.
Every new Firestone design goes through rugged tests
of safety and strength far exceeding any driving
condition you'll ever encounter.
We prove them in our test lab,
on our test track,
and in rigorous day-to-day driving conditions.
All Firestone tires meet or exceed the new
federal government testing requirements
(They have for some time.)
Firestone—The Safe Tire.
At 60,000 Firestone Safe Tire Centers.
At no more cost than ordinary tires.

Firestone, in *Firestone Tire & Rubber Co.* v. *FTC*, 481 F.2d 246 (6th Cir. 1973), admitted that it was technologically impossible to assure that a tire was free of defects. By implying an unqualified assertion of safety, they created a deceptive ad. While Firestone made no explicit claim about the safety of its tires under all driving and road conditions, it did imply a claim. The court said: "[Firestone's] advertisement asserts flatly that the Firestone tire is 'The Safe Tire' and describes the exacting rugged tests . . . which the tires are put through to assure this safety. [Firestone's] advertisement gives no indication that there is any limit to the safety of this tire." As a result of this case Firestone was required to disclose clearly and conspicuously, in close proximity to any safety claim, that "the safety of any tire is affected by conditions of use, such as inflation pressure, vehicle weight, wear, and other operating conditions."

THE USE OF TECHNICAL LANGUAGE AND VAGUENESS

Deception can be accomplished through the use of technical language that the consumer is not likely to understand, or by making vague or ambiguous statements. Technical language or complicated verbiage cannot be expected to be understood by the average consumer.

Using a Foreign Language

About 1840 Edouard Pinaud opened a business in Paris, France, to manufacture perfumes. His goods, as well as his name, became very well known. Ed. Pinaud for many years built a reputation for the quality of his products. After Pinaud's death in 1868, the Klotz Company took over the Pinaud line.

From 1891 to 1895 a Mr. Hecht worked for Klotz. After leaving, Hecht began manufacturing in the United States his own line of toilet preparations. Hecht's bottles, contents, stoppers, and labels were all made in the United States. The labels however were printed in French. The labels contained the sentence:

Preparee par M. Hecht,
Dernierement avec Parfumerie Ed. Pinaud, Paris.

Roughly translated the line means "Prepared by Mr. Hecht, formerly with perfumer Ed. Pinaud, Paris." The court in *Koltz* v. *Hecht,* 73 F. 822 (2d Cir. 1896), stated that using foreign words, although literally true, can be considered deceptive. Hecht admitted at the trial that it, in fact, was his intent to mislead the public into believing that his domestic perfume was made in France, therefore trading on the reputation of French perfume and the name of Ed. Pinaud. While it was true that nowhere on the bottle was it stated that the product was foreign made, Hecht ingeniously conveyed that impression through his labeling—especially if the purchaser was not fluent in French.

Deception by Implying a Technical Term

Let's look at another example. The following ad ran in trade magazines (directed toward mattress manufacturers) by a manufacturer of mattress cloth:

STERITIZED FABRIC has a proven sales idea,
proven in shoes, proven in clothes, proven in hats.
The sales appeal of a STERITIZED FABRIC has been proven
in many other fields.
We are not guessing when we say that what has been done
in the shoe, the hat, and the dress industries
can also be done in the mattress industry.
In the Nation's Greatest Stores,
other merchandise has shown sales jumps by using the same
Germ-Repellent Method.
STERITIZED FABRIC—Repellent to Bacteria. Repellent to Water.
STERITIZED mattress ticking avoids perspiration, stains, and odor.
STERITIZED FABRIC is absolutely noninjurious.
STERITIZED FABRIC Repels Germs,
Helps protect all the family against spread of infection,
is positively nonirritating, guards against odors.
STERITIZED Mattress Fabric . . .
Tested under standards stated in Circular 198,
U.S. Department of Agriculture,
made by Blumenthal Print Works, New Orleans, U.S.A.
Blumenthal Print Works, Converters of Cotton Cloth.

In the *Matter of Blumenthal*, 43 F.T.C. 158 (1946), the use of the word *Steritized* created a problem for the advertiser because the buyer perceived the word to say *sterilized*. This was a natural assumption. Why was this a problem if the fabric lived up to the claims? Well, there's the rub. It didn't. The steritized fabric didn't do any of the things that the ad claimed it could. It was not sterile, sanitary, antiseptic, odorless, bacteriostatic, or bacteria-, germ-, or water-repellent. It would not prevent perspiration odors, wear longer, or guard against the spread of infection. People would believe that, by some new sterilizing process, the Blumenthal fabric could have all of the claimed qualities. Blumenthal simply made up a name for its product, which bore an amazing resemblance to another word.

Deception through Technical Language

In *Chrysler Corp.* v. *FTC*, 561 F.2d 357 (D.C. Cir. 1977), we see an example of confusing technical language. During the

1973–74 energy crisis, Chrysler ran ads for their Dodge Darts. A typical ad ran as follows:

THE SMALL CAR VS. THE SMALL CAR
You can buy a Chevrolet Nova OR
you can buy a small car that can beat
it on gas mileage*. . . .
* * * * *
The answer is a small car at your
Chrysler-Plymouth and Dodge dealers. . . .
* * * * *
See all the Darts at your Dodge/Dodge Trucks dealer.
See the Dusters and Valiants at your
Chrysler-Plymouth dealer.

The asterisk in the ad referred to a footnote which read: "Gas mileage figures based on October 1973 *Popular Science* magazine. Tests performed by *Popular Science* for its report were conducted on '73 vehicles with figures adjusted by *Popular Science* for 1974 model changes and the results of EPA tests."

That was one of a series of ads, all with the same message. The *Popular Science* tests that are referred to in the ad showed that the Plymouth Valiant and Dodge Dart equipped with 6-cylinder engines got better gas mileage than a Chevrolet Nova equipped with either a 6-cylinder or a V-8 engine. The same report also showed that Valiants and Darts equipped with V-8 engines got worse mileage results than Novas equipped with V-8s or 6-cylinder engines. In essence, the ads claimed that, based on the magazine report, all Chrysler small cars got better gas mileage than all Chevrolet Novas. In reality, however, the report covered only those cars equipped with 6-cylinder engines. But that was not stated clearly in the ad.

DECEPTIVE TRUTH

Up to this point, we have dealt with deceptive untruths. But what about deceptive truth? There is a common element to all of the cases involving statements of deceptive, literal truth. That is, there is always some element missing, or a conclusion is inferable that is short of the truth.

In *Donaldson* v. *Read Magazine, Inc.,* 333 U.S. 178 (1947), the court discussed advertisements that, as a whole, may be misleading even though every sentence taken separately is literally true. This may occur when things are omitted or when advertisements are composed in such a way that they mislead.

Donaldson, who was the Postmaster General, sued *Read Magazine* based on its puzzle contests. Donaldson sued because he felt that *Read's* contest was "a scheme . . . for obtaining money through the mails by means of false and fraudulent pretenses, representations, and promises."[7]

In 1945 *Read Magazine* advertised its *Facts Magazine* Hall of Fame Puzzle Contest. Customers were led to believe that they would be eligible to win prizes by paying a $3 fee. In reality they would have to pay up to $42. Customers were also led to believe that the contest was a puzzle contest. It was not. The puzzles were so easy to solve that most people would solve all of them. The prizes were awarded, if the truth be known, based on a tie-breaking letter-essay contest.

Read Magazine argued that it had explained all of these facts in its ads. The ads contained wording that specified that the first $3 puzzles might result in a tie. This would require a second and third series of $3 puzzles. Ultimately, if no winner appeared, one would be selected based on essays on "The Puzzle I Found Most Interesting and Educational in This Contest."

There were sentences in *Read's* advertisements which, taken alone, would have conveyed to a deliberate reader all of these details of the contest. But they were not sentences standing alone. They were small and inconspicuous bits of lengthy descriptions. *Read's* ads were very long, and its form letters to contestants were even more lengthy.

In bold one inch type their ads barked:

$10,000 FIRST PRIZE PUZZLE CONTEST

Pictures of sample puzzles covered the page. The ads left little doubt that the contest presented an opportunity to win large

---

[7]39 U.S.C. 259, 732.

prizes (remember, this was 1947) by solving the puzzles. In the lower left corner of the ad appeared the "Official Rules of the Contest." There were 10 rules. About the middle of the ninth rule appeared the only reference to the possible need for essay letters as a means of tie-breaking. While all of the information was in the ad, and no claims were made that were not factual, the ad was still deceptive. Granted there is a fine line here, but there is still a line.

CONCLUSION

Having now studied the various problem areas involving Section 5 of the Federal Trade Commission Act, the advertiser will be better equipped to avoid creating a deceptive ad. Advertisers and their agencies, with this knowledge in mind, must carefully and objectively evaluate their advertising to avoid trouble.

CHAPTER 4

ADVERTISING'S PART IN PRODUCTS LIABILITY

It's such a perfectly imperfect human thing.
—*Charles Bragg*

"This is a stickup. Open the safe." Startled, John Klages turned toward the voice from the other side of the registration counter. Klages worked as a night clerk at Conley's Motel in Hampton Township, Pennsylvania. It was about 1:30 A.M. on an otherwise quiet March morning, and two armed men stood across the counter. Klages indicated that he didn't have the combination to the safe. In an instant, one of the robbers pointed a gun at him and fired. The gun, fortunately, was only a starter pistol, and Klages suffered only minor injuries.

The day after the robbery attempt, Klages decided that he needed something to protect himself from future holdups. After reading some literature, a fellow employee, Bob McVay, suggested that they investigate mace as a weapon. McVay gathered four brochures from Markl Supply Company. The manufacturer of the mace weapon was General Ordnance Equipment Corporation. Klages selected the MK–II model because it was easy to conceal yet had the stopping power that he felt he needed.

The literature claimed that the product:

Rapidly vaporizes on face of assailant effecting
instantaneous incapacitation . . . .
It will instantly stop and subdue entire groups . . . .
Instantly stops assailants in their tracks . . . .
An attacker is subdued—instantly, for a period
of 15 to 20 minutes . . . .
Time magazine stated the chemical mace is

"for police the first, if not the final,
answer to a nationwide need . . ."
A weapon that disables as effectively as a gun . . .
and yet does no permanent injury.
The effectiveness is the result of a unique
incapacitation formulation (patent pending)
projected in a shotgun-like pattern of heavy liquid droplets
that, upon contact with the face, cause extreme tearing,
and a stunned, winded condition, often accompanied
by dizziness and apathy.

McVay and Klages read the brochure and, after discussing it with their boss, purchased an MK–II mace weapon from Markl Supply.

About 1:40 on the morning of September 22, 1968, two men entered the motel office where Klages was again on duty. The two men requested a room. Klages handed them a registration form and turned to reach for the room key. One of the men announced that it was a holdup, pulled out a gun, and demanded that Klages open the safe.

Klages moved over behind the cash register where the mace was kept and, using the register as a shield, squirted the mace directly into the robber's face. Klages quickly ducked behind the counter. Unfortunately, the robber followed and shot him in the head—this time with a real gun, with real bullets. He survived the attack, but the bullet wound left Klages blind in his right eye.

Klages sued General Ordnance for damages. On March 4, 1974, a jury trial began in *Klages* v. *General Ordnance Equipment Corp.*, CCH Prods. Liab. Rep. Paragraph 7664 (Pa. Super. 1976). When it was over, the jury ruled in favor of Klages, awarding him $42,000.

This case is an example of products liability. Granted, the advertising did not cause the injury. The advertising was the machinery that created the image in the mind of the consumer—an image that the product would perform in a certain way. The manufacturer made a product for a specific purpose. The consumer purchased the product for that purpose. When the product failed to live up to it, the manufacturer was liable for the injury that resulted.

A manufacturer, through its advertising, implies that its product is safe for—and/or will perform—its intended use. The manufacturer makes a promise or representation about his product. In the Klages case the manufacturer sold a product designed solely as a device to deter would-be assailants. Its sole use was to protect the purchasers from harm under extremely dangerous conditions. Klages bought the product with these specific purposes in mind. The product failed to live up to its promise, and the injury that resulted made the manufacturer liable.

PRODUCTS LIABILITY AND ITS EFFECT ON ADVERTISING

Products liability is an area of law that deals with a product's failure to perform whatever function it was sold for. In this chapter we explore the connection between a company's advertising and products liability lawsuits.

The manufacturer's advertising or promotion may be a direct reason to bring a suit or it may become evidence during a suit, evidence that can establish what the consumer expected from the product. The advertising may demonstrate the manufacturer's inability to live up to the representations made in the advertisement.

In the eyes of the law, a manufacturer is liable for any deficiency in its product. The point here is that in products liability lawsuits, the advertising somehow lulled the consumer into a false sense of security about the product's safety or capability—enough to induce him into its purchase or use. This was the case with Klages.

Theories of Products Liability

To assess the role that advertising plays in products liability litigation, we should understand that there are a number of legal theories under which a products liability lawsuit can be brought. Those theories are briefly described below with specific illustrative cases, which you'll find discussed later in the chapter.

Negligence exists when there is a failure to exercise reasonable care to protect others against high risks. A manufacturer may be negligent for an act (such as poor quality control) or for a failure to act (such as not testing the product). See *Baxter* v. *Ford Motor Co.* on page 69.

Deceit occurs when there is intent to mislead regarding the existence or nonexistence of a material fact and the consumer relies on the misleading information and damages result. A good example is *Bahlman* v. *Hudson Motor Car Co.* on page 74.

Fraudulent concealment covers situations in which the manufacturer withholds information when he has a duty to speak. A case in point is *Hasson* v. *Ford Motor Co.* on page 80.

Negligent misrepresentation allows the consumer to bring suit when the manufacturer's statements become misrepresentations that he should have known were untrue or inaccurate. Again, this deals with the duty of reasonable care. See *Leichtamer* v. *American Motors Corp.* on page 78.

Strict liability holds the manufacturer liable for a consumer's physical injury resulting from a misrepresentation about the product. In these cases the consumer does not need to prove that the misrepresentation was made negligently or fraudulently. An example is *Procter & Gamble Mfg. Co.* v. *Superior Court* on page 71.

Express warranty is any specific warranty that becomes a part of the purchase. Any act, representation, affirmation of fact, or promise made by the manufacturer about the product becomes a part of the bargain.[1] This creates an express warranty that the product will live up to the act, representation, and so on. See *Greenman* v. *Yuba Power Prods., Inc.* on page 71.

Implied warranty exists by operation of law. Simply stated, it is implied in the sale of the product. One such warranty is for merchantability.[2] There is also a warranty of fitness for a

---

[1] Uniform Commercial Code, Section 2-313.
[2] Uniform Commercial Code, Section 2-314.

particular purpose.[3] Two good examples are *Ford Motor Co.* v. *Lonon* on page 73, and *Filler* v. *Rayex Corp.* on page 76.

Strict tort liability occurs when the product is defective and that defect causes injury or damage. It is not necessary to prove that the manufacturer or seller was negligent.[4] A good example is *Greenman* v. *Yuba Power Prods., Inc.,* on page 71.

These theories form the basis for all of the cases in this chapter. In one form or another, all products liability litigation stems from these areas of law.

Placing Liability on Advertising Claims

In *Rogers* v. *Toni Home Permanent Co.,* 167 Ohio St. 244, 147 N.E. 2d 612 (1958), Ms. Rogers purchased a Toni Home Permanent set marked "Very Gentle." She bought the product because of the manufacturer's claims in its advertising and on its packaging. After following the directions supplied with the kit, Rogers's hair became "cotton-like . . . and . . . gummy." Her hair would not dry, and when the curlers supplied with the kit were removed, her hair fell out, leaving only one-half inch of hair remaining.

This case is important because it was the first time the court made an effort to change how a manufacturer's liability was viewed. Originally, a consumer could sue only the seller of a product for breach of warranty. It was considered that no contract existed between the ultimate consumer and the manufacturer, and therefore no warranty existed. The only contract was between the consumer and the store where the item was purchased. The manufacturer could not be sued directly, except for cases of negligence.

In recent years, however, the courts have taken the position that the consumer could sue the manufacturer directly for breach of warranty actions (otherwise known as products liability). The court said:

---

[3]Uniform Commercial Code, Section 2-315.
[4]Restatement of Torts (Second), Section 402A.

Today, many manufacturers of merchandise, including the defendant herein, make extensive use of newspapers, periodicals, signboards, radio, and television to advertise their products. The worth, quality, and benefits of these products are described in glowing terms and in considerable detail, and the appeal is almost universally directed to the ultimate consumer. Many of these manufactured articles are shipped out in sealed containers by the manufacturer, and the retailers who dispense them to the ultimate consumers are but conduits or outlets through which the manufacturer distributes his goods. The consuming public ordinarily relies exclusively on the representations of the manufacturer in his advertisements. What sensible or sound reason then exists as to why, when the goods purchased by the ultimate consumer on the strength of the advertisements aimed squarely at him do not possess their described qualities and goodness and cause him harm, he should not be permitted to move against the manufacturer to recoup his loss. In our minds no good or valid reason exists for denying him that right. Surely under modern merchandising practices the manufacturer owes a very real obligation toward those who consume or use his products. The warranties made by the manufacturer in his advertisements and by the labels on his products are inducements to the ultimate consumers, and the manufacturer ought to be held to strict accountability to any consumer who buys the product in reliance on such representations and later suffers injury because the product proves to be defective.

Basically, products liability cases involve the performance that the consumer can reasonably expect from a product and also any resulting injury because of a consumer's expectations.

Products liability is not an area in which a manufacturer can be sued because of an advertising claim. However, products liability cases can be made using the advertising as proof of what the consumer expected from the product. Since advertising imparts an image, that image can become a large part of what the consumer expects when he or she purchases the product. If it fails, the advertising can be brought in to substantiate what the consumer expected and if the manufacturer is liable for any injury that resulted.

Now let's take a closer look at some cases that involve products liability issues and advertising.

THE SHATTERPROOF GLASS CASE

In one case, the literature about an automobile claimed that the windshield of the car was shatterproof. The case was *Baxter* v. *Ford Motor Co.*, 12 P.2d 409, aff'd on rehearing, 15 P.2d 1118 (Wash. Sup. Ct. 1932). During the month of May in 1930, Mr. Baxter purchased a Model A Ford town sedan from St. John Motors, an authorized Ford dealer. Baxter had read and relied on statements made in Ford's promotional literature— statements that the windshield was made of glass that would not break or shatter. Baxter recovered damages because on October 12, 1930, while driving the car, a flying rock shattered the windshield of his car, causing small pieces of glass to destroy his left eye. The literature that Baxter read contained the following:

Triplex Shatterproof Glass Windshield

All of the new Ford cars have a Triplex shatterproof glass
windshield—so made that it will not fly or shatter under the
hardest impact. This is an important safety factor because
it eliminates the dangers of flying glass—
the cause of most of the injuries in automobile accidents.
In these days of crowded, heavy traffic, the use of this
Triplex glass is an absolute necessity.
Its extra margin of safety is something that every motorist
should look for in the purchase of a car—
especially where there are women and children.

In essence, Ford should have known that the statements were true or it should not have made them. In other words, Ford was negligent. The court said:

If a person states as true material facts . . . to one who relies and acts thereon to his injury, if the representations are false, it is immaterial that he did not know they were false or that he believed them to be true.

The automobile was represented as having a shatterproof windshield. By examining the car, the average consumer would not know if that representation was true. Statements of the manufacturer would have to be relied on.

Since the concept of caveat emptor (buyer beware) was first created, the complexity of doing business has undergone many changes. Advertising has become a major factor in creating the demand that causes goods to flow from manufacturer to ultimate consumer. As we discussed earlier, the manufacturer is bound to a form of strict liability to the buyer. Strict liability places absolute liability on the advertiser for a consumer's physical injury resulting from a misrepresentation about the product. The manufacturer is liable to the buyer for representations that are proven to be false whether in advertisements, literature, or in a document that is passed along to the consumer by the dealer.

Let's look at a hypothetical situation. Acme Company manufactures hoists for cars. Acme distributes a manual that contains statements about the hoist's strength, lifting capacity, and so on. Mr. Jones goes into a local auto parts store and, after reading the literature, buys an Acme hoist. Jones uses the hoist to lift his car. The hoist does not have the lifting capacity that was stated in the literature, and as a result, Jones's car crashes to the floor injuring him. Acme is subject to strict liability to Jones.

Similar situations may occur in almost any form. But the form that the representation takes is not important. In fact, a representation may be in the form of an advertisement on the radio or television, in the newspaper, or in other literature (labels on the product, packaging material, and so on). It can be written or oral. For strict liability to exist, there must be an issue of fact in the advertising claim. In other words, the representation that the consumer relied on must be presented as a fact. This type of claim is more than just puffing, fantasy advertising, and the like. To illustrate this concept, let's go back to our earlier hypothetical example.

What if the hoist was advertised in the newspaper as "strong and safe for most uses," "the best available," or "the best for the price," or even "the most desirable." Could these types of statements give rise to a legal action if the product fails? There is no definite answer, but the advertiser must be cautious. Even general statements can be considered to carry implications of fact. Such statements as a detergent being "kind to the hands" or a power tool being "rugged" have involved implications of fact, as we see in this chapter.

In *Procter & Gamble Mfg. Co.* v. *Superior Court*, 268 P.2d 199 (Cal. App. 1954) the claim of a detergent being kind to the hands was at issue. On February 3, 1953, Loretta and Robert Jones filed suit in the Marin County Superior Court of California asking for $60,000 in damages. Loretta had been injured, as she alleged, while using Procter & Gamble's product Cheer. Her injury was "a severe dermatitis and dermatosis, causing nervousness and illness and inability to perform her household duties for a six-month period, as well as permanent disfigurement of her hands, which prior to that time were beautiful and smooth."

Claims of Quality Construction

In *Greenman* v. *Yuba Power Prods., Inc.*, 377 P.2d 897 (Cal. Sup. Ct. 1963) a claim of a power tool being rugged was discussed. Mr. Greenman saw a demonstration of a product called a Shopsmith. The Shopsmith was a combination power tool used as a drill, saw, and wood lathe. After studying a product brochure, Mr. Greenman decided that he wanted a Shopsmith. He told his wife this, and she purchased one for Christmas in 1955.

In 1957 Greenman purchased an attachment that would allow him to use the Shopsmith as a wood lathe. While working on a wood piece, it suddenly flew out of the lathe, striking Greenman in the head and causing serious injuries.

The jury returned an award for $65,000 in favor of Greenman. The court determined that Yuba Power Products had negligently constructed the Shopsmith. Expert witnesses determined that the set screws used to hold sections of the machine together were not adequate. Normal vibration would cause the screws to loosen, allowing the tailpiece of the lathe to move away from the spinning piece of wood and eventually allowing the wood to fly out of the lathe at high speed.

Here again, we see that the statements made in the manufacturer's product brochure were instrumental in determining the nature and extent of any express warranty that Yuba had made. As we saw earlier, an express warranty is created when any description, sample, model, fact, or promise is made by the seller to the buyer that relates to the goods and becomes part of the basis of the bargain. The express warranty is that the goods will live up to the promise. It does not matter that the advertiser knew or should have known that the express warranty was a misrepresentation.

The following information was contained in the Shopsmith brochure:

When Shopsmith Is in Horizontal Position—

Rugged construction of frame provides rigid support
from end to end.
Heavy, centerless-ground steel tubing ensures perfect
alignment of components.
SHOPSMITH maintains its accuracy because
every component has positive locks that hold adjustments
through rough or precision work.

The court wrote: "A manufacturer is strictly liable . . . when an article he places on the market, knowing that it is to be used without inspection for defects, proves to have a defect that causes injury to a human being." Simply because the Shopsmith was placed on the market, the consumer could assume that it was safe for the jobs for which it was built. Those jobs were detailed in the product brochure on which the consumer who purchases the product would rely. It does not matter that the manufacturer did not intend to mislead or cause harm. The harm occurred, and the manufacturer was liable. This holds true as long as the injury results from a defect in the product that appears when the product is being used as intended.

Liability for Commercial Loss

In February of 1962, Mr. Lonon purchased a Fordson Major Diesel tractor from the Haywood Tractor Company. Lonon was a farmer and needed a large tractor capable of performing certain tasks. He had visited the Ford tractor dealers in the area and had read the sales literature. He also had seen the many advertisements that Ford published in farm magazines and on television. The literature contained information about the live power take-off, the power steering lift, and other full specifications.

Over a period of time the tractor failed to perform the functions that were claimed it could perform. The tractor was taken in for repairs on many occasions with no effect. It was defective from the time that it was purchased. Lonon sued Ford after failing to receive any satisfaction. In *Ford Motor Co.* v. *Lonon,* 398 S.W.2d 240 (Tenn. 1966), the jury award of $4,000 was upheld. Lonon received $4,000 plus court costs for a tractor that originally cost him $4,243.10.

What makes this case interesting is that, unlike other products liability cases, there was no injury to the plaintiff. Most of the decisions hold the manufacturer liable for physical injury that was a direct result of the manufacturer's breach of warranty. In this case, we see that the courts can apply the same principle to commercial losses (losses of time and work as opposed to physical injury) that result from a defectively manufactured product.

THE SEAMLESS STEEL ROOF CASE—
IMPLIED SAFETY CLAIMS

Mr. Bahlman, a traveling shoe salesman, bought a 1936 model Hudson Eight Sedan from the Hudson Motor Car Company, based in part on the claim that the car had a seamless steel roof. The manufacturer, in its promotional literature, had represented that the car had that feature. In fact, the Hudson was touted as "A Rugged Fortress of Safety." However, in reality the roof was made of two separate parts. Typical of the advertising claims that Mr. Bahlman read were:

> Beneath the bigness and beauty, the safest car on today's
> highway, with the world's first safety engineering.
> Safeness combined with the first bodies all of steel.

> Bodies introduced last year by Hudson and now brought to new
> heights of strength and beauty with an improved
> seamless steel roof.
> * * * * *
> How, What, Why about the 1936 Hudsons and Terraplanes.
> A steel top which is a smooth, solid unit with the body shell.
> There are no seams or joints in the roof and body structure,
> just a complete steel body made from a single sheet of steel.

In *Bahlman* v. *Hudson Motor Car Co.,* 288 N.W. 309 (Mich. 1939), the court held for the plaintiff. Bahlman was injured by a jagged edge of the welded roof when his car overturned. Hudson had obviously conveyed an impression of a safety characteristic in its literature by claiming that the roof was one piece and therefore stronger than a welded roof.

The construction of the roof of the car was represented as a specific safety feature, and specifically as protection against the type of injury that Bahlman suffered. The fact that Bahlman's own negligent driving caused the accident was not significant because the safety feature existed to protect the people in the car from what actually took place. The safety features in a car are provided in the event of an accident regardless of who or what caused the accident.

THE ABSOLUTELY HARMLESS TOY CASE

On the packaging of the Ronson revolver, a toy pistol, was a picture of a small boy firing a Ronson revolver.

> In looks and action
> just like the real thing.
> B-A-N-G! F-L-A-S-H! S-M-O-K-E!
> Absolutely harmless.

Shortly before Christmas in 1926, William Crist was demonstrating a Ronson revolver in the Crist Department Store window in Circleville, Ohio. William, a child of less than 10, was dressed in a Santa Claus suit, complete with beard. When William fired one of the Ronson revolvers, the sparks from the toy ignited the soft cotton material of the Santa Claus suit. In seconds the boy was enveloped in flames and seriously injured. The court in *Crist* v. *Art Metal Works,* 243 N.Y. Supp. 496 (1st Dep't 1930), described the boy's injury as ". . . serious, painful, and permanent injuries, both externally and internally, about his head, face and limbs, . . . and . . . serious permanent disability and shock to his nervous system."

The interesting aspect of this case was that no defect in the product was alleged or discussed. In fact quite the contrary, the toy revolver operated perfectly. It was the claim that the toy was "absolutely safe" for a child that gave rise to the law suit. The advertising convincingly relieved all fear of possible injury to a child user. Here was a key example of where advertising plays a strong role in establishing the expectations of a product's performance. The product did not fail, but it failed to live up to its claim of safety.

There are cases in which the advertising or literature only suggests a safety quality. Other times a reference to safety is specific and direct, as in the case we just discussed. What is important for the advertiser to know is that the courts tend not to differentiate between these when looking at liability.

THE BASEBALL SUNGLASSES CASE

Richard Beck, the baseball coach at Oak Hill High School in Marion, Indiana, would not allow his players to wear sunglasses because he thought they were too dangerous. However, before the 1966 season he read the following advertisement for sunglasses in *Sporting News:*

PLAY BALL!

and Flip for Instant Eye Protection with
RAYEX
baseball
SUNGLASSES
Professional
FLIP-SPECS

> Scientific lenses protect your eyes with a flip
> from sun and glare anywhere . . .
> baseball, beach, boat, driving, golfing, fishing,
> just perfect for active and spectator sports
> —world's finest sunglasses.

The product packaging stated: "Simply flip . . . for instant eye protection," and "Rayex lenses are guaranteed for life against breakage."

After reading the advertisement and packaging, coach Beck purchased Rayex flip-down sunglasses for his team. One of the teenage boys on the team, Michael Filler, wore the glasses while playing in a game. A batted ball struck the boy in the face, breaking the glasses. The shattered glasses splintered and damaged one of the boy's eyes so badly that it had to be removed. The court in *Filler* v. *Rayex Corp.*, 435 F.2d 336 (7th Cir. 1970), in awarding damages in excess of $101,000 said about the product:

> Since they lacked the safety features of plastic or shatterproof glass, the sunglasses were in truth not fit for baseball playing, the particular purpose for which they were sold.

There was no explicit advertising claim about the shatterproof quality of the glasses. The ad copy referred only to protection against sun and glare. But they were advertised in a sporting magazine, directed to athletes, and stated that they were safe for use in baseball. The obvious implication was that they were safe for use in that sport, even though the manufacturer had not made adequate tests to support that claim. This was a case of a safety claim being implied, but a safety claim none the less. And along with the sale, an implied warranty was created.

Regarding a point that we covered earlier, an implied warranty means that the warranty is implied with the sale of the product. As we have discussed, there are warranties of merchantability and fitness for a particular purpose. Merchantability refers to the fitness of the product for the ordinary purposes for which such goods are used. Fitness for a particular purpose implies a specific use by the buyer which is peculiar to the nature of his business.

THE OVERTURNED GOLF CART CASE

The Missouri Supreme Court upheld a $94,000 award in *Blevins* v. *Cushman Motors*, 551 S.W. 2d 602 (Mo. 1977), involving a man being pinned under a golf cart that had overturned. Advertisements had appeared in golfing magazines promoting the Cushman golf cart. Typical of the ad's copy was:

> Talk about a turned on ride. Smooooth.
> With a beefier, low-slung 3-point rubber suspension.
> New rubber suspensions between power frame and main frame
> lets the GC tool through turns with super ease, super safety,
> super stability.
> Low ground-hugging center of gravity makes for wide stance,
> razor-honed handling.
> Fat, ground-gripping, turf-protecting 9.50 × 8 Terra Tires
> are standard.
> This baby floats the course.

On the afternoon of July 15, 1969, Albert Blevins and a friend met for a round of golf at the Stayton Meadows Golf Course. The two men began play using their Cushman Golf Cart. On the 13th hole the cart was being driven at about five miles per hour when it crossed a wet, shaded area. The cart skidded and turned over, throwing Blevins's friend clear of the cart. Blevins, however, fell on the ground and was pinned and injured by the overturned cart.

In order to win his case, Blevins needed to establish that the accident and damage resulted from a use of the product that was "reasonably anticipated." Blevins was required to show that the golf cart was used as that—a golf cart which could negotiate a golf course. Here the advertising clearly convinced the court that that use was not only anticipated but encouraged. The advertising showed a "justified use and reliance by the driver" of the cart. In fact, the advertising tended to draw the purchaser into a false sense of security as to the use of the cart and its safety.

PUNITIVE DAMAGES

Increasing indications show that advertising is being considered heavily as an influential factor in imposing punitive damages in certain law suits. Punitive damages are, in fact, damages awarded to punish the wrongdoer. They are also a strong deterrent for others to consider.

In *Leichtamer* v. *American Motors Corp.*, 424 N.E. 2d 568 (Ohio 1981), a four-wheel-drive vehicle overturned while going down an incline. On April 18, 1976, Paul Vance and his wife Cynthia invited Carl and Jeanne Leichtamer to go for a ride in the Vances' Jeep CJ–7. The Vances belonged to an off-road club located near Dundee, Ohio, which was an off-road park converted from an old strip mine.

While the Vances' Jeep was descending a double-terraced hill, the vehicle's rear end pitched over. The Jeep had cleared the first embankment; and after clearing the second, it landed on the front wheels. At that point, the rear end continued over the front end of the Jeep. The Jeep landed upside down pointing back up the hill. Paul and Cynthia Vance were killed. Carl Leichtamer sustained a skull fracture, and Jeanne Leichtamer became a paraplegic.

During the trial it was acknowledged that Paul Vance's negligence caused the accident. However, it was claimed that the Leichtamers' injuries were "substantially enhanced, intensified, aggravated, and prolonged" as a result of the failure of the factory-installed roll bar on the Jeep. The roll bar was offered as optional equipment on the Jeep CJ–7 and was promoted solely for protection in the event of a rollover. The roll bar was not structurally sound enough to withstand the pitchover that the Vances went through.

Jeep, a division of American Motors Corporation had produced a multimillion dollar television campaign that encouraged people to buy a Jeep:

> Ever discover the rough, exciting world of mountains,
> forests, rugged terrain?
> The original Jeep can get you there,
> and Jeep guts will bring you back.

This case illustrates the role advertising can play in the imposition of liability. The expectations that the consumer develops about the safety of a product are formed largely through the product's advertising. The manner in which a product's use is advertised is relevant to the use that the product is intended for.

The Jeep commercials depicted its qualities and safety in an off-road situation and stressed the Jeep's ability to negotiate steep hills. One particular spot challenged a young man, accompanied by his girl friend:

> "You guys aren't yellow, are you?
> Is it a steep hill?
> Yeah, little lady, you could say it is a steep hill.
> Let's try it.
> The King of the Hill is about to discover the new Jeep CJ-7."

The advertising clearly depicted the Jeep going up and down steep and rugged terrain safely. Even the owner's manual claimed that the Jeep could "proceed in safety down a grade which could not safely be negotiated by a conventional 2-wheel-drive vehicle."

The court felt that the advertising was a significant factor in supporting a finding for punitive damages since it showed the probable use of the vehicle while ignoring the danger that could likely result from that use. The court said:

> The commercial advertising clearly contemplates off-road use of the vehicle. The salesman's guide to the vehicle described the roll bar in the following terms:
> "Surround yourself and your passengers with the strength of a rugged, reinforced steel roll bar for added protection. A very practical item, and a must if you run competition with a 4WD club. Adds rugged good looks, too."
> Given the foreseeability of roll-overs and pitch-overs, the failure of appellants to test to determine whether the roll bar

"added protection" represents a flagrant indifference to the probability that a user might be exposed to an unreasonable risk of harm. For appellants to have encouraged off-the-road use while providing a roll bar that did little more than add "rugged good looks" is a sufficient basis for an award of punitive damages.

The Ohio Supreme Court granted a $2.2 million damage award in the case. Over half of the damages were punitive.

The Extent of Punitive Damages

Recently, the California Supreme Court affirmed a $9.2 million award in *Hasson* v. *Ford Motor Co.,* 19 Cal. 3d 530 (1977), CCH Prods. Liab. Rep. paragraph 9398 (Sept. 16, 1982). About $4 million were in punitive damages. The case developed because of a catastrophic brain injury suffered by the driver of a 1965 Lincoln Continental when the brakes failed on a hill. The driver established that the manufacturer failed to warn dealers and owners of a known problem with the brakes, and how to correct it, because it was protecting the model's reputation among customers. The manufacturer deliberately failed to test the problem and failed to install a dual master cylinder, which would have overcome the defect.

Deceit and fraudulent concealment—which we discussed at the beginning of this chapter—occur when the advertiser intends to mislead the consumer regarding a material fact about the product and the consumer relies on that information to his detriment. If the advertiser expressly misstates a fact, it is deceit. If the advertiser withholds information when he should give it out, it is fraudulent concealment.

The issue here was Ford's knowing disregard for the safety of the vehicle, something that its advertising convinced otherwise. Ford management had a policy of advertising that the Lincoln Continental was free from the need for service for a large portion of its components.

CONCLUSION

Advertisers must be aware of all areas of product liability. The portrayal of the product in advertising or promotional literature can be a major factor in claims against the integrity of the product. The stakes are high today in products liability litigation. Now, proof of liability has become facilitated by recent legal activity in this area. Claims are higher. Awards are higher. Juries are more willing to award substantial punitive damages.

CHAPTER 5

THE RIGHTS OF PRIVACY AND PUBLICITY

Civilization is the progress toward a society of privacy.
—*Ayn Rand*

The year is 1913. The place is an empty horse barn recently converted into a "factory where pictures that move are made." It's daytime, but the inside of the big empty barn is dark. Only bright sunlight streams through a window at the end of the room. A few stagehands move camera equipment around in the distance. The air is dusty. The floor is covered with straw.

As the television commercial we're watching continues, a man's feet step into view. A megaphone sits on the floor in front of his feet. The name *Mr. DeMille* is stenciled on it. The legendary director rocks in place in his knee-high riding boots, tense in anticipation.

The camera moves around him while he clutches a pair of leather gloves behind his back. His hands squeeze the gloves with nervous excitement. DeMille takes in the activity happening within the room. We see, almost as if a ghost, the image of an early 1900s train approaching from the distance. Then we see the image of an early 1900s camera crew on the set.

We hear a recognizable voice: "In 1913, a young director prepared to step off the train in Flagstaff, Arizona. But it was raining. So he stayed on to the end of the line and shot his feature-length Western in a rented barn in a quiet farming town . . . called Hollywood."

The last of the crew members have moved away and the director moves out of the picture. Through the stark light of the window emerges the figure of a man. He walks toward us and becomes recognizable as Gene Barry the actor. "Now, at the barn where it all began, you can relive those early days when Hollywood first met the movies." He turns toward DeMille. "Ready, Mr. DeMille." The actor finishes: "The Hollywood Studio Museum. Where the legend lives on."

What you've just read is a script from a recent television commercial that I produced promoting the site of the first feature-length motion picture—a little yellow barn, located in Hollywood and preserved as a historical landmark. The place where, literally, "Hollywood" began.

I've used this example (and we'll return to it later) because the commercial involves the subject of this chapter—the right of publicity and the right of privacy. Both rights protect a person against the unauthorized use of his or her identity. As we see in this chapter, each area of law covers different injuries and promotes different values. Whenever an advertiser uses an image, likeness, or name of another person in an ad or for trade, certain rights must be considered. Here, we explore two of these rights.

THE RIGHT OF PRIVACY

We start with the oldest of the two rights, the right of privacy. The concept of a specific right of privacy began to take shape in the late 1800s to protect individuals who truly desired privacy, mainly private citizens.

Here's a little sociology lesson. Individuals, being a part of society, give up many rights and privileges that they would be free to exercise in nature. In exchange for this, they receive the benefits of being part of society. But all rights are not given up. There are matters that are private that any intelligent member of society can recognize, and there is a right of privacy in those matters.

The intent of the right of privacy laws is to protect the essence of the individual person. To put it another way, privacy laws protect his or her persona from being taken and used without his or her knowledge or permission for the profit of

another. The words Shakespeare wrote for Iago were straight
to the point:

> Good name in man or woman, dear my lord,
> Is the immediate jewel of their souls;
> Who steals my purse steals trash; 'tis something,
>   nothing;
> Twas mine, 'tis his, and has been slave to thousands;
> But he that filches from me my good name
> Robs me of that which not enriches him,
> And makes me poor indeed.

Individuals have the right to live their lives in any way
they see fit so long as it does not invade the rights of others or
violate public laws or policies. People may make themselves
visible to the public when they desire and may withdraw from
the public when they wish.

In Roman law we see the beginnings of what would become
the right of privacy. Anyone who brought public attention to
another on a public road or on the other's own private grounds
would be punished. Shouting until a crowd gathered or following an honest woman or child were banned under Roman law.
In those days the law recognized a right "to be let alone." Even
though, at the time, it was considered a property right, and
property was an extremely valuable commodity.

In Semayne's case[1], one of the oldest English cases to be
reported, we first find the legal maxim applied that "the house
of every one is to him as his castle and fortress, as well for his
defense against injury and violence as for his repose." Today,
we find Semayne's maxim recognizable in our phrase "every
man's home is his castle."

The unreported case of *Manola* v. *Stevens,* heard before the
Supreme Court of New York (1890), was the first case in this
country where the right of privacy idea was used in an attempt
to persuade the court that the right existed. The complainant
claimed that while the plaintiff performed on the Broadway

---

[1](5 Coke, 91), 1 Smith's Lead. Cas. 228.

stage in tights, she was photographed with the use of a flash-light. This was done without her knowledge or consent by the defendant sitting in a box seat. While the court permanently enjoined the display of the unauthorized photo, they steered clear of labeling this a right of privacy.

Right of Privacy—The Early View

In 1902 the New York Court of Appeals rejected the existence of common law right of privacy in *Roberson* v. *Rochester Folding Box Co.,* 171 N.Y. 538, 64 N.E. 442 (1902). Abigail Roberson—at the time a child—sued for the unauthorized use of her photograph in posters (promoting a flour product) that were displayed in stores, warehouses, saloons, and so on. Even though the posters were complimentary—describing her as "The Flour of the Family"—the publication of the photo subjected her to "scoffs and jeers . . . causing her great distress and suffering both in body and mind."

In spite of this, the court refused to rule in favor of Roberson. They feared that this would open the flood gates once the principle of a privacy right was established. The court said: " . . . the so-called right of privacy has not yet found an abiding place in our jurisprudence, and, as we view it, the doctrine cannot now be incorporated without doing violence to settled principles of law by which the profession and the public have long been guided."

However, the public reacted very strongly to what it considered to be an injustice and demanded that the legislature change the law. The New York legislature quickly enacted a statute prohibiting the use of a person's name, likeness, or picture, without prior written permission, for trade or advertising purposes.[2] This became the model law that other states have since followed.

---

[2] 1903 N.Y. Laws Ch. 132, sections 1–2 (codified as amended; N.Y. Civil Rights Law sections 50–51 (1976)).

The Right of Privacy Becomes Law

The first court case to specifically recognize the right of privacy was *Pavesich* v. *New England Life Ins. Co.,* 122 Ga. 190, 50 S.E. 68 (1905).

Paolo Pavesich's picture was published in a life insurance company's ad that had run in the *Atlanta Constitution* newspaper. His picture, that of a healthy and well-dressed man, appeared next to one of a sickly and badly dressed one. The caption above Pavesich read, "Do it now. The man who did." Above the sickly person ran the caption, "Do it while you can. The man who didn't." Below both pictures was the statement, "These two pictures tell their own story." Under Pavesich's picture was the following copy:

> "In my healthy and productive period of life
> I bought insurance
> in the New England Mutual Life Insurance Co.
> of Boston, Mass.,
> and today my family is protected
> and I am drawing an annual
> dividend on my paid-up policies."
> —Thomas B. Lumpkin, General Agent.

The photo was used without Mr. Pavesich's knowledge or consent. The statement under his picture was also false; he never had a life insurance policy with the company. Pavesich asked for $25,000 in damages. He got it. In essence the court allowed Pavesich to recover damages for injured feelings.

The Pavesich case for the first time established precedent for future actions under a right of privacy, and the court, in an opinion over 30 pages long, addressed the issue in detail. In its conclusion to the case it said:

> So thoroughly satisfied are we that the law recognizes within proper limits, as a legal right, the right of privacy, and that the publication of one's picture without his consent by another as an advertisement, for the mere purpose of increasing the profits and gains of the advertiser, is an invasion of this right, that we venture to predict that the day will come when the American bar will marvel that a contrary view was ever entertained by judges of eminence and ability. . . .

Since the time of the Pavesich decision and the passage of the New York statute, every state has developed (in one form or another) a right of privacy. The U.S. Supreme Court, in fact, established that the right of privacy stems from the specific guarantees in the Bill of Rights.[3] All right of privacy laws protect against one of four forms of violations: (1) the unauthorized use of another person's name or likeness for another's benefit, (2) the invasion into an individual's seclusion, (3) the public disclosure of embarrassing private facts, and (4) the presentation of an individual in a false light in the public view. The common denominator between these four is the right to be left alone.

Waiver of Privacy Rights

The right of privacy, like every other right of an individual, may be waived by voluntarily allowing one's image to be used in an ad. An advertiser must get written permission for such use in order to avoid a violation. Also, a person may imply that he or she waives privacy rights. A good example of this is when a private citizen runs for public office. Here, the person's rights are waived in order to allow the public to investigate how the candidate's private life is conducted. This is allowed to determine the person's qualifications for the office that the candidate wishes to hold. But the waiver of rights applies only to matters that affect competency for the office being sought. This type of implied waiver, however, is rarely involved in advertising situations.

THE RIGHT OF PUBLICITY

The right to privacy had its limitations however. As years progressed, many people actually wanted publicity, not privacy. The right of publicity grew out of the need to aid people such

---

[3]See *Griswold* v. *Connecticut*, 381 U.S. 479, 484 (1965).

as celebrities, entertainers, and athletes who wanted to protect the use of their marketable image.

Development of the Right of Publicity

Prior to the establishment of a right of publicity, it was not illegal for others to use entertainers' names or likenesses. Because entertainers sought publicity, they were making their lives public, and as such, waived their rights to privacy.

In *O'Brien* v. *Pabst Sales Co.*, 124 F.2d 167 (5th Cir. 1941), a well-known football player claimed a violation of his right of privacy after Pabst used his picture on a calendar promoting its beer. While at Texas Christian University, David O'Brien was selected by Grantland Rice on his *Collier's* All American Football Team in 1938. O'Brien was probably the most publicized football player of the 1938–39 season. After graduating from TCU, he would play for the Philadelphia Eagles.

Pabst Brewing Company published a calendar every year with the schedule of the entire football league included. Inland Lithographing Company printed 35,000 calendars for 1939 that used the picture of O'Brien in uniform. The headline read, "Pabst Blue Ribbon Football Calendar, 1939."

O'Brien claimed that he had not given his permission for the use of his picture. In fact, he did not even know that it had been used until quite some time after its release to stores. He claimed that he was greatly embarrassed by the publication of his picture in connection with the sale of beer, a product that he personally was against using.

The court, however, stated that: " . . . as a result of his activities and prowess in football, his chosen field, and the nationwide and deliberate publicizing with his consent and in his interest, he was no longer . . . a private but public person, and as to their additional publication he had no right of privacy."

The court decided that O'Brien had no case. He could not recover under a right of privacy claim because O'Brien was a famous national football league figure and had purposefully publicized his name and photos. Because of this, he had waived his right of privacy. In fact the court said, "the publicity [he] got was only that which he had been constantly seeking."

Establishment of the Right of Publicity as Law

Essentially, celebrities had little chance of recovering damages for the appropriation of their names or likenesses for commercial use. However, this dim outlook was soon changed by the Court of Appeals for the Second Circuit. For the first time, a right of publicity was recognized in *Haelan Laboratories* v. *Topps Chewing Gum, Inc.,* 202 F.2d 866 (2d Cir. 1953).

Haelan was a chewing gum company that had obtained the exclusive right to use a baseball player's photograph in connection with the sale of gum. The defendant Topps claimed that it had a contract for the use of the same ballplayer's photograph during that same time. Topps had, in fact, deceptively persuaded the ballplayer to enter into a contract with it while he was still bound by the contract with Haelan.

In this case, the courts admitted that, in addition to rights of privacy, a person has a right of publicity. It protects a person's commercial interest in his or her identity, and a person has the right to authorize the publication of a picture. When this happens, it is an exclusive grant, and other advertisers are not allowed to use the picture. Haelan won its case because it owned the publicity rights to the ballplayer. Topps's contract was invalid.

Public Figures Do Not Waive Their Right of Privacy

Public figures who do not market themselves commercially may suffer injury by being associated with commercial products. These people have not waived their rights of privacy simply by being public figures.

A good example of this occurred when Jacqueline Onassis won an action under a right of privacy claim in *Onassis* v. *Christian Dior, New York, Inc.,* 122 Misc.2d 603, 472 N.Y.S.2d 254 (Sup. Ct. 1984). What made the case unique was the way that Dior violated her right of privacy. Dior, through its ad agency J. Walter Thompson, produced a campaign of 16 ads. Dior spent $2.5 million in publications including *Esquire, The New Yorker, Harper's Bazaar,* and the *New York Times.*

The ads featured a trio known as the Diors (one female and two men) who were to be the essence of the idle rich, decadent, and aggressively chic. The intent was to develop a group of characters that would become the most memorable personalities since Brooke Shields refused to let anything come between her and her Calvins. The copy for one of the ads read:

When the Diors got away from it all,
they brought with them nothing except
The Decline of the West
and one toothbrush.

The ads led the reader through a progression of various situations that would include the marriage of two (but not the exclusion of the third), the birth of a baby, and their ascent to Heaven. One of the ads, the one for the wedding, ran the headline:

Christian Dior: Sportswear for Women
and clothing for Men.

The copy continued:

The wedding of the Diors was everything
a wedding should be:
no tears, no rice, no in-laws, no smarmy toasts,
for once no Mendelssohn.
Just a legendary private affair.

The ad showed the trio along with their wedding party. Included in the group were movie critic Gene Shalit, model Shari Belafonte Harper, actress Ruth Gordon, and a secretary named Barbara Reynolds who bears an amazing resemblance to Jacqueline Onassis. All were obviously delighted to be at the event.

Dior knew that there was no chance of Ms. Onassis consenting to being in the ad. She has never permitted the use of her name or picture to be used in connection with the promotion of any commercial products, but only for public service, art, educational, or civic projects. So, the agency and photographer Richard Avedon contacted Ron Smith Celebrity Look-Alikes to supply someone who resembled Onassis. That they did with Barbara Reynolds. The use of look-alikes requires the permission of the actual celebrity, nonetheless.

Even though Onassis's name was not used in the ad, and the image was not of Onassis, the public would naturally assume that it was Onassis. A visual pun was used to catch the reader's eye and draw attention to the ad. What they had was a recognizable likeness, which was not consistent with reality.

Dior also contended that having Onassis attend the wedding of the Diors was "no more than a touch of humor" and therefore was protected as a form of free speech. However, simply claiming that a statement was intended to be funny does not make it permissible to make the statement. In this case, the humor was used only to promote Dior products, so absolutely no freedom of speech privilege existed for its use.

What is ironic about this case—as the court noted—was that Dior was attempting to "pass off the counterfeit as a legitimate marketing device," when it had in the past, so adamantly tried to prevent others from deceptively obtaining the "fruits of another's labor." For example, in a previous case, *Dior* v. *Milton*[4], Dior complained bitterly of the misappropriation of its good name and reputation that had taken so long to develop. Now the shoe was on the other foot.

Although Onassis is a public figure, even a celebrity, she purposely avoided any connection with commercial products. Embarrassment and annoyance were her injury rather than loss of economic opportunity.

As a side note, we'll look at another aspect of celebrity look-alikes in Chapter 9. There, comparative advertising has also become involved in situations using look-alikes.

When Freedom of the Press Overcomes the Rights of Privacy and Publicity

In 1978, the movie *Magic* was released and subsequently grossed over $13 million. One of the stars of the movie was Ann-Margret. For only the second time in her career she ap-

---

[4] 9 Misc.2d 425, 155 N.Y.S.2d 443, aff'd. 2 A.D.2d 878, 156 N.Y.S.2d 996.

peared in a scene nude. She made the decision to disrobe for artistic reasons and to do so only if there was a minimal crew at the filming and if no still photos were taken.

High Society magazine runs photographs of well-known women caught in revealing situations. In one particular issue, five pages were devoted exclusively to Ann-Margret. One of the photos was taken from the movie *Magic* and showed her nude from the waist up. After learning of this photo, suit was brought in *Ann-Margret* v. *High Society Magazine, Inc.*, 498 F.Supp. 401 (1980), for violation of her right of privacy and right of publicity.

There is no doubt that Ann-Margret is considered a celebrity, and simply because she is a celebrity she has not given up her rights to privacy. However, she chose to appear in the motion picture, partially nude, knowing that the public would see her performance. The reproduction of scenes from that performance were faithful and accurate and not distorted, and therefore not an invasion of her privacy.

The court said: "Undoubtedly, the plaintiff is unhappy about the appearance of her picture in [the] magazine. And while the court can sympathize with her feelings, the fact that she does not like either the manner in which she is portrayed, or the medium in which her picture is reproduced . . . [does] not expand her rights or create any cause of action . . . "

As far as her claim of violation of her right of publicity, the court felt that it also had no merit. There is only an action when the use is for "advertising purposes or for the purposes of trade." (The fact that the magazine is sold for profit does not constitute such a use.) The mere use of the photos in an editorial context is acceptable. The case was dismissed.

When the Rights of Publicity Exceed Freedom of the Press

"Ladies and gentlemen, children of all ages, I present the great Zacchini." Hugo Zacchini practiced a form of entertainment developed by his father and performed by his family for over 50 years. Zacchini was a human cannonball, and over the years he performed at many public fairs and events.

In August and September of 1972, Zacchini performed his act at the Geauga County Fair in Burton, Ohio. The performance took place in a fenced area surrounded by grandstands. He was shot from a cannon into a net 200 feet away, and the performance lasted 15 seconds.

A freelance reporter for Scripps-Howard Broadcasting—owner of the local television station—visited the fair on August 30 where Zacchini was performing. Zacchini spotted the reporter carrying a video camera and requested that he not tape the performance, but on the next day the reporter returned and videotaped the feat anyway. The event was broadcast on the 11 o'clock news along with a commentary, which was very complimentary. When Zacchini learned of the unauthorized broadcast, he sued for damages for showing and commercializing his act without his consent. This was the first case involving the right of publicity to reach the United States Supreme Court: *Zacchini* v. *Scripps-Howard Broadcasting Co.,* 433 U.S. 562 (1977).

Scripps-Howard argued that its broadcast of the event was protected under the 1st and 14th Amendments—freedom of the press. The TV station had the right to broadcast items of legitimate public interest. However, the TV station broadcast the entire act, from start to finish, along with a description of the event. If the station had broadcast that Zacchini was performing at the fair, commented on the performance, and showed his picture on TV, this could have been a very different case.

But as the Court said: Zacchini "had a right of publicity that gave him personal control over commercial display and exploitation of his personality and the exercise of his talents. This right . . . was said to be such a valuable part of the benefit, which may be attained by his talents and efforts, that it was entitled to legal protection."

Zacchini did not sue to stop the broadcast of his performance; he simply wanted to be paid for it. The Court agreed that Zacchini's commercial interest in his act was protected under his right of publicity.

DESCENDIBILITY OF THE RIGHT OF PUBLICITY

The right of publicity is a property right, separate from the right of privacy. The right of privacy is a personal right and is nondescendible; it terminates at death. The right of publicity is a property right, on the other hand, and can be inherited by or assigned to someone.

While some courts disagree, the trend is clearly toward descendibility. Since it is a property right, it survives after the death of the owner. A valid reason exists for recognizing this survivability. It motivates celebrities' efforts and creativity in encouraging them to develop their image so that their heirs will also benefit. It's money in the bank, so to speak. It may take many years to develop a reputation that will create large economic returns. Along those lines others not related should not be able to benefit from the efforts that celebrities put into developing their own images.

In practice, the various state courts have adopted one of three views regarding descendibility (see Table 5–1). One view says that the commercial use of the person's name or likeness shifts to the public domain after death. In other words, the right of publicity is never descendible.

TABLE 5–1
State Interpretation of the Descendibility of the Right of Publicity

State	Always Descendible to Heirs	Descendible If Exploited during Life	Never Descendible (Public Domain)
Alabama	✓		
Alaska		✓	
Arizona		✓	
Arkansas			✓
California		X	
Colorado		✓	
Connecticut	X		
Delaware	✓		
Florida	✓		
Georgia	X		

TABLE 5–1 *Concluded*

State	Always Descendible to Heirs	Descendible If Exploited during Life	Never Descendible (Public Domain)
Hawaii		√	
Idaho		√	
Illinois			√
Indiana			√
Iowa			√
Kansas	√		
Kentucky			X
Louisiana	X		
Maine	√		
Maryland	√		
Massachusetts	√		
Michigan			X
Minnesota			√
Mississippi	X		
Missouri			√
Montana		√	
Nebraska			√
Nevada		√	
New Hampshire	√		
New Jersey	√		
New York	X		
North Carolina	√		
North Dakota			√
Ohio			X
Oklahoma			√
Oregon		√	
Pennsylvania	√		
Rhode Island	√		
South Carolina	√		
South Dakota			√
Tennessee			X
Texas	X		
Utah		√	
Vermont	X		
Virginia	√		
Washington		√	
Washington, D.C.	√		
West Virginia	√		

X = States where the descendibility issue has been decided.
√ = States where no apellate decisions have been made regarding descendibility. These states should be checked, since the accuracy of the position of these states may vary.

Another view recognizes descendibility only if the right of publicity has been sufficiently exploited before death. What constitutes sufficient exploitation? Generally, it must be exploited by the celebrity through the creation of a second business or through the use of his or her name or likeness in connection with a product or service promoted by the person.

Finally, some courts recognize the descendibility of the right of publicity without any other conditions. Let's take a closer look at the three views. It is important to remember that the theory that applies to each case is determined by the state law used to decide that case.

Nonsurvivable Theory—The Statue of Elvis

The strict view of descendibility is illustrated in *Memphis Development Foundation* v. *Factors Etc. Inc.*, 616 F.2d 956 (6th Cir. 1980). This is an example of when the right of publicity is not descendible. Under Tennessee law the courts hold the opinion that the celebrity's right of publicity is not inheritable.

Elvis Presley died on August 16, 1977, in Memphis. In his honor, the Memphis Development Foundation, a nonprofit corporation, wanted to build a large bronze statue of Elvis in downtown Memphis. The foundation would collect the needed money from contributions. Contributors of $25 or more received an eight-inch pewter replica of the full-size statue.

The defendant, Factors Etc., was the assignee of Presley's right of publicity, and the company claimed that Memphis Development had taken away its right to market Presley's name and likeness. Memphis claimed that Factors's license did not allow for the distribution of the statuettes.

The court decided that, based on Tennessee law, Factors could not inherit Presley's right of publicity. It reasoned that "the basic motivations are the desire to achieve success or excellence in a chosen field, the desire to contribute to the happiness or improvement of one's fellows, and the desire to receive the psychic and financial rewards of achievement." Essentially, the court felt that this right should not be survivable to the heirs because the celebrity alone did not have complete control over developing the notoriety in the first place.

The court felt that the public was an integral element in the creation of an image. Therefore it had "serious reservations about making fame the permanent right of a few individuals to the exclusion of the general public." In conclusion, the court said: "Fame falls in the same category as reputation; it is an attribute from which others may benefit but may not own." In other words, the right of publicity is not descendible but rather becomes public domain after death. At least this is the case in Tennessee and other states that have adopted the same philosophy.

Descendibility If Exploited during Life

The second option is seen in California where there is no descendibility unless the right was sufficiently exploited during life. To illustrate, let's look at a case involving Bela George Lugosi and his well-known character, Count Dracula, the legendary character created in 1897 by author Bram Stoker. In September of 1930, Lugosi entered into an agreement with Universal Pictures to star in the lead role in the film classic *Dracula*. The case was *Lugosi* v. *Universal Pictures*, 25 Cal. 3d 813 (1979), during which Justice Mosk rather sardonically stated, "not unlike the horror films that brought him fame, Bela Lugosi rises from the grave 20 years after death to haunt his former employer."

In this case, the heirs of Lugosi, his son and widow, claimed that Universal had taken property rights that the studio had not been given in the agreement for the production of *Dracula* in 1930. Between 1960 and 1966 Universal licensed many companies to manufacture items using the Count Dracula character. There was no doubt that the merchandising of the Count Dracula character was patterned after the likeness of Lugosi. It may well be true, also, that Lugosi is readily recognized as having been Count Dracula, even though Max Schreck, Christopher Lee, John Carradine, Lon Chaney, and others also have appeared in the role.

Yet, Lugosi never exploited commercially the character of Dracula during his lifetime. He also never exploited his own identity commercially. Let's assume that, for the sake of argument, Lugosi had opened a company named Lugosi/Dracula Enterprises. This company made T-shirts and hats with a picture of the actor made up as Dracula. Under the picture was printed "Dracula Lives . . . signed Bela Lugosi." This product created a large public awareness of the business. If the business existed and had not been sold before Lugosi's death in 1956, his heirs may have had a claim if the Dracula image was later misappropriated.

However, under California law, the right to profit from one's name and likeness is personal and must be exercised during lifetime in order for the right to survive after death. Since Lugosi hadn't used his name or likeness as Count Dracula in association with any business, service, or product (other than the part in the movie), he had no claim under the California interpretation of publicity rights. As a result, his heirs lost the case.

It is important to note that this case does not concern Lugosi's right of publicity for his likeness, but rather that of a character he played. Unless there is a contract to the contrary, merely playing a role creates no inheritable property rights— any more than George C. Scott has any rights to the character of General Patton, James Whitmore to that of Will Rogers, Gregory Peck of General MacArthur, or Charlton Heston of Moses.

The United States Court of Appeals for the Second Circuit agreed with the Lugosi decision when it decided a case involving three brothers—Adolph, Julius, and Leo Marx. This case concerned the brothers' public image for which they were known as Harpo, Groucho, and Chico, respectively. The case was *Groucho Marx Productions, Inc.* v. *Day and Night Co., Inc.*, 523 F. Supp. 4851 (S.D.N.Y. 1981), rev'd, 689 F.2d 317 (2d Cir. 1982).

At the New End Theatre in London, a play opened in January of 1979 called *A Day in Hollywood/A Night in the Ukraine*. In May of 1980, it came to Broadway. The second half of the play featured performers who simulated the Marx Brothers' unique style, appearance, and manner.

The Marx Brothers had assigned the rights to their names, likenesses, and style prior to their deaths; and subsequently their heirs transferred that right to Groucho Marx

Productions, the plaintiff. The Marx Brothers, it can be said, made a profession of capitalizing on the unique characters that they created. Their fame arose directly from their efforts to create their instantly recognizable characters. The Marx Brothers' characters bore little resemblance to their actual personalities. This was a key issue in the case.

The Marx Brothers capitalized on the commercial value of the artificial personalities they created. Every appearance and advertisement they took part in demonstrated their awareness of the commercial value of their images as Chico, Harpo, and Groucho. In fact, the Marx Brothers had promoted many products during their lifetimes, including Plymouth cars and Smirnoff vodka.

The play created a duplication, as faithfully as possible, of the Marx Brothers' performances. Granted, it devised a new situation and used new lines. But the essential style of humor of the Marx Brothers was accurately reproduced. The court said: "Although the [plaintiffs] may have intended to comment 'about 1930s Hollywood, its techniques, its stars, and its excesses,'. . . the content of the relevant portion of the play attempts to accomplish that objective exactly as would the Marx Brothers themselves."

The court found that indeed the Marx Brothers had established a commercial use of their names, likenesses, and images during their lifetimes. This allowed their right of publicity to survive them, to be passed on to their heirs. They had won their case.

Always Descendible Theory

The third approach makes the right of publicity always descendible. The case we see here was easier to determine than the Lugosi case because it featured actors playing themselves. Stanley Laurel and Oliver Hardy developed their own characters, which were theirs alone and certainly not fictional.

The heirs of Laurel and Hardy brought suit for $250,000 against Hal Roach Studios who claimed that the studio had been given the exclusive rights to the Laurel and Hardy characters. Roach contended that it had acquired the rights through contracts between the studio and the comedy team in

1923. However, the rights acquired were those of copyright for the Laurel and Hardy films, not the unlimited usage of the Laurel and Hardy names and likenesses. We'll look more closely at copyright in Chapter 6.

Roach then claimed that the names and likenesses of the comedy team are in the public domain. The court in *Price* v. *Hal Roach Studios, Inc.,* 400 F.Supp. 836 (S.D.N.Y. 1975), disagreed. Its only question was whether the right of publicity terminated on the death of Laurel and Hardy, or was it descendible.

The court felt that there was no reasonable basis to assume that the right was not assignable or that it should terminate with the death of the person. The court decided that the heirs of Laurel and Hardy were entitled to the commercial rights to the names and likenesses of the team. It also determined that the heirs were entitled to the actual damages sought in the lawsuit—for the appropriation of that right by Roach.

A further extension of the right of publicity for celebrities involved the late Dr. Martin Luther King, Jr., a public figure but not a celebrity. From 1955, Dr. King was the prime leader of the civil rights movement in the United States. For his efforts, he was awarded the Nobel Peace Prize in 1964. On April 4, 1968, Dr. King was assassinated.

American Heritage Products manufactured plastic products for funeral accessories. It developed the idea of marketing a bust of the late Dr. King. Although the company had asked permission for the endorsement of the product of the Martin Luther King, Jr. Center for Social Change (the nonprofit corporation that holds the rights to the King estate), it refused to participate.

Regardless, American Heritage hired an artist to produce a mold for the bust. It also hired an agent to promote the product. American bought two half-page ads in the November and December 1980 issues of *Ebony Magazine.* The ad offered:

An exclusive memorial.
An opportunity to support
the Martin Luther King, Jr. Center for Social Change.

* * * * *

> A contribution from your order goes to
> the King Center for Social Change.

American also printed 80,000 brochures that were inserted into newspapers across the country. Two hundred busts had been sold with orders for 23 more when the lawsuit was initiated in *Martin Luther King, Jr. Center for Social Change, Inc. v. American Heritage Products, Inc.*, 694 F.2d 674 (11th Cir. 1983).

Generally, the right of publicity is the distillation of celebrities' exclusive rights to the use of their names and likenesses. These celebrities are most often actors, musicians, athletes, comedians, or other entertainers. In this case Dr. King was none of these. However, he still had the right to control the use of his image for trade purposes and advertising.

Indeed a public figure, Dr. King avoided having his name exploited during his life, and he is protected from having it exploited after death. Under Georgia law, individuals do not have to commercially exploit their names or likenesses during their lifetimes in order to have the right of publicity extend beyond life to their heirs. The center won its case against American Heritage.

PROBLEMS RELATING TO CONSENT

The most appropriate method of avoiding suits involving right of privacy or publicity is to obtain the person's prior consent. Generally, this consent must be in writing, and it involves more than just the authorization to use a person's name, likeness, or image. Involved are questions of how the image is used, the media, the form, where and when it is used, and so on. The advertiser must make certain that these questions are answered by the consent release to avoid liability later.

Let's look at the different areas where consent problems are common.

Consent for a Specific Use

As a very successful fashion model, Christie Brinkley's photos have appeared on the covers of most major magazines including

Mademoiselle, Ladies Home Journal, Harper's Bazaar, and *Sports Illustrated.* In September of 1979, John Casablancas, the president of Elite Model Management (Brinkley's agent), signed a licensing agreement with Galaxy Publishing. The agreement was to produce a series of posters of several models, including Brinkley.

Brinkley verbally agreed to the project and picked her own makeup artist, hair-stylist, and bathing suit for the photo session. Photographer Michael Reinhardt photographed Brinkley for the poster. Home Box Office (a cable TV company) filmed the photography session for use in a special entitled: "Beautiful, Baby, Beautiful," on the careers of this country's top models. Brinkley gave her written permission to appear in the broadcast—in the same pose and suit that was to be used for the poster.

After the session, Brinkley reviewed the photos and requested some retouching be done on the specific shot she had intended for the poster. This was done. At that point, Galaxy proceeded to print the posters. The problem was that Brinkley never signed a model release authorizing the publication of her pictures in a poster. Brinkley stated that she "agreed to participate in a shooting from which a poster *may* have been the result, depending of course on my final judgment of the final product." She claimed that the printing and distribution of pinup posters was an unauthorized exploitation, for commercial purposes, of her name and image. The court agreed.

In *Brinkley* v. *Casablancas,* 80 A.D.2d 428, 438 N.Y.S.2d 1004 (App. Div. 1981), Brinkley's consent for the use of her photo for a cable television show did not include consent for a poster of a different photo taken at the same session. There was no written permission given for that particular photo to be used as a poster.

Consent for a Specific Length of Time

Another area where a problem can arise is the time span allowed for the usage. In 1973 Charles Welch, an actor, appeared in a television commercial for Mr. Christmas, a manufacturer of artificial Christmas trees. Welch was paid the sum of $1,000 for the commercial. According to the contract the $1,000 fee allowed the commercial to be run for no more than one year. However, the contract further provided an additional year's option with the payment of an additional $1,000. Regardless of the fact that Mr. Christmas had not paid Welch the additional year's fee, it allowed its distributors to air the commercial in 1974.

Welch found out about this and agreed to a financial settlement for the 1974 option. In March of 1975 Mr. Christmas was contacted by the Screen Actors Guild and cautioned that the spot could not be aired any longer without further negotiations. In spite of this warning, the commercial aired during 1975.

In the lawsuit that resulted, *Welch* v. *Mr. Christmas Inc.*, 57 N.Y.2d 143, 440 N.E.2d 1317 (1982), the plaintiff was awarded compensatory damages of $1,000 and exemplary damages of $25,000. Here, the time limit was part of the original consent agreement. Using the commercial after the authorized period expired is the same as airing the commercial with no consent at all.

Mr. Christmas used as a defense in its case that *it* did not use the commercial. The company claimed that its dealers were expected to purchase their own air time and that it did not know or have control over the spots used by them. However, Mr. Christmas encouraged its dealers to get the maximum use of the commercial, and it made no attempt to notify the dealers that the usage period had ended. All of this made Mr. Christmas liable.

As we have seen before, not taking action when you have a responsibility to do so is also negligent. (We'll discuss such responsibilities in greater detail in Chapter 11, The Client/Agency Relationship.) Since the agreement was with the actor and Mr. Christmas, those are the parties who are responsible to each other. If the dealers had aired the spot after they were notified in writing not to by Mr. Christmas, this may have been a different situation.

Usage in a Medium that Was Not Authorized

Frank Dzurenko is a model who participated in a photo session for Jordache jeans. At the end of the photo session, Dzurenko signed a model release inserting the phrase "magazine ad use only." His reason for adding the limitation was that in the photos he had posed with a female model who was wearing only a pair of jeans.

After the session one of those photos was blown up and produced as a poster, which was then distributed to retailers. This violated Dzurenko's right of publicity because the photo's use exceeded the limitations of the release. In *Dzurenko* v. *Jordache, Inc.,* 59 N.Y.2d 788, 451 N.E.2d 477 (1983), the court determined that a release can cover not only the use of a name, picture or likeness, but also the time, form, and media of its use. Dzurenko won the case.

Another interesting issue here was that Jordache brought up as a defense that Dzurenko didn't sign the release with the limitation until after the photos had been taken. However, this didn't matter. Dzurenko had the absolute right to limit the usage of the photos in any way he desired, regardless of when the release was signed.

When Parental Consent Is Revocable

One other problem regarding consent can occur when a child's parent gives consent and then the child, on becoming an adult, wants to withdraw it. This can pose a unique problem for advertisers. That was exactly what happened with Brooke Shields and Garry Gross.

In 1975 Brooke Shields was 10 years old. At the time she was registered with the Ford Model Agency, working as a child model (and a very famous one at that). One of the jobs she did was for Playboy Press that required her to pose nude in a bathtub. The intent was that the photos would be published in a publication called *Sugar and Spice.*

Before the photo session, Teri Shields, Brooke's mother, signed a consent for the photographer Garry Gross to "use, reuse and/or publish, and republish" the photos. Brooke's photos appeared in *Sugar and Spice* as well as on posters and in other publications. Brooke even used the photos in a book about herself with the permission of the photographer. Gross, in fact, had shot Brooke on many occasions for *Penthouse* magazine,

New York Magazine, and advertising for the Courtauldts and Avon Company.

In 1980 Brooke learned that the *Sugar and Spice* photos had appeared in the French magazine *Photo.* At that point, she became disturbed by the publication of the photos and attempted to buy the negatives from Gross. When that failed, she brought suit: *Shields* v. *Gross, 58 N.Y.2d 338 (1983).* The suit claimed, among other things, that her right of privacy had been violated and sought to cancel the consent given by her mother in 1975.

According to New York's Civil Rights Law, section 50, once the written consent is obtained, the photos can be published as agreed. If that person is a minor, his or her parents may give the consent. Under common law, infants can disaffirm their own or their guardian's consent. However, where a specific statute permits a class of agreements to be made by a child, the discussion is ended, and the agreement is valid. Consent had been given, and it would stand under its original terms. Brooke lost her claim.

FORMS OF DEPICTION THAT CAN CAUSE LIABILITY

What type of depictions can cause trouble for advertisers? As we'll see, there are many. There is a difference between the right of privacy and the right of publicity regarding what depictions create a problem. The right of privacy is very specific, while the right of publicity is more broad.

Upholding Privacy Rights Requires Recognizability

The right of privacy generally requires a visually recognizable likeness of the person if the name is not used. This right is narrower in scope than publicity rights because it protects citizens where there is a recognizability by others.

What constitutes a recognizable likeness? The New York Court of Appeals defined just that in *Cohen* v. *Herbal Concepts, Inc.*, 63 N.Y.2d 379, 472 N.E.2d 307 (1984). In 1977 on the July 4th weekend, a woman and her daughter were photographed while bathing in a stream in Woodstock. The photo of Susan Cohen and her four-year-old daughter Samantha was shot from behind while they bathed nude in the stream located on their friend's private property. Ira Cohen, the husband and father, saw the photographer taking pictures, became incensed, and chased him away.

The photo showed the nude mother and daughter from behind and to the right in a full-length pose. The shot did not show their faces, but their backs and right sides are clearly visible as was the mother's right breast. The photo later appeared in ads that ran in *House and Garden, House Beautiful,* and *Cosmopolitan* magazines.

The ad for Au Naturel, manufactured by Herbal Concepts, promoted a product intended to help eliminate body cellulite. As the ad said: "those fatty lumps and bumps that won't go away." While leafing through one of the magazines that contained the ad, Ira Cohen "recognized [his] wife and daughter immediately."

The issue here was whether a photograph of the nude mother and child constitutes a sufficiently identifiable likeness without showing their faces. The court established that it does. Features such as the mother's and child's hair, bone structure, body shape, stature, and posture all together could make the people in the photograph identifiable by someone familiar with them.

The court ruled that the photo need not show the face. The plaintiff need only show that the photograph is reasonably recognizable. The photo was clear and sharp with no objects blocking the subjects. In New York, privacy claims are based on sections 50 and 51 of the Civil Rights Law. This statute, as with many other states, was designed to protect a person's identity, not only his name, portrait, or picture. The plaintiff must be "identifiable." The fact that Susan and Samantha were identified by Ira Cohen was acceptable.

THE MANY FORMS THAT CAN VIOLATE PUBLICITY RIGHTS

As for publicity rights, almost any form that can be devised can potentially cause trouble. Because of this, the advertiser must be very careful when using any form of celebrity or public figure in an ad. Name, image, likeness, voice imitations, commonly associated phrases, look-alikes, cartoons, even identifiable situations are potential problem areas. Now, let us explore some of these areas in detail.

Use of a Phrase

The use of a familiar phrase can be an infringement. In 1962 Johnny Carson began hosting "The Tonight Show" for NBC Television. Carson was introduced five nights a week with the phrase "Here's Johnny." Johnny Carson is a well-known entertainer, and a large segment of the television viewing public associated him with the particular phrase.

In 1967 Carson authorized the use of this phrase by another business. He allowed it to be used by a restaurant chain called "Here's Johnny Restaurants." In 1970 Carson formed a clothing manufacturer and used the phrase "Here's Johnny" on its clothing and in its advertising. And in 1977 Carson authorized Marcey Laboratories to use the phrase as a name for a line of toiletries.

However, in 1976 a Michigan corporation was formed to rent and sell a product it called "Here's Johnny" portable toilets. The owner developed a clever tag line for the product: "Here's Johnny Portable Toilets. The World's Foremost Commodian." The owner claimed that this made "a good play on a phrase."

Not long after this, Carson brought suit for, among other things, infringement of his right of publicity in *Carson* v. *Here's Johnny Portable Toilets, Inc.*, 698 F.2d 831 (6th Cir. 1983). Here was a case of an appropriation of Carson's identity without the use of his name. The phrase is so recognizable that when the public heard it, no one else but Carson came to mind.

The phrase "Here's Johnny" is a symbol of Carson's identity, just as is a name or picture. The president of the toilet company even admitted that he used the name because it identified Carson.

A celebrity's right of publicity is invaded when his identity is intentionally appropriated for commercial purposes. The fact that the defendant did not use Carson's last name does not lessen the offense. In fact, no violation would have occurred if his name had been used.

The court gave as examples names that would not have violated Carson's right of publicity: "J. William Carson Portable Toilet," "John William Carson Portable Toilet," and "J. W. Carson Portable Toilet." The reason that these uses of his name would not have been violative of Carson's right is simple—there would have been no appropriation of Carson's identity as a celebrity. Even if his real name was used, the public would not have associated the two as the same.

Use of an Object

Here's another example of appropriation of an identity without the use of a name. This case involved an object commonly associated with a celebrity.

Lothar Motschenbacher was an internationally known race car driver. Part of his income came from product endorsements. Since 1966 all of Motschenbacher's cars were individualized to set them apart from other cars and to make them more recognizable as his. Each was red with a narrow white pinstripe, unlike any other car. The white background of his racing number 11 was always an oval, unlike the circular ones on other cars.

In 1970 R. J. Reynolds Tobacco Company and its agency William Esty produced a television commercial that used a stock photo showing several race cars on the track. Motschenbacher's car was in the foreground. The driver could not be identified in the photo.

The ad agency altered the photograph for the commercial. They changed the numbers on all of the cars; Motschenbacher's number 11 was changed to 17. A spoiler (wing) was attached to the car displaying the name of the product, Winston. All other product names were removed from the other cars.

The agency then filmed the slide adding a series of comic-book-type balloons with messages. Over Motschenbacher's car the balloon said: "Did you know that Winston tastes good, like a cigarette should?" The commercial was broadcast nationally.

Motschenbacher filed suit in *Motschenbacher* v. *R. J. Reynolds Tobacco Co.*, 498 F.2d 821 (9th Cir. 1974). The court agreed that the plaintiff himself was not recognizable. However, the decoration of the car in the picture left little doubt that the car was that of Motschenbacher, and it implied that he was driving. R. J. Reynolds lost the case.

Use of a Performer's Style

Appropriation of a performer's style is another way that one's right of publicity can be violated. Guy Lombardo had invested 40 years in developing his image as Mr. New Year's Eve. Add to this the combination of New Year's Eve, balloons, party hats, and "Auld Lang Syne" in the right context and you have an image that is unmistakable, and one that can be exploited commercially.

Doyle Dane Bernbach, the ad agency for Volkswagen, entered into negotiations with Lombardo in late 1974 to obtain his appearance in a television commercial. The negotiations, however, fell through. Regardless, the ad agency went ahead and produced the commercial featuring several products of the car manufacturer all set against the background of a New Year's Eve party.

Lombardo's name was never mentioned, but the actor used to portray the bandleader conducted the band using the same gestures and choice of music. Even the set resembled the one that Lombardo had become so associated with. The case that resulted was *Lombardo* v. *Doyle Dane Bernbach, Inc.*, 58 A.D.2d 620, 396 N.Y.S.2d 661 (App. Div. 1977). Lombardo won.

Use of Three-Dimensional Objects

Eleanor Brown Young was, in 1941, a professional model of junior misses' clothes. She was employed by a department store and was asked to pose for the making of a mannequin. She allowed Greneker Studios to mold the mannequins in her image—her form, features, and likeness—for the exclusive use of her employer.

Later, it was learned that Greneker sold the mannequins to other people. *Young* v. *Greneker Studios, Inc.,* 175 Misc. 1027, 26 N.Y.S.2d 357 (Sup. Ct. 1941), was the case that followed. Young alleged that Greneker manufactured and sold mannequins in her likeness, without her permission, for the purposes of trade. Under New York Civil Rights Law, section 51, an action may be brought by "any person whose name, portrait, or picture is used . . . for advertising purposes or for the purposes of trade without the written consent first obtained."

Even though Young gave her permission for her employer to make and use the mannequins in her image, she had not given permission to the company who manufactured them to sell to anyone else.

What this case points up is that the courts give broad latitude to what form constitutes a portrait or picture of a person. A picture is not limited only to a photograph of the person, but to any representation of that person. The representation can be two-dimensional or, as in this case, three-dimensional. The words *picture* and *portrait* are general enough to encompass any form from a photograph to a painting to a sculpture.

Use of Photo-Illustrations

Another form that can create a problem involves photo-realistic illustrations. On February 15, 1978, Leon Spinks defeated Muhammad Ali in a 15–round split decision. Until then, Ali had been the heavyweight boxing champion of the world. In the February 1978 issue of *Playgirl* magazine a picture ran with an article entitled "Mystery Man," showing a nude black man seated in a corner of a boxing ring. The illustration fell somewhere between cartoon and realistic art. The article was not editorial, but rather fictional writing, using, as the court determined, the picture of Ali solely "for the purposes of trade."

There was no question that the portrait was of Ali. In the court's words: "The cheekbones, broad nose, and wideset brown eyes, together with the distinctive smile and close-cropped black hair are recognizable as the features of . . . one of the most widely known athletes of our time." In *Ali* v. *Playgirl, Inc.*, 447 F. Supp. 723 (S.D.N.Y. 1978), the court agreed that Ali's right of publicity had been violated.

One important thing to note here is that not only was the magazine liable for the violation of the right of publicity, but the artist who drew the portrait was named as a defendant as well.

Use of Modified Photos

When a photograph or picture is modified or altered slightly, but still identifiable as a specific person, a problem can result. A situation such as this happened quite some time ago in 1917 when Gladys Loftus, a 22-year-old Ziegfeld Girl, appeared in the rose garden scene in *Midnight Frolics* wearing a special costume known as the rose costume made by Lady Duff-Gordon.

Loftus had her picture taken wearing the rose costume by Alfred Johnson, a photographer employed to take pictures of some of the girls in that play in costume. Loftus became readily recognizable in her costume, and the public became very familiar with Johnson's photograph of her.

Sometime later The Greenwich Lithographing Company, a designer of theatrical and movie posters, was hired to produce a poster for the photoplay *Shame*. The posters were distributed throughout the city of New York. The name *Shame* appeared very large on the poster along with copy that read:

Coming
Soon
to your
local
theatre
John W. Noble presents
the photoplay of the hour
SHAME
featuring
Zena Keefe
(A story of the world's unjust condemnation.)

On the poster was a picture of a man pointing his right hand in scorn at a woman who had her head slightly bowing. Greenwich admitted that it had copied the photograph of Loftus to use as the model of the woman in the poster. The artist, Ira Cassidy, used the rose costume picture when he painted the poster art for *Shame,* making only slight variations— changing the tilt of the head; lowering the hair; altering the outline of the nose, chin, and neck; and removing the right arm from view. All other aspects of the photo were duplicated in the painting.

The court determined in *Loftus* v. *Greenwich Lithographing Co., Inc.,* 192 A.D. 251, 182 N.Y.S. 428 (App. Div. 1920), that the poster was not a direct copy of the photo, but the image of Loftus was duplicated in such a way as to make it easily identifiable as being Loftus. Loftus won her case.

Use of a Voice Impersonation

Here again, the advertiser must be careful. A very popular trend, especially in radio commercials, is to produce spots using voice impersonators. At the end of these spots an announcer states "celebrity voice impersonated." This is done to clarify that the voice is an imitation and to avoid a violation of the celebrity's right of publicity.

THE HOLLYWOOD STUDIO
MUSEUM COMMERCIAL

At the beginning of this chapter, I wrote about a television commercial that I had produced for The Hollywood Studio Museum. Now that you have read the chapter, I'm sure that you can see why I used the story to begin.

Let's analyze that commercial to see if and where a problem could arise. First, there is the image of C. B. DeMille. Do we have to be concerned with invasion of his privacy rights? What about his rights of publicity? Secondly, we must consider the rights of Gene Barry.

DeMille's privacy rights ended at the time of his death, so there is no problem. Regarding publicity rights, did we need the permission of the DeMille heirs to use his name and likeness? As we know, publicity rights are survivable under certain conditions. Under California law (that's where jurisdiction would be), the publicity right is descendible, but only where it was exploited commercially during life. DeMille exploited his name and likeness during his life for commercial purposes. He was a very famous motion picture director, and his name alone sold many movies. Permission of the DeMille heirs was required and obtained.

As for Gene Barry, consent was required. Obviously, his appearance in the commercial was evidence of his consent to have his name and image used. However, there were questions of usage. Barry, through the Screen Actors Guild (SAG), authorized use for only one year. The consent was for television and radio use only. Another restriction Barry required was that we clearly identify the spot as "a public service message." This was to clarify that he had donated his time and name and thereby not diminish his worth for commercials other than public service messages. Noncompliance with any of these restrictions could give rise to a lawsuit for breach of his publicity rights.

CHAPTER 6

COPYRIGHT REGULATION

Life is a copycat.
—*Heywood Broun*

Let's examine a situation involving an advertising agency. We'll call the agency Doufus-Wazoo Advertising. One of its clients, Acme Chemicals, made swimming pool chlorine and asked the agency to create a television commercial for its product. The creative team got together and devised a spot showing different shapes and styles of pools with the tag line: "No matter what the shape of your pool, Acme will keep it in shape."

The agency writer and creative director took the idea to Mr. Wazoo, the agency president (and Acme account executive), and explained that this could be a terrific spot with the right pools, scenes, and camera angles. Mr. Wazoo loved the idea. He wanted to produce an impressive commercial, but knew that the client didn't have much of a budget. Therefore, filming the commercial was out of the question.

So, Mr. Wazoo told the creative director to get a selection of the best pool shoots he could find from a stock photo house. The creative director ordered a group of 104 color slides. When the slides came in, Mr. Wazoo and the creative director looked them over and picked the best 14. But the fee for using the photos was $300 each. Mr. Wazoo ordered all 104 slides to be sent out and duplicated. Then, he instructed the creative director to use the 14 best in the commercial.

The creative director explained that the agency should not have duplicated all of the slides without permission from the stock photo house. He also explained that the agency could not use the photos in the commercial unless it had permission and paid the appropriate fee. Since the slides were copyrighted, this would be illegal.

Mr. Wazoo claimed that the client did not have $4,200 to pay for all 14 slides, but here's what he did. He sent the slides back to the stock photo house, but told them that the agency only needed to use—and pay for—one slide in the commercial. The agency, however, used all 14. Mr. Wazoo boasted, "They'll never find out, and if they do we'll just pay the fee."

The creative director, under protest, produced the commercial using the 14 slides, 1 of which was paid for. The commercial aired, and Acme was thrilled with the results. Doufus-Wazoo beamed with pride at its creative work. Mr. Wazoo gloated at producing the commercial for next to nothing and for making the client happy. Everyone—except the creative director, who saw the light from the oncoming train—was very pleased.

Not too long after, a United States Marshall walked into the agency and handed Mr. Wazoo a summons. The agency, the photo lab that duplicated the photos, the editing company that made the commercial, the distributors who were listed on the commercial, and the client were all being sued for copyright violations. The stock photo house claimed over $5 million in damages. And then depression set in.

Could such a blatant violation of copyright really happen? Would an agency be naive enough to think that it could get away with such a thing? Could this story be real? Absolutely. I know, because I was the creative director. Ultimately, the case was settled out of court.

This type of copyright abuse occurs quite often—in fact, too often. In many cases, the agency just doesn't understand what can and can't be done legally. Some know the rules and still ignore them. As in the situation I just explained, some learn the hard way. Since forewarned is forearmed, let's take a look at the areas of copyright law that affect advertisers. Keep in mind as you read this chapter and the next (on trademark) the differences between the two areas of law. Each is based on different principles and, therefore, must be thought of separately.

THE COPYRIGHT ACT OF 1976

The Copyright Act protects the creators of artistic works as an incentive to pursue their creative talents. The United States Constitution—Article 1, Section 8—provides that Congress shall have the power: "To promote the Progress of Science and useful Arts, by securing for limited Times to Authors . . . the exclusive Right to their . . . Writings . . . ." The original Copyright Act was passed by the first Congress in 1790, shortly after the signing of the Constitution. The act has been amended over the years in 1831, 1870, 1909, and most recently in 1976.

In 1976 Congress updated the Copyright Act, which went into effect on January 1, 1978. Any work produced after that date was covered by the new law. Works created prior to that date are covered by the Copyright Act of 1909. In this chapter we deal with the current act.

REQUIREMENTS TO QUALIFY FOR COPYRIGHT PROTECTION

It is important to understand what can qualify to be copyrighted. There are conditions that must be met in order to apply for protection under copyright law. Then, to qualify, a work must be the product of the original author and meet the requirement of originality. It must also be considered a "writing" and be fixed in a tangible medium. Let us look at each of these requirements separately.

Definition of a *Writing*

To be eligible for copyright protection, an item must be fixed in writing. The common definition of a writing is much different than the legal definition. Under the Copyright Act, the definition of *writings* is quite broad. Basically, a writing is anything that is "fixed in any tangible medium of expression, now known or later developed, from which [the original] can be perceived, reproduced, or otherwise communicated, either directly or with the aid of a machine or device."[1]

At the time when the Copyright Act was first written, about the only means of performance was the stage. There were, of course, books, maps, and so on, which were specifically listed in the original act. But other than those forms of creative expression, the stage was all that was left. In those years, the only medium to record the stage performance was the mind of the audience. Today, a performance can be recorded in many ways with incredible realism. Protection of the creative work, therefore, has had to expand with technology to keep pace with the times.

Between 1970 and 1971 Mr. Goldstein and his associates purchased copies of record albums or tape cassettes at local record stores. They took these recordings and duplicated them on tape and distributed them to retail stores to be sold to the public. Goldstein never asked for permission from, and made no payments to, the artists, writers, performers, producers, or any other person involved with the original recordings. No payments were made for the use of the artist's name or the title of the original album.

Eventually the State of California, where this occurred, arrested and prosecuted Goldstein in *Goldstein v. California,* 412 U.S. 546 (1973), for record piracy: the unauthorized duplication of major artists' performances. In this case, the United States Supreme Court established that a writing covered "any physical rendering of the fruits of creative, intellectual, or aesthetic labor." Records and tape recordings certainly qualified.

Fixed in a Tangible Medium

As we saw earlier, in order for an original work to be considered a writing, the work must exist in some tangible entity. A tangible entity can be paper, video tape, film, computer disk,

---

[1]17 U.S.C. section 102(a)(1982).

record, recording tape, or almost anything else capable of maintaining its form. Under the copyright statute, material is protected when it is created and fixed into a concrete medium so that it can be perceived by others.

David Brown wrote a term paper for Professor Hagendorf's law course in 1977. In the fall of 1978, Hagendorf adopted Brown's paper in an article he wrote for Commerce Clearing House, a legal publisher. Brown sued—and won—for copyright violation in *Hagendorf v. Brown*, 699 F.2d 478 (9th Cir. 1983). Even a term paper can be protected by copyright. It is a tangible form that can be perceived by others.

Definition of *Author*

Only the original author of a work can receive copyright protection. This was first discussed in *Burrow-Giles Lithographic Co. v. Sarony*, 111 U.S. 53, 58 (1884). In this case, photographer Napoleon Sarony took a picture of Oscar Wilde in January of 1882. Sarony claimed that he was the author of the copyright to that picture, entitled "Oscar Wilde No. 18." Sarony printed a copyright notice on each copy of the photograph which read: "Copyright, 1882, by N. Sarony."

Burrow-Giles had printed reproductions of the Oscar Wilde picture without Sarony's permission. Burrow-Giles argued that a photographer cannot be considered an author and therefore cannot hold the copyright to the photo. However, the court disagreed and awarded Sarony $600 in damages (remember, this was 1883). At the time of this case, photography was a rather new medium and did not exist at the time the original copyright act was created.

From this case an *author* is defined as the person "to whom anything owes its origin; originator; maker . . . ." Lord Justice Cotton defined an author this way: "In my opinion, *author* involves originating, making, producing, as the inventive or master-mind, the thing which is to be protected, whether it be a drawing, or a painting, or a photograph."

In addition, the author of a work protected under copyright has a variety of rights. These include the rights to make and distribute copies of the work, to create adaptations, and to publicly display and perform the work.

Requirement of Originality

Copyright protection is available only to original works. But what is the definition of *original?* An original work must be the result of an independent effort. Here's an example.

United Card Company and Roth Greeting Cards were both in the business of manufacturing greeting cards for sale through gift and card stores. United president, Mr. Koenig, and vice president, Mr. Letwenko, produced a series of seven cards that bore an amazing resemblance to seven cards already produced by Roth. When Roth found out about this, *Roth Greeting Cards* v. *United Card Co., 429 F.2d 1106 (9th Cir. 1970),* resulted.

Roth's suit was for copyright infringement. While United claimed that the cards it produced were its own creations, it admitted to "visiting greeting card stores and gift shows in order to observe what was going on in the greeting card business." In addition, Roth had a complete staff of writers and artists, while United had none. In fact, most of United's work was done by Koenig and Letwenko themselves.

Although the United cards were not exact duplications of the Roth cards, they were "in total concept and feel the . . . same as the copyrighted cards of Roth." The United cards were far too similar to the Roth cards, even to the casual observer. Since the Roth cards were the originals, they were protected by copyright. As a result, United lost the case.

THE SCOPE OF COPYRIGHT PROTECTION

Anyone who deals with advertising needs to understand copyright and what it protects. Certain works can be copyrighted, others cannot. Now we take a closer look at what can and cannot be protected.

Under the current definition, almost any form of expression can be covered under the Copyright Act. For the advertiser, the most common forms of copyright works include:

1. Photographs, television commercials, videos.
2. Illustrations, renderings, cartoons, prints, charts, models, mock-ups, drawings.

3. Sound recordings, radio commercials, music.
4. Ads, billboards, brochures, displays.
5. Literary works.

Generally, items that are not eligible to be copyrighted include the following:

1. Works that have not been fixed in a tangible form. For example, if a person creates a song in his mind, it must be put in writing or some other tangible form to be copyrighted. The thought is not tangible because others cannot perceive it.
2. Titles, names, short phrases and slogans, symbols, or design elements. These items could be protected under trademark law in certain cases. See Chapter 7.
3. Ideas, procedures, methods, systems, processes, concepts, principles, discoveries, devices, and machines. These would be protected under patent law if the item qualified.
4. Works that are only common property information and have no original authorship. This includes items like calendars, rulers, public lists, and so on.

Copyright Protects Only a Specific Item

Copyright, as we have seen, protects the work from unauthorized duplication or copying. The work might be in any form from a brochure, to a photograph, a drawing, a sign, or a television commercial. However, copyright protects only the tangible medium used. As an example, if a photograph of a house is copyrighted, only the specific photograph is protected, not the house that it depicts.

This situation actually occurred in *Modern Aids, Inc.* v. *R. H. Macy & Co.*, 264 F.2d 93 (2d Cir. 1959). Modern Aids ran newspaper ads for a massage machine that it made. Macy duplicated the machine almost exactly, which was legal since there was no patent on the machine. However, Macy also copied Modern Aids' ad, which was illegal. The Modern Aids ad was copyrighted and therefore protected. Yet the machine shown in the ad was not protected by copyright.

Objects of Use Are Not Copyrightable

Objects which are only *objects of use* are not copyrightable. Things like time cards, account books, diaries, bank checks, score cards, address books, order forms, and the like fall into this category. In other words, items that do not in and of themselves convey information are considered items of use. While a blank account book cannot be copyrighted, a specific one with entries in it can be.

Copyright of Compilations, Derivative Works, and Collections

A compilation, collective work, or derivative work may be copyrightable in some cases. A derivative work can include a work that is based on one or a number of preexisting works: translations, abridgements, fictionalizations, a motion picture adapted from a novel, reproductions, and condensations. Collective works also include periodicals, anthologies, or encyclopedias where a number of separate works are brought together into one entity.

A compilation is a collection or assembling of preexisting works. According to the Copyright Act a compilation is "data that are selected, coordinated, or arranged in such a way that the resulting work as a whole constitutes an original work of authorship."[2] It is important to keep in mind that in order for the derivative work or collection to be copyrightable, it must have enough originality in itself to merit protection. Also, it must not infringe any other existing copyrights. To avoid violations, permission must be obtained from the original authors.

A person who assembles these separate works into one unit would be considered the author of the collective work, and, if the work is copyrightable, that person may be the owner of that copyright. But the owner of the collection of works only owns the rights to the collection, not to the individual works that it is composed of.

---

[2] 17 U.S.C. section 101.

Rand McNally, in 1978 and again in 1982, produced the *Rand McNally Mileage Guides* for sale to the public. These guides listed mileage figures between various cities throughout the United States. Rand McNally gathered the distance figures for its guide from various city, county, and state maps that were in the public domain. It also examined road conditions, compensated for variations between map sources, and broke down the distances into smaller segments. Unavailable mileage figures between some cities were developed from scales between other cities. *Rand McNally Mileage Guides* were compilations and were copyrighted. As we saw earlier, individual facts cannot be copyrighted, yet certain compilations of facts can be protected under copyright.

A problem arose when Fleet Management System copied virtually all of the figures listed in the *Rand McNally Mileage Guides* to produce mileage guides of its own. This all came to light in *Rand McNally & Co. v. Fleet Management Sys. Inc.,* 600 F.Supp. 933 (N.D. Ill. 1984). In this case, the court determined that Rand McNally had valid copyrights to the compilation and that Fleet Management had infringed on its copyright. Keep in mind that it was not the individual figures that were protected under the copyright. But it was the collection of data that had been copied almost in total that caused the violation.

PROTECTION OF COPYRIGHT

To be protected by copyright, the author must abide by certain rules.

Notice of Copyright

When something is considered important enough to protect, it should be identified by a copyright notice. The notice must consist of three items: a *C* with a circle around it for visual works or a *P* with a circle around it for audio works (or the word *copyright* can be used), the year of first publication, and the copyright owner's name. Under the Copyright Statute, the following format should appear:

Copyright 1987, John Doe & Company.
or
©1987, John Doe & Company.

Ideally, each copy of the material should have this notice clearly and conspicuously showing. Proper notice shows the world that the owner claims the copyright to the work. Typically, copyright notice should be placed on:

- A photograph—printed on the back of the print.
- A slide or negative—attached to the sleeve.
- A TV commercial or video—legibly displayed on the screen at the beginning or end of the spot for at least two to three seconds.
- A magazine or newspaper ad—printed in the corner of the ad legibly.
- A radio commercial—printed on the label on the box and on the tape reel.
- Original artwork—printed on the back of the original.
- A book, report, or other literary work—printed on the title page at the front of the work.

Publication of Copyrightable Work

Legally, *publication* is defined as "the distribution of copies . . . of a work to the public by sale or other transfer of ownership, or by rental, lease or lending. The offering to distribute copies . . . to a group of persons for purposes of further distribution, public performance, or public display, constitutes publication."[3]

In other words, when someone gives a copy of an original work to another in connection with a proposal, the original is considered published. So, it is important that the original and any copies clearly display the copyright notice. Unless this is done, an inadvertent publication by another may cause loss of protection.

---

[3]17 U.S.C. section 101.

Registering for Copyright

Ideally, copyright should be registered as soon as the work is fixed in a concrete form. But in any case, a person must register the copyrightable work with the Copyright Office within five years of the date of publication. If notice was not placed on the work, the author must make a reasonable attempt to add the notice to all works distributed after discovery of the omission.

Although registering a work is not required to secure protection under copyright, there are valid reasons why the author should. Most importantly, registration of the copyright protects the author by providing evidence of ownership. This is a crucial point for legal support of an author's claim to copyright protection. If a work is infringed upon, prior registration is required before a lawsuit can be filed.

To register a copyright, the appropriate form must be completed. This form, along with copies of the work and a fee (currently $10) must be sent to the Register of Copyrights, Copyright Office, Library of Congress, Washington, D.C. 20559. That office can be contacted to obtain the required forms. Remember that there are different forms for different types of works, and it is important to use the proper one for registration. Here's a list of the current forms:

- TX: Nondramatic works, literary works.
- SE: Serials, successive items bearing numerical or chronological designations (newsletters, magazines, annuals, etc.).
- PA: Performing arts (musicals, dramatic works, motion pictures, audiovisual works, etc.).
- VA: Visual arts (pictorial, graphic works, sculpture, advertisements, etc.).
- SR: Sound recordings.
- RE: Renewal registration.
- CA: Corrections or amplifications.
- GR/CP: Group contributions to periodicals.

Duration of Copyright Protection

Copyright protection begins when the original work is fixed in some tangible form by the original author. Protection continues for the life of the author and for 50 years after his or her death. In works-for-hire situations (which we will discuss later in the chapter), the duration of protection is 75 years from the first publication date or 100 years from creation, whichever is shorter.

TRANSFER OF COPYRIGHTS TO OTHERS

The rights to a copyright are transferable, usually by assignment or licensing. The transfer of exclusive rights (where only the grantee can use the rights) is only valid if it is put in writing and signed by the holder of the copyright. Transfer of nonexclusive rights need not be in writing. Remember though, whenever a copyright is transferred or licensed, it must be recorded with the Copyright Office.

Compulsory Licensing of Copyright

Compulsory licensing covers certain works that others can use after the payment of a fee that is set by the Copyright Office. This is instead of the copyright owner agreeing to the use. This practice is common in the music industry. Here's how it works. If an agency wants to use a musical piece in a commercial, notice is served on the owner of the copyright, and monthly royalties are paid to the owner. Cable television can also obtain a compulsory license for the transmission of copyrighted works. Royalties are paid as a percentage of the gross receipts of the cable system to the Copyright Royalty Tribunal and later distributed to the owners.

Assignment of Rights

Many authors assign their rights to organizations who, in turn, authorize usage by others for a fee. Organizations such as

ASCAP (American Society for Composers, Artists and Publishers) hold copyrights for many musical works. Broadcasters and commercial users are required to pay a fee to ASCAP for the use of material, which is then distributed to the owners.

THE WORKS-FOR-HIRE RULE

When an employer, or other person or company, has an employee or agent perform work, the employer is considered the author and the owner of the copyright of that work. In other words, when the work is made by an employee, the actual person who created it does not own the copyright. The person who employed the worker does.

Works for hire include items produced by an employee as part of his employment. It also covers works specifically ordered or commissioned for a particular purpose if there is an agreement in writing that the work was for hire. However, a work for hire does not normally include routine professional services on behalf of a client (unless there is an agreement to the contrary).

To illustrate, if a photographer is hired by a company to photograph a product made by that company, the photographer is the copyright owner. This is not considered a work-for-hire situation unless there is an agreement to the contrary. However, if an employee of the company is asked to photograph that same product, the company is the owner of the copyright. In this situation it is a work for hire.

COPYRIGHT AND PROTECTION OF IDEAS

One point about copyright must be made clear. Copyright does not protect an idea, per se. It does, however, protect the expression of an idea. If the expression of the original idea is recognizable in another work, enough to create an infringement, a lawsuit may result.

I'll clarify this point. If Widget Manufacturing Company designed and built a new widget refurbisher, the company cannot copyright the machine. We saw earlier that devices are not copyrightable. If anything, the machine would need to be protected under patent law. Now, to produce a brochure for its new product, Widget Manufacturing had a photograph taken of the machine. That picture could be copyrighted. It's an expression of the idea. But the copyright only protects the photo, not the widget. Now, we take a closer look at this concept.

Copyright Does Not Protect Ideas, Per Se

As we saw in the previous section, copyright is limited in scope. It does not protect against the use of an idea. Copyright protection does not cover "any idea, procedure, system, method of operation, concept, principle, or discovery, regardless of the form in which it is described, explained, illustrated, or embodied in such work."[4]

Copyright Protects the Expression of an Idea

Copyright might be used to stem an unauthorized expression of an idea. An expression of an idea can take almost any form. An advertisement, a movie, a book, even a video game can all be expressions of ideas. Unlike a patent, copyright protects only the expression (tangible fixed form used to allow others to perceive it) of an idea—not the idea itself.

Atari (and Midway) own the exclusive copyrights for a video game called PAC-MAN. Atari markets a home video version of the game. Shortly after PAC-MAN hit the market, another company, North American Philips Consumer Electronics, hired independent contractor Ed Averett to create a video game, which was named K. C. Munchkin. Averett was very well qualified for the task since he had developed over 21 other

---

[4]17 U.S.C. section 102.

such games. Mr. Staup, who was the head of North American's video game development department, and Averett got together and visited various sites to see and play PAC-MAN.

The two men discussed the PAC-MAN game, its strengths and weaknesses, and decided to develop a version of the game for North American's Odyssey line of home video games. Averett began work on the project; and when it was completed, he showed it to North American. It examined the game and determined that it was totally different from PAC-MAN. However, its legal counsel told North American that the game should be changed even more to avoid any potential liability. Averett made a few changes to the game, and it was then produced and marketed to the public.

Stores in various cities ran advertisements promoting the new game. Typical of these ads were those in the Chicago *Sun–Times* and the *Tribune,* which described the K. C. Munchkin game as "a PAC-MAN type game." The ads also claimed that it was "as challenging as PAC-MAN." When Atari learned of the new game, it produced its own response: *Atari Inc.* v. *North American Philips Consumer Elecs.,* 672 F.2d 607 (7th Cir. 1982).

Atari sued for copyright infringement because North American's game was so similar to PAC-MAN. Atari argued that an ordinary consumer would assume that K. C. Munchkin was taken directly from PAC-MAN. Atari needed to prove that K. C. Munchkin was "substantially similar" to PAC-MAN. And it did that.

The problem in cases like this is that there is no concrete rule or test to determine if an idea or the expression of an idea has been taken. It is a very subjective decision. This was addressed in the Atari case. "Obviously, no principle can be stated as to when an imitator has gone beyond copying the 'idea,' and has borrowed its 'expression.'" The video board game "idea" can not be protected. But the specific form, PAC-MAN, which is the expression of the game (idea), can be protected. It is the individual features of the game—shapes, sizes, colors, sequences, arrangements, and sounds—taken as a whole that form an expression.

Exact duplication or almost exact duplication is not necessary. "[A]n infringement . . . includes also the various modes in which the matter . . . may be adopted, imitated, transferred, or reproduced, with more or less colorable alterations to disguise the piracy."[5] The main consideration given by the courts in these situations is the overall similarities, not the minute differences between the works.

The features of K. C. Munchkin are very similar to PAC-MAN. Those of you who have played the game would instantly recognize it as a copy. The main "Gobbler" characters in both games are very similar in shape, mouth, and movement, as well as the sounds that they make. The same applies to the other characters of the two games. The board field is also very similar as is the method of play and the rules and object of the game. The K. C. Munchkin game uses the same role-reversal and regeneration characteristics of PAC-MAN as well. There was no doubt in this case that there was copyright infringement. Atari won a permanent injunction and substantial damages.

THE FAIR USE DOCTRINE

All holders of copyright are susceptible to the *fair use doctrine,* which permits certain copying of copyrighted material for purposes of criticism, news reporting, teaching, or research. But generally, copying for commercial use violates the rights of the copyright holder. The fair use doctrine will not protect advertisers who try to use copyrighted material for commercial purposes without paying for it.

Fair use was developed to balance the authors' rights to protection of their copyrights (and accompanying economic compensation) and the public's desire for a free flow of ideas and information. Basically, the doctrine tries to achieve a safe area between copyright protection and freedom of speech.

---

[5]*Universal Pictures Co. Inc. v. Harold Lloyd Corp.,* 162 F.2d 354, 360 (9th Cir. 1947).

Fair Use Protection against Infringement

The main issue that the courts look to in determining if the use falls under the fair use doctrine is whether the usage substantially diminishes the value of the work.

One of the most notable examples of fair use was shown in the landmark case involving Universal City Studios and its suit against Sony. This case discussed an area of copyright— copying by home video recorders—that Congress could not have conceived would occur when it enacted the first Copyright Act. Sony manufactures millions of its Betamax video tape recorders and sells them through many retail outlets.

Universal owns the copyrights to many of the movies, television programs, and other programming that is broadcast over public television stations across the country. In *Sony Corp. v. Universal City Studios,* 52 U.S.L.W. 4090 (U.S. Jan 17, 1984) rev'g 659 F.2d 963 (9th Cir. 1981), Universal claimed that by Sony providing the means to record these shows from television, people were violating copyright laws. Universal was claiming essentially contributory infringement in its suit. In other words, Sony could not infringe on Universal's copyrights directly, but Sony contributed to it through consumers who bought and used the video recorders. However, Universal's argument was not valid under the Copyright Act. Contributory infringement did not exist here anymore than it would for a camera manufacturer or a photocopy machine manufacturer.

In addition to the fact that people could copy movies and television shows, Sony argued that the video recorders allowed the consumer to time-record a show. This allowed the consumer to watch the show when it was more convenient. Actually this expanded the television viewing audience that would watch the program. Therefore, the copyright holder could not object to the home recording of copyrighted material. The key here was whether the home recording impaired the commercial value of the work now or in the future. In this case it did not.

The court determined, in a 22-page opinion, that noncommercial home recording of copyrighted material broadcast over public television was fair use. It did not constitute copyright infringement. *Noncommercial* is the operative word here because there would be no reduction in the market for the original work.

Although every commercial use of material that is copyrighted is a copyright infringement, noncommercial uses are a different matter. In order to uphold a claim of infringement through noncommercial uses, it must be shown that allowing the use could cause some harm or could damage the potential market for the work. If the copyrighted material is used for commercial use, the likelihood is *presumed,* but for noncommercial use it must be *shown.* Universal tried to argue that by allowing its shows to be recorded at home, "live television or movie audiences will decrease as more people watch Betamax tapes as an alternative." The court disagreed and Sony won.

Here's an example that relates to advertising directly. The *Miami Herald,* published by Knight-Ridder Newspapers, developed an ad campaign to promote the new format of its television magazine supplement to the newspaper. The Sunday supplement was introduced in the newspaper in November 1977. The campaign included print ads and television commercials.

The whole focus of the *Miami Herald*'s campaign was to compare its TV magazine to *TV Guide* magazine. The print ads showed the covers of both magazines in actual size, with the headline which read:

> The *Herald*'s new TV book.
> It's a little bit bigger
> and a little bit better.

The message in the ad was that the *Miami Herald*'s book was bigger, had more listings, was easier to read, and was more up-to-date than *TV Guide* magazine. In the television commercials, the message was the same. A typical spot, based on the Goldilocks and the Three Bears theme, went like this:

Narrator:

> This is the story of Sidney Bear, Cindy Bear, and Junior Bear. They all loved to watch TV, but . . . .

Older man:

> This TV book is too small.

Child:

> This TV book is too big.

Older woman:

> This TV section is just right.

Narrator:

> It was the Sunday *Herald*'s new TV book at no extra cost. The three bears loved the new, just-right size with its up-to-date and more complete listings. 'Til one day this little blonde kid—uh, but that's another story. Something for everybody. Everyday of the week.

When Triangle Publications, the owner of *TV Guide* magazine, heard about these ads, it sued in *Triangle Publications* v. *Knight-Ridder*, 626 F.2d 1171 (5th Cir. 1980). In that case, Triangle objected to the reproduction of a *TV Guide* cover in both the print ads and in the television commercials. The issue was whether the use of the *TV Guide* cover in the *Herald*'s ads was allowed under the Fair Use Doctrine.

The court determined that the *Herald*'s ads did not copy the essence of *TV Guide,* that is the articles, schedules, and features contained inside. The *Herald* reproduced only the cover of the magazine. This, the court reasoned, was not enough to consider that the commercial value of *TV Guide*'s copyright would be diminished. In fact, if the *Herald*'s ads drew customers away from *TV Guide,* it would have been because of the validity of the message—the difference between the two publications—and not from showing the *TV Guide* cover.

The court concluded by saying that *TV Guide* "suffered no economic injury whatever from the alleged infringement of its copyright." The *Herald* won its claim of fair use.

When Fair Use Does Not Protect against Infringement

The fair use doctrine has been used to allow certain forms of parody. In other words, when the "style of . . . [a] work is closely imitated for comic effect . . ."[6] But the advertiser must understand what limits the fair use doctrine has. To determine whether the use made of a copyrighted work can be considered fair use, the following needs to be considered:

1. The purpose and character of the use, including whether such use is of a commercial nature or is for nonprofit educational purposes;
2. the nature of the copyrighted work;
3. the amount and substantiality of the portion used in relation to the copyrighted work as a whole; and
4. the effect of the use upon the potential market for or value of the copyrighted work.[7]

On the other hand, in the advertising area, a parody can fall outside the fair use doctrine when another company's theme, tag line, or primary characteristic is taken. Sambo's restaurants found this out when Dr. Pepper sued it for copyright infringement.

Dr. Pepper developed its "Be a Pepper" campaign in 1978. Within four years the company had spent over $100 million on the campaign and had realized tremendous results. Dr. Pepper was so pleased with the results that it planned for the campaign to run for 10 years.

In many cases, success breeds imitation. Here, Dr. Pepper was the success, Sambo's was the imitation. While the Dr. Pepper campaign was in its fourth year, Sambo's ad agency, Bozell & Jacobs, developed a campaign called *Dancing Seniors*.

Both commercials started with one person (the leader) dancing and singing the beginning of a jingle. "I drink Dr. Pepper and I'm proud. I'm part of an original crowd." As opposed to "I eat at Sambo's Restaurants every day. I get a special deal on my dinner meal." Both commercials used people dancing along with the leader to a chorus: For Dr. Pepper,

---

[6]*Webster's New Collegiate Dictionary* (Springfield, Mass.: Merriam-Webster Inc., 1976).
[7]17 U.S.C. section 107.

"Wouldn't you like to be a Pepper, too?" For Sambo's, "Don't you want to be a senior, too?"

The Sambo's commercials first aired in late 1980, and when Dr. Pepper learned of this in January 1981, it sued in *Dr. Pepper Co. v. Sambo's Restaurants, Inc.*, 517 F. Supp. 1202 (1981). Dr. Pepper held copyrights to its television commercials and to the "Be a Pepper" jingle. As a defense to the case, Sambo's claimed that it was entitled to parody the Dr. Pepper commercial under the fair use doctrine.

However, any commercial use has a tendency to contradict the fair use doctrine. This is a very risky area for advertisers. Because of Sambo's use of the essence and substance of the Dr. Pepper commercial, it diminished that spot's value, uniqueness, and originality. This took the infringement out of the fair use arena. Sambo's impact on the useful life of the "Be a Pepper" campaign was an infringement. Sambo's lost.

As we have just seen, the more unique the concept of the commercial, the greater the protection required against infringement. If the commercial is based on more general situations, greater latitude will be allowed. Any car commercial may use a showroom as its setting with a car salesman speaking to the audience. However, if the bulk of the commercial shows a salesman announcing claims about the car, which are obvious and blatant lies, and subtitles are shown (as in the recent Isuzu commercials), the courts will be more inclined to consider this type of use an infringement.

COPYRIGHT PROTECTON RELATING TO ADVERTISEMENTS

Copyright law can, as we just saw in the Dr. Pepper case, be used against an ad or commercial that is derived substantially from another commercial. This goes back to the "expression of an idea" concept we discussed earlier—that is, if the other commercial takes the same basic feeling or premise. Devising a concept for an advertisement is an idea. A specific ad is an expression of that idea, and it can be copyrighted.

When an Ad Takes the Expression of Another Ad

To illustrate this point, let's take, for example, McDonald's campaign developed directly from the H. R. Pufnstuf cartoon characters. When McDonald's agency, Needham, Harper & Steers, developed the McDonaldland concept, it was patterned after the characters in the H. R. Pufnstuf TV show. The Pufnstuf television series, which began in 1969, featured a boy named Jimmy, who lived on "Living Island"—a fantasyland inhabited by mayors with large round heads and oversized mouths, Keystone-Cop-type assistants, crazy scientists, multiarmed evil creatures, animated trees having human faces, and talking books. The McDonaldland image used the same location, characters, and elements.

McDonald's even used the people who designed and constructed the sets and costumes for Pufnstuf, as well as some of the same voice people for the campaign. The set itself was the same Living Island concept used in Pufnstuf. In January 1971, the McDonaldland commercials began to air.

The Pufnstuf cartoon characters had previously been licensed for Kellogg's cereal, the Ice Capades, as well as other toys and games. In fact, the Ice Capades actually replaced the Pufnstuf characters with the McDonaldland characters after the McDonald's campaign began.

The creators of Pufnstuf sued McDonald's for copyright infringement in *Sid & Marty Krofft* v. *McDonald's*, 562 F.2d 1157 (1977). Even though the specifics of the McDonald's campaign were not identical, they were substantially similar enough to have captured the look and feel of the Pufnstuf characters. McDonald's lost, was required to stop using the ads, and had to pay $50,000 in damages. The credibility of the Pufnstuf characters had been eroded. Pufnstuf even showed loss of licensing (Ice Capades) as a direct result of the McDonaldland ad campaign.

When There Is Not Enough Similarity of Expression

On the other hand, certain cases show a lack of similarity and therefore no infringement of copyright. The creators of the

Pink Panther character tried at one time to sue Lincoln-Mercury for copyright infringement. When Lincoln-Mercury developed an animated cat character for use in its ads, the creators of the Pink Panther sued because of the similarities between the Lincoln-Mercury cat and the Pink Panther. It was claimed that both of the cats had human characteristics and mannerisms as well as elongated tails. But this was not enough to cause infringement.

However, Lincoln-Mercury had used a live cougar as its identity for many years prior to the alleged infringement. Also, the Lincoln-Mercury cat had a strong masculine personality as opposed to the glitzy Pink Panther personality. In fact, many companies have used animated cats including Exxon, B. F. Goodrich's Tigerpaws tires, Kellogg's Tony the Tiger, Le Tigre shirts, and others.

LEGAL REMEDIES

Obviously, one should not take the copyrighted work of someone else and use it without permission. The legislature, in creating the Copyright Act, felt that there were two good reasons for making this unauthorized use illegal. First, the author may have future plans to license the work. And infringement could severely interfere with these plans. We saw this in the Dr. Pepper case. Second, the author may consider that commercial exploitation of his work may demean his creative efforts and thereby erode its credibility. This is especially true in the case of literary works, although we saw the advertising version of this in the Pufnstuf case.

If actual damages cannot be shown, the statute provides for not less than $250 or more than $10,000 per infringement. This can be increased up to $50,000 for willful infringement. There is a wrinkle to the "per infringement" fine. If we go back to the Doufus-Wazoo story at the beginning of this chapter, you'll recall that the agency was slapped with a $5 million lawsuit. In that case the TV commercial used 14 copyrighted slides, and the use was willful; that's $50,000 multiplied by 14.

Also, each time the commercial airs another 14 infringements occur. It adds up fast!

Remedies for copyright violaton include injunction, seizure, impounding and destruction of infringing items, damages and profits, and in many cases attorney's fees. Indeed, advertisers should be careful where copyright infringement is concerned. The penalties are very severe, as we have seen.

CHAPTER 7

TRADEMARK REGULATION

I hate the man who builds his name
On ruins of another's fame.
—*John Gay*

Within 20 years after the Civil War, a Columbus, Georgia pharmacist named John S. Pemberton had invented, manufactured, and sold a variety of products. These ranged from Globe of Flower Cough Syrup and Indian Queen Hair Dye to Triplex Liver Pills, Gingerine, and Extract of Styllinger.

Pemberton later moved to Atlanta where he created a drink that combined an extract of kola nut, fruit syrup, and extract of coco leaf. In 1886 he took his syrup to Jacob's Drug Store in Atlanta where, on a trial basis, he was allowed to sell his drink at the soda fountain. The drink became modestly popular with the patrons of Jacob's Drug Store.

Eventually, Pemberton became disillusioned with the drink and sold out to a man named Asa Chandler. Pemberton made $1,750. With his new product in hand, Chandler first advertised the drink as a "Wonderful Nerve and Brain Tonic and Remarkable Therapeutic Agent." By 1893, Chandler had sold 48,427 gallons of his tonic. A year later, soda water was added to the mixture, and it was bottled.

Chandler's tonic grew in popularity. In fact, the more a person drank, the more that person wanted. In part this was because of the caffeine and small amounts of cocaine that remained in the syrup after the brewing process. As sales of the drink grew, it became apparent to Chandler that he needed to market the product on a larger scale. So in 1906 he hired the Massingale Agency in Atlanta to advertise his product. From that point on, Chandler's drink (which was named by the Jacob's Drug Store bookkeeper) soared into marketing history on the wings of a trademark the likes of which has not been seen since. The drink was Coca-Cola.

The strength and value of a trademark to identify goods and distinguish them from others cannot be overstressed. As Coca-Cola proved, a successful business gets that way by investing much of its efforts in building a favorable identity for itself and its products. This can be called *reputation,* and in many cases it is called *good will.* The public's knowledge of this image—what we in advertising work so hard to build and maintain—will draw first-time buyers and continue to bring others back.

Once the buyer, let's say Ms. Jones, is satisfied with a product, she will seek it out to buy again. Ms. Jones seeks out the same product because of qualities she found in it before, and hopes to find again. Sociologists tell us that these qualities can range from actual product performance to ego gratification. Regardless, the consumer finds a fulfillment in some form. This satisfaction in a brand also draws attention to new products introduced by the same manufacturer. It can create a built-in satisfaction with the product, even before it's purchased.

Take, for instance, the Chevrolet Corvette. Since the car's inception in 1953, its popularity has grown steadily. In the mid–1970s when oil prices were climbing, the 55 MPH speed limit was invoked, and the V–8 engine was dying, demand for the Corvette continued to grow. Over the years, this demand has increased. Today, even before a new Corvette model is released, many people place orders for one. This demand exists, in large part, because of the reputation that the Corvette name has built up over the years. I know from personal experience that this is true. I've owned eight of them.

Trademarks are an important part of indicating the origin of the product. They make the product recognizable and identifiable by the consumer. Often, the trademark can say more than any photo or amount of ad copy. The old adage claims that pictures speak louder than words. Well, a reputable trademark can speak louder than both. Take the Volkswagen ads in the early 1970s. One such ad ran the headline: "Here's What to Do to Get Your Volkswagen Ready for Winter." The rest of the page was blank—except for the Volkswagen logo. That shows how strong the Volkswagen trademark is.

When a consumer sees a product with a particular trademark on it, that person should be able to rely on the image that the name conjures up and to trust the quality of a product that carries a certain trademark. After all, the trademark laws were created to support that trust. A trademark is intended to distinguish one manufacturer's goods from others'. That's why a company must protect its trademark and also why a company must be careful not to let its trademark infringe on another company's mark. These are concerns the advertiser and its agency need to pay close attention to.

While reading this chapter, the advertiser should be most concerned with how to protect its own mark and not infringe another's mark. It is not my desire here to teach the reader how to search trademarks. That should be left to a competent trademark attorney.

QUALITIES OF A TRADEMARK

There are many aspects of trademark law that advertisers must understand. One of the first is what qualities need to exist in a trademark. The following section discusses this important issue.

The Difference between a Trademark and a Trade Name

Under the federal Trademark Act of 1946, trademarks may be registered but trade names may not. Trademarks are defined as any "word, name, symbol, or device or any combination thereof adopted and used by a manufacturer or merchant to identify his goods and distinguish them from those manufactured by others." Trade names, however, are "individual names and surnames, firm names and trade names used by manufacturers, industrialists, merchants, agriculturalists, and others to identify their businesses, vocations, or occupations."[1]

In other words, a trademark refers to products or services, and a trade name refers to the business entity itself. For example, Beatrice (the company) is a trade name while its product, Hunt's Ketchup, is a trademark; Kodak is a trademark while Eastman Kodak Company (the manufacturer) is a trade name.

Types of Trademarks

The term *trademark* actually covers a number of marks of various uses. There are trademarks, service marks, certification marks, and collective marks. A trademark, as we have just discussed, is used in connection with a product.

A service mark is used when referring to the sale of a service. Since services rarely have anything concrete to place a name or mark on, the service mark generally identifies the business itself. In this case, what would usually be considered a trade name would be registered as a service mark. As an example, if Acme Auto Repair Service, Inc. desired to protect its name, it would have to register it as a service mark. These services are identified with an *SM* symbol. The category of service marks also includes slogans, titles, characters, and symbols.

Another form of mark is called a *certification mark,* which calls attention to the origin, material, nature, method of manufacture, accuracy, quality, or labor source. Examples include the Good Housekeeping Seal of Approval, the mark used for the AFL–CIO, or the mark used by the cotton industry to designate 100 percent cotton.

Collective marks, another form of trademark, are marks used to show membership in an organization or group. A collective mark has no relation to a specific product or service, but merely shows affiliation with the group. The marks used

---

[1]Trademark Act of 1946, section 45, 15 U.S.C., section 1127 (1976).

by the Elks' Lodge or the American Association of Advertising Agencies are prime examples.

STRONG MARKS AND WEAK MARKS

As far as trademarks are concerned, there are two strengths of marks: strong and weak. The law offers different protection for each type; it is, therefore, important for the advertiser to be aware of the difference between a strong and a weak mark.

Strong Marks

Strong marks can receive protection under trademark law simply because they are distinctive. Marks in this category can include those that are suggestive of the product. A strong mark is coined or fanciful, such as *Kodak, Xerox,* or *Exxon. Sure* for deodorant, *Raid* for insect spray, and *Drano* for clogged sinks are other examples of strong marks. Strong marks, while they are suggestive, are more than just descriptive of the product.

Weak Marks

Weak marks do not automatically qualify as trademarks. But weak marks will be permitted protection if the Trademark Office allows it. A weak mark would be composed of words that praise or describe a quality like *best* or *premium*. However, a weak mark, as such, will be granted protection as a trademark only if it has acquired a secondary meaning. This implies that the consumer makes an automatic connection between the product or service (that the mark refers to) and its source. In other words, the consumer must associate the product and the mark with the manufacturer. If this connection can be shown, then protection can be afforded the mark. For example, when you hear the term *Big Mac,* what do you think of? McDonald's of course. That's *secondary meaning*.

Another category of weak marks includes the use of geographical names. Unless secondary meaning could be established, names using *Swiss* for watches, *Columbian* for coffee, *California* for oranges, and so on would not be protected under trademark law. These names only designate the geographic origin of the item, and a manufacturer cannot take such a designation for its own to the exclusion of others.

Weak marks also include surnames. Common names like Johnson, Smith, White, and Jones have probably already been trademarked at some time. If another company has already trademarked a surname, a manufacturer runs the risk of infringing on that mark. Even if the name is the person's legitimate one, it can still infringe on another's trademark.

Let's say that Smith's Oil begins manufacturing its product and trademarks the name. It runs a high risk that another trademark already exists under that name. If time goes by, and no claims are brought up, consumers may become accustomed to associating Smith's Oil with the product. In this case the name develops a secondary meaning. At that point, if another manufacturer begins selling an oil product under that same name, in the same marketing area, it would be infringing on Smith's trademark.

Marks that use descriptions of praise as trademarks also fall into the weak mark category. *Premium, World's Finest,* and others are very weak unless secondary meaning can be attributed to the trade name. However, this does occur, as we see later. Products such as Pabst Blue Ribbon beer, Gold Medal Flour, and others have achieved this secondary meaning status and are protected under trademark.

REGISTRATION OF MARKS

Trademarks are registered with the U.S. Patent and Trademark Office in Washington, D.C. The importance of registering a mark is that this act notifies others that the owner of the mark *claims* the exclusive rights to its use. But registering the mark alone is not enough to protect it. Notice of registration must be used along with the mark. Keep in mind that registering a mark does not create an unlimited legal right to ownership; rather it's a claim of ownership. To be protected, the mark must not infringe on another's mark. These points are discussed more fully later in this chapter.

Length of Registration

Once a trademark is registered, the claim is established for 20 years. Registration may thereafter be renewed for unlimited 20-year periods. An application must be filed within six months before the expiration of a trademark. As an alternative, it can be renewed up to three months after a mark expires if a penalty is paid.

Trademark Registers

Trademarks can be recorded in one of the two registers of the Trademark Office—the Principal Register or the Supplemental Register. All applications for registration go first to the Principal Register. If the mark does not meet the requirements of that register, it is passed on to the Supplemental Register for possible acceptance. This is an automatic process that the Trademark Office uses.

Unlike copyright, it is important to note that registering a mark does not provide any rights of ownership in a trademark. Any such right exists through common law as a property right. Because of this, many marks that are not registered are still afforded trademark status. Also, others that are registered can be denied trademark status if challenged by a previous holder of the mark. The registers only provide a place where marks can be listed for public record. This doesn't mean that there are not good reasons to register a mark. Indeed there are, and we look into these reasons later.

The Principal Register accepts only marks that meet certain standards. But keep in mind that the Trademark Office does not provide a search for similar marks that have already been registered. The applicant must perform its own search or hire someone (such as a trademark attorney) to do this. The Trademark Office only judges a mark against its standards for acceptance, not against other marks already registered (that's the applicant's responsibility). Standards for acceptance include:

1. The mark must be distinctive.
2. The mark must not be immoral, deceptive, or scandalous.
3. The mark must not consist of a flag, emblem, or insignia of the United States or other country.
4. The mark must not consist of the picture or signature of an individual without prior consent.
5. The mark must not resemble another mark.
6. The mark must not be merely descriptive of the product.
7. The mark must not be geographically descriptive of origin.
8. The mark must not be a surname.

The Supplemental Register is more lenient. There are four requirements for registration.

1. The mark must be unqualified for registration on the Principal Register.
2. The mark must be able to distinguish the product.
3. The mark must not fall into any category above for the Principal Register except numbers 6, 7, or 8.
4. The mark must have been used in commerce for one year without opposition.

NOTICE OF REGISTRATION

It is important to place a notice of registration along with a trademark. A notice of registration of a mark allows damages to be recovered if the mark is infringed on. Damages cannot be received otherwise. Only the infringing usage of the mark may be stopped. Notice also lends a certain amount of credibility, which should help deter potential infringers. Last, registration notice helps establish that the mark is a trademark and not a generic term.

The Trademark Act states that " . . . a registrant of a mark . . . *may* give notice that his mark is registered by displaying with the mark as used . . . the letter *R* enclosed within a circle." The Act goes on to say: " . . . in any suit for infringement under this chapter by such a registrant failing to give such notice of registration, no profits or damages shall be recovered . . . *unless the defendant had actual notice of registration . . .* " (emphasis added).[2] For the record, there are two alternate notice forms, which are acceptable but seldomly used because of their sheer bulk: "Registered in U.S. Patent and Trademark Office" and "Reg. U.S. Pat. & Tm. Off."

Marks that are not yet registered, but for which application has been made, can be identified with a *TM*. Please be aware that it is legal to use a notice of actual registration only after a certificate of registration has been issued.

The registration notice may be placed anywhere in relation to the mark and in any type style. If a trademark is used more than once in an ad, it is not necessary for the notice to appear every time the mark appears. But it should appear with the mark that is first or most prominent. Also, the notice itself should be large enough to be readily recognizable and readable.

Another important item to note is when using another company's trademark in your ad, always use the appropriate notice with the mark. Also, when you use someone else's trademark in an ad, capitalize the mark. For example, use *XEROX* or *Xerox,* not *xerox.* In other words, capitalizing lets the reader of the ad know that the mark is the trademark of another company. This may need to be clearly identified elsewhere in the ad if there is any chance of confusion, such as: "Acme® is the registered trademark of Widget Manufacturing Co."

Using a Trademark Notice with a Mark that Has Not Been Registered

If a notice is placed with a trademark that is not registered, severe problems can result. First, the right to register the

---

[2]15 U.S.C., section 1111.

mark in the future can be lost. A trademark known as *Four Roses* is a good example. In 1925, Small Grain Distilling Company applied for and was granted the trademark *Four Roses* for its high-grade whiskey. Four Roses was a widely known brand name at the time.

Early in 1926 another company, Four Roses Products, began placing a notice of registration on its product of malt syrup used in making liquor. The name *Four Roses* was used on the product packaging along with the notice "Trade-Mark Reg. U.S. Pat. Off." When Small Grain learned of this, it brought the case to court in *Four Roses Products Co. v. Small Grain Distilling & Drug Co.*, 29 F.2d 959 (DCC 1928).

The fact was that Four Roses Products had never received a registration of the trademark for *Four Roses*. It had applied for registration but had been denied. Four Roses Products used the registration notice even though it knew it had no registration. The court determined that Small Grain's trademark of *Four Roses* was legitimate and Four Roses Products's mark was not. Essentially, Four Roses Products tried, through the use of the registration notice, to imply that its product was authentic and that any other, including Small Grain's, was an infringement. This was not accurate.

Since Four Roses Products used the registration notice on an unregistered mark, it lost the case, had to pay damages for infringement, and lost any chance for future registration. As a side note, this must have been a heated case in court considering the time. It occurred not long after the 18th Amendment to the Constitution was adopted. The amendment repealed prohibition.

There is another reason not to use a registration notice if the mark has not been registered. The right to stop another company from using the same mark can be lost. Fox Photo learned about this in 1972. The company provided photo developing and finishing services to the public. The Fox Photo logo consisted of a red running fox with the name Fox Photo across it. Fox Photo also used, as part of its logo, a red *R* in a circle.

Sometime later, Harry Otaguro began publishing a photo magazine called *FOX*. Fox Photo decided that Otaguro's magazine infringed its trademark because of the similarity in the names and the fact that both products were in the same field—photography. *Fox-Stanley Photo Products, Inc.* v. *Otaguro,* 339 F. Supp. 1293 (D. Mass 1972), resulted. Unfortunately Fox Photo had never registered the Fox Photo mark. That, however, did not deter it from placing a registration notice with the logo to imply registration of the mark.

Fox Photo lost its case at the outset because it simply did not own the trademark. Because it had used a registration notice on a mark that had not been registered, Fox also lost its right to be granted a trademark registration for its logo in the future.

ANOTHER FORM OF ERRONEOUS USE OF A TRADEMARK

Other than the situations described above, there is an additional form of trademark misuse that can cause problems. This involves using a mark with goods different from those it was registered for. A trademark can be used only with the product line that it was registered for. In other words, registering a mark for use with a specific product does not automatically allow that mark to be used with other products. Here's an example. If Bonzo Company manufactures and owns a trademark for its line of cars, it cannot use that trademark for its new line of dishwashers.

In 1965 Cumberland Packing Company wanted to register the mark for *Sweet 'N Low*. The low-calorie sugar substitute was to be marketed to the public in packet form. Cumberland had been assigned the rights from the inventor, May MacGregor.

Another company who sold only to the trade, Duffy-Mott Company, also owned a trademark to use the name *Sweet 'N Low*. It too had been assigned rights to the name by MacGregor for use of her sugar-substitute formula in canned, frozen, and fresh fruits, vegetables, pudding, and cake mixes. Duffy-Mott opposed the registration of the mark for Cumberland's packet version of *Sweet 'N Low*, claiming that it would infringe Duffy-Mott's use of the mark. *Duffy-Mott Co.* v. *Cumberland Packing Co.,* 154 USPQ 498 (TTAB 1967), was the case.

Duffy-Mott argued that by allowing registration of *Sweet 'N Low* for the sugar substitute sold in packets, its mark would be eroded. However, the court reasoned that the issuance of a registration for Cumberland would not infringe on the mark used by Duffy-Mott. Cumberland's mark would be directed to the public in raw form. On the other hand, Duffy-Mott's mark was directed to the trade to be included in a finished product. Since the product lines and markets were different for each company, the court allowed registration for Cumberland.

GENERICIDE: WHAT CAN HAPPEN
WHEN A MARK IS MISUSED

Ultimately, when a mark is misused, it can be lost to the forgotten world of generic terms. The consumer may begin to consider a trademark as the name of the product line in general. Then the trademark no longer identifies and distinguishes the product of a particular manufacturer. Instead of standing for one particular *brand* of the product, it stands for the *type* of product. This is called genericide.

When a trademark is not handled properly, it can be weakened to the point that it is not protected as a trademark any longer. Therefore, an advertiser must be very cautious. The manufacturer's own promotion, labeling, and advertising are at fault when this happens. Genericide has been the demise of many trademarks, which we now consider product lines, including *cellophane, celluloid, kerosene, lanolin, linoleum, milk of magnesia, dry ice,* and (as we'll soon see) *aspirin, thermos bottles, escalators,* and *PROMS.* These trademarks were allowed to deteriorate to the point that they became synonymous with the product and not the manufacturer.

The key is this—genericide happens in the mind of the consumer, not to the product. Yet, there is something that the advertiser can do to control how the consumer perceives the trademark. The easiest way to avoid genericide and to protect a trademark would be to use the word *brand* in connection with the name and product. In other words, *Xerox brand copiers* or *IBM brand computers.* This helps forestall any assumption by consumers that the trademark is generic.

The Headache that Aspirin Caused

How many brands of aspirin can you think of? Bayer, Johnson & Johnson, Excedrin, Bufferin, and Anacin are some of the major ones. This is the problem that Bayer had to deal with in the early 1920s, because originally *aspirin* was a trademark.

Aspirin was the trademark for the drug acetyl salicylic acid, a powder that was patented by Bayer Company in 1898. In 1904 the name of the drug was changed to *momoacetica-cidester of salicylic acid*. Bayer began to allow chemists, druggists, and physicians to make the powder into tablets and sell them under names such as *Squibb Aspirin, Smith, Klein & French Aspirin*, or *United Drug Company Aspirin*. United Drug, in particular, sold over 19 million tablets in its first two years. The consumer could not possibly have known the manufacturer of the drug, only the name on the bottle.

It wasn't until 1915 that Bayer changed its policy and discontinued selling to other manufacturers. From that time on Bayer prohibited others from manufacturing or selling the drug. It began selling aspirin itself in tablets to the general public. Tablets were sold in tin boxes with the legend:

The Trademark "Aspirin"
(Reg. U.S. Pat. Office)
is a guarantee that the momoaceticacidester of salicylic acid
in these tablets is of the reliable Bayer manufacture.

But it was too late. The harm had been done. Because of this change in policy, United Drug sued Bayer claiming that the name *aspirin* had become a descriptive name, free for anyone to use. The case was *Bayer Co. v. United Drug Co.*, 272 F. 505 (SDNY 1921). While the druggists knew that *aspirin* was a trademark, the general public did not. Its only knowledge of the product was through the over-the-counter brands that were available, especially since many manufacturers had used the name alone in labeling and advertising—all allowed by Bayer.

Bayer understood that the term *aspirin* had become generic. When it began to sell to the public in 1915, its labels read: "Bayer—Tablets of Aspirin." This meant that the tablets were Bayer's make of the drug known as *aspirin*.

The public could not have known that *aspirin* was a trademark for momoaceticacidester of salicylic acid; it thought that *aspirin* was the name of the drug. By allowing this confusion to occur, Bayer failed to protect the trademark as such, and the Trademark Office declared the trademark not valid as of 1918. The court in its decision agreed with the Trademark Office and United Drug and determined that the name *aspirin* had become a generic term.

The Moving Stairway

Trademark registration number 34,724 was registered to Charles D. Seeberger in 1900. The trademark was for the term *escalator.* Seeberger had invented the device and assigned the trademark to the Otis Elevator Company a number of years later. Otis manufactured not only elevators but escalators as well.

A typical ad for Otis from a 1946 issue of *Architectural Forum* magazine contained the following:

Otis (logo)
THE MEANING OF THE OTIS TRADEMARK.
To the millions of daily passengers on the
Otis elevators and escalators, the Otis
trademark or name plate means
safe, convenient, energy-saving transportation.
* * * * *
To the thousands of building owners and managers,
the Otis trademark means the utmost in safe,
efficient, economical elevator and escalator operation.

Obviously, the Otis name was treated as the trademark, and the names *escalator* and *elevator* were merely descriptive of the product. This was plain from the ad copy. As a result, the Haughten Elevator Company attempted, in the late 1940s, to have the name *escalator* declared generic.

Haughten succeeded with its efforts in *Haughten Elevator Co. v. Seeberger,* 85 USPQ 80 (Comm'r 1950). Here, the court determined that the term *escalator* was a generic term for a moving stairway. The court reasoned that the term *escalator* described any moving stairway made by any company. Otis, in large part, allowed this to occur through its literature and advertisements. The term *escalator* was not used by Otis to identify it as the originator and only source of an escalator. The word *escalator* became a generic term for any moving stairway. Trademark number 34,724, held by Otis, was cancelled.

Keeps Hot Things Hot and Cold Things Cold

A German company named Thermos-Gessellschaft M.B.H. manufactured vacuum-insulated containers that were adopted from Dewar's vacuum flask invention of 1893. In 1907 the German company sold out to a new American company named The American Thermos Bottle Company. This company produced the now well-known thermos bottle. Initial sales were $114,987 in 1907, and by 1960 the company grossed $13,280,164 for the year.

As early as 1910, American Thermos was promoting the fact that *Thermos* had become a household word. The term *Thermos* was used as a synonym for *vacuum-insulated,* thus Thermos bottle. The public adopted this term and began referring to the thermos bottle as if it were a type of product.

A competitor, Aladdin Industries, also manufactured vacuum-bottles. When it started calling its product a thermos bottle, American Thermos sued to stop this use in *American Thermos Products Co.* v. *Aladdin Industries, Inc.,* 169 USPQ 85 (D. Conn. 1970). Here, it was determined that *thermos* had become the generic term for the vacuum bottle. American Thermos used the combination of *Thermos bottle,* not *Thermos-brand bottle,* or *Thermos vacuum-insulated bottle.* American Thermos could still use the name, but so could anyone else.

The court stated that American Thermos, during the early 1900s, welcomed the public's conception that *Thermos* was synonymous with *vacuum-bottle.* American Thermos "recognized this as an 'enormous amount of free advertising' worth, at that time, between three and four million dollars . . . " On the other hand, it paid a high price for the free advertising; it lost its trademark protection forever.

The PROM that Never Was

Most losses of trademark protection to genericide occurred in the years when marketing and advertising techniques were young. As we have seen, many early trademarks were lost because of poor handling. But today's company is still at risk when it comes to trademark protection. Today's high-tech market clearly shows this with a recent example involving the computer revolution and one of its components, the PROM.

High-tech afficionados love to use initials for the names of components. For computer memories, RAM stands for Random Access Memory, SAM for Simultaneous Access Memory, CAM for Content-Addressable Memory, ROM for Read-Only Memory, and PROM for Programmable-Read-Only Memory.

The Harris Semiconductor Division of Radiation Inc. developed the first *field* programmable-read-only memory. Harris adopted the acronym *PROM* for the product and put that name on its merchandise. Soon after, other companies developed similar programmable-read-only memories and also used the designation *PROM*. Harris attempted to stop the other manufacturers from using the name and claimed that *PROM* was a trademark for its own products. Harris then attempted to register the term *PROM* as its trademark.

When this occurred, Intel (one of the other competitors) brought an action to stop Harris from acquiring the trademark. In *Intel Corp.* v. *Radiation Inc.,* 184 USPQ 54 (TTAB 1974) it was discussed whether or not the term *PROM* should be trademarked. Essentially, the court determined that *PROM* was merely the "descriptive letters [that] constitute the initials or abbreviations of the common name of the product . . . "

In fact, the trade had already become well-acquainted with the term *PROM*. The acronym had been used extensively by publications within the trade and in promotional materials from the various manufacturers. It was common practice in the electronics industry to use abbreviations as an easy method for identifying the different components. And it was also well-known that these acronyms did not denote the manufacturer of the component. Indeed, *PROM* was only a descriptive name or acronym for the specific type of memory. Harris was not granted a trademark for the term *PROM*—it was a generic name.

HOW TO AVOID GENERICIDE

Al Ries and Jack Trout, in their inspiring book *Positioning: The Battle for Your Mind,* extoll the virtues of positioning a product so that the brand name becomes generic with the product. It's the basis for positioning strategy, and anyone in advertising knows it. Let's take a short step back to our Bayer case. In their book Trout and Ries use it as an example to discuss the power in a name. To today's consumer, "The tablets in a bottle of aspirin are Bayer. Not aspirin manufactured by a company called Bayer. . . . The great strength of a generic brand name is this close identification with the product itself. In the consumer's mind, Bayer is aspirin, and every other aspirin brand becomes 'imitation Bayer.' "[3]

The strength of positioning strategy cannot be questioned. But what is good for marketing image may be terrible for protection of a trademark. The advertiser must be careful not to destroy a trademark in the process of building brand awareness.

The best method an advertiser can use to avoid genericide is to treat a trademark as a trademark. In other words, distinguish it from the type of product. How can you accomplish this? For copywriters, a trademark should always be an adjective that modifies the product name. It is not a noun; the noun names the type of product. Actually, the trademark is a proper adjective modifying a proper noun—allowing both words to be capitalized.

As an example, let's take a fictitious company called Metropolis Manufacturing. It makes a car called the Metro-

---

[3]Al Ries and Jack Trout, *Positioning: The Battle for Your Mind* (New York: McGraw-Hill), p. 105.

mobile. Now *Metromobile* is a trademark. In its advertising, to protect the trademark, Metropolis must not refer to its car merely as a Metromobile. It should refer to it as a Metromobile Automobile or Metromobile Car. (Also, note that a trademark is not a verb since you can't Metromobile to work.)

Here's the test to see if a trademark is treated as a trademark therefore avoiding possible genericide. A typical advertisement headline to accomplish this might read: "Enjoy the Freedom of the Road in a Metromobile Car." If you eliminate the trademark, *Metromobile,* does the remaining sentence make sense? Aside from the fact that it would be a horrible headline, it would read: "Enjoy the Freedom of the Road in a Car." The headline still makes sense grammatically. Compare this to an incorrect usage of the mark. If the type of product were left out, the headline would read, "Enjoy the Freedom of the Road in a Metromobile." Now remove the trademark from this version, and the headline would make no sense: "Enjoy the Freedom of the Road in a _____." The sentence must make grammatical sense if the trademark is removed.

But let's be realistic. Not all advertisers follow these rules. One reason is that some trademarks are so strong the consumer invariably knows exactly what product is being referred to. How is it that a consumer can drive a Ford, smoke a Salem, use a box of Tide, drink a Coke, or wear a pair of Nikes? It happens because some trademarks are very well understood by consumers. They know exactly what product is being referred to. This is the secondary meaning we discussed earlier. The consumer places the generic name with the trademark automatically in his mind. We saw this earlier when we discussed positioning. Yet, all trademarks are not so fortunate as to have that status.

Only in cases where the generic term is understood so thoroughly can the advertiser feel secure that the trademark can stand alone. For new products, or lesser-known ones, habitual use of the trademark without mention of the generic product should be avoided. When Bayer first heard people ask, "What brand of aspirin do you use?" it should have seen what was coming.

SLOGANS

In some cases slogans may be trademarked. But those situations are controlled by strict guidelines. Slogans, if they qualify for protection, fall into the category of service marks. A trademark may consist of any slogan, but it is allowed protection only if it distinguishes the product.

In 1932 American Enka adopted the mark of a black rectangle with a thread extending through it. Below the logo was the name American Enka. Above the logo was the slogan, "The Fate of a Fabric Hangs on a Thread." By 1939 Enka had modified its mark. The slogan remained, but the logo became a tag with the words *Fashion Approved* in it. Underneath the tag were the words *Enka Rayon*.

Then in 1947 Enka applied for registration of its mark with the slogan. The Commissioner of Patents and Trademarks, John Marzall, declined to register the slogan. Enka then filed suit in *American Enka Corp.* v. *Marzall*, 92 USPQ 111 (DDC 1952), to decide the matter.

The court determined that Enka could register its slogan with the logo. Enka was the only user of the slogan, and it had become widely known to identify its rayon yarn from any other. The slogan unquestionably indicated the origin of the mark. Indeed, certain word combinations can operate as trademarks when they are so distinctive. The fact that the words comprise a slogan does not bar them from trademark status.

"We Smile More"

Marriott had been using the slogan, "We Smile More," as an advertising and promotional line since 1964. In 1968 the hotel chain applied for registration of the slogan as a trademark after it learned that Ramada Inns had begun using the same line.

The case went to trial *In re Marriott Corp.*, 517 F.2d 1364 (CCPA 1975), where it was determined the slogan did qualify to be registered. A slogan does not have to be unique in verbiage to qualify. "[A] capability of identifying and distinguishing the source of goods or services is all that is required to support registration."

The court went on to say that "the function of a . . . mark is to indicate continuity of quality of services, i.e., that the quality of services rendered in connection with a particular mark is controlled by a single entity." Marriott showed that customers were aware of the slogan and recognized the mark as belonging to it. These consumers substantiated that they knew the slogan referred to Marriott, and only to Marriott. Indeed, the slogan indicated the source. The court allowed the registration of "We Smile More" as a trademark.

The Slogan that's a Mouthful

Everyone in advertising will no doubt remember McDonald's campaign in the mid-1970s that used the slogan: "TWOALL BEEFPATTIESSPECIALSAUCELETTUCECHEESEPICKLES ONIONSONASESAMESEEDBUN."

McDonald's began using the slogan in its advertising in late 1974. It spent over $2 million in advertising, using the slogan as its theme through the end of 1975. The advertising campaign included almost every media available from TV, radio, newspaper, magazine, billboards, through point-of-purchase, contests, and premiums. In essence, McDonald's saturated the market with "TWOALLBEEFPATTIESSPECIALSAUCELET-TUCECHEESEPICKLESONIONSONASESAMESEEDBUN."

McDonald's applied for registration of its slogan as a trademark in 1975, and *In re McDonald's Corp.*, 199 USPQ 490 (TTAB 1978), resulted. At the hearing, the argument was made in opposition to the application, that the phrase was no more than a descriptive list of ingredients of a Big Mac sandwich. However, the phrase is a unique "and somewhat catchy arrangement and combination which in its entirety creates a commercial impression quite different from that of the individual words as they are ordinarily used."

Through its massive advertising campaign, McDonald's also met the second requirement for registration, that of knowledge of origin by the public. At the time, everyone who knew the name McDonald's knew the slogan. There was little doubt, the public knew that the phrase meant only McDonald's.

"America's Freshest Ice Cream"

When a slogan is a mere statement, puff, or irrelevant phrase, it will not be allowed protection. A good example of this is evident in the case, *In re Carvel Corp.*, 223 USPQ 65 (TTAB 1984), involving Carvel Ice Cream. Carvel wanted to register its slogan "America's Freshest Ice Cream." The company had been using the slogan since 1978 along with its logo. However, as the court put it, the mark "is not a mark capable of distinguishing [Carvel's] goods from like goods of others . . . "

Carvel attempted to argue its point that because it used the word *fresh* in relation to ice cream it is a distinctive mark. It felt that the word *fresh* was not normally associated with ice cream, and therefore it was distinctive. The court was not convinced. This simple expression of praise was not capable of functioning as a trademark. A common expression, such as the one Carvel used, could not indicate anything other than a motive toward high quality. It certainly could not indicate the origin of the mark to the general public. Hypothetically though, if it could have been proven that the slogan was well-understood by the public to mean Carvel, and only Carvel, the outcome may have been different.

Strictly speaking, the Trademark Act does not prohibit expressions of praise (even if they are self-inflicted) from being registered. But in order for one to be registered, there must be enough originality or uniqueness to set it apart from other marks in the consumer's mind. It must distinguish the origin (owner) of the mark for the consumer. Clearly, Carvel's slogan failed to accomplish this and therefore was refused registration.

Typical Slogans that Have Been Refused Registration

The following list presents a few more examples of typical slogans that have been refused registration.

"Best and Biggest Cigar"	Lewis Cigar Company
"America's Finest Overall"	Levi Strauss
"Tender Fresh"	Nash-Finch Fresh Cut Chicken
"Sudsy"	Parsons Ammonia
"Champagne"	Demos Salad Dressing with Champagne
"The Professional Health Care People"	Career Employment Services
"More Gun for the Money"	Mossberg Firearms
"America's Most Luxurious Mattress"	Englander Mattress Company
"For a Day, a Week, a Month or More!"	Brock Residence Inns

CONSIDERATIONS IN CHOOSING A TRADEMARK

When a company develops a new product, generally it creates a new name for it—and possibly a trademark. In many cases the ad agency is involved in choosing the name, so it's important to know what to consider in selecting a trademark.

Marks that Infringe Existing Marks

The most important concern in developing a new mark is establishing that it does not infringe on an existing mark. The new mark must not be the same as another existing mark or be confusingly similar to an existing mark.

Believe it or not, there is no single place where the applicant can look to find a list of all trademarks. Simply checking with the trademark office isn't enough. One reason for this is that some marks may be registered in a particular state (we look at this later in the chapter). Another reason is that a mark may have been used for many years without being registered. The original mark would be allowed protection in many cases under common law. Refer to the section "Trademark Registers" on page 144 for an explanation. There are, however, professional trademark search services. These services are fairly thorough and use a number of sources to determine if the mark already exists as a trademark. But beware. They are not 100 percent conclusive.

It is very important to check new trademarks before putting them into use as Goodyear found out. Goodyear is the world's largest tire manufacturer. In 1974 its net sales reached over $5.25 billion. A minor competitor, Big O Tire Dealers, manufactured a private label tire of its own. In late 1973 Big O named its line of tires *Big Foot*. The name appeared on the sidewall of each tire.

In July of 1974 Goodyear adopted the name *Big Foot* for its new Custom Polysteel Radial tire. Here the name also appeared on the side of the tire. Goodyear hired a trademark search firm to investigate any existing trademark conflicts. None were shown. Feeling secure, Goodyear developed an advertising campaign to promote its new tire, Big Foot. Within a year, Goodyear had spent over $9.6 million on the advertising of this one product. Typical headlines from Goodyear ads were:

> Bigfoot, the new Polysteel Radial
> only from Goodyear.
>
> * * * * * *
>
> Bigfoot. The Polysteel Radial that keeps
> its feet even in the rain.
> Only from Goodyear.

In August of 1974, Goodyear learned of the existing and previous trademark held by Big O Tires. Goodyear tried to buy the rights to use the name from Big O, but the offer was never accepted. When Big O refused the offer, it mentioned the possibility of a lawsuit if Goodyear did not stop using the trademark *Big Foot*. Goodyear informed Big O president Norman Affleck, that if Big O did bring suit, "the case would be in litigation long enough that Goodyear might obtain all the benefits it desired from the term *Big Foot.*

In fact, Big O Tires did sue in *Big O Tire Dealers, Inc.* v. *Goodyear Tire & Rubber Co.,* 561 F.2d 1365 (1977). The problem occurred because Goodyear—through their search firm—failed to verify that there was an existing trademark for *Big Foot*. Since there was, it lost the case.

At the trial it came to light that when Goodyear learned of the Big O trademark, not only did it not discontinue its ad campaign, which claimed exclusiveness, it continued to willfully infringe the existing mark. Goodyear basically thumbed its huge corporate nose at Big O. Because of Goodyear's action and its disregard for Big O's trademark, the court awarded $678,302 in compensatory damages and $4,069,812 in punitive damages.

Marks that Cannot Be Registered

There are a few areas that could disqualify a mark from registration. These were listed earlier in the section on the two registers and their requirements to qualify for registration. Now let's take a closer look.

Confusing or Deceptive Marks. Marks cannot be registered that are "likely . . . to cause confusion, or to cause mistake, or to deceive."[4] This could also occur through the use of a similar or exact duplication of another trademark.

Marks that Are Descriptive of a Place or Function. Marks cannot be registered as trademarks if they are only functionally or geographically descriptive, or if the mark is only a surname. In other words, the mark must be distinctive.

Use of Flags or Insignias. Marks cannot use flags, coats of arms, insignia of cities, states, the federal government, or foreign countries.

Use of Names or Personal Identities. Marks cannot use the name, image, or signature of a person, unless written permission is given.

Use of Immoral Marks. Marks cannot be "immoral" or "scandalous."[5] This includes names that are contemptuous or disparage a person, institution, established belief, or national symbol.

---

[4]15 U.S.C., section 1052(d).
[5]15 U.S.C., section 1052(a).

Protection Only for a Specific Category of Use

Keep in mind that a mark can only be registered for the specific category in which it is used. We saw this illustrated earlier in the Sweet 'N Low case. The Patent and Trademark Office maintains records for the classification of trademarks under the specific category of goods or services for which the mark is used.

The name Johnnie Walker has meant high quality Scotch Whiskey since 1880, when the trademark was created. I think I can safely say almost every adult knows the name Johnnie Walker and quickly associates it with whiskey. Since its inception, the name was heavily advertised and promoted. As a result, the name Johnnie Walker has gained an excellent and very recognizable reputation.

In the early 1950s, Tampa Cigar Company began marketing one of its cigars under the name *Johnnie Walker.* This irritated John Walker & Sons (the whiskey company) enough to file a law suit: *Tampa Cigar Co.* v. *John Walker & Sons, Ltd.,* 222 F.2d 460 (5th Cir. 1955), 110 USPQ 249 (Com. Pat. 1956). Clearly, the use of *Johnnie Walker* on cigars was an infringement. Tampa tried to take advantage of the fame and reputation built up in the Johnnie Walker name. In effect, Tampa Cigar tried to create the impression that the makers of the whiskey were the makers of the cigars. This is called *palming off.*

Tampa argued that because the products were different, it should be allowed to use the name. "That," the court said, "we decline to do." While the products, whiskey and cigars, are different, they are often sold to the public at the same time and in the same stores. Bars, liquor stores, restaurants, markets, convenience stores all sell these items. Johnnie Walker whiskey and cigars could literally be placed side by side and sold to the same person at the same time. This was a case where, even though the products were different, the cigar's use of the mark was an infringement.

On the other hand, there are cases where no infringement exists. A good example of this can be seen in *Holiday Inns, Inc.* v. *Holiday Out In America,* 481 F.2d 445 (5th Cir. 1973). Holiday Inns had developed a considerable reputation with the public for its chain of travel motels. Its reputation was one of consistent high quality. Keeping close watch over its marks of *Holiday Inn, Holiday Inns of America,* and *The Nation's Innkeeper,* Holiday Inns, Inc., guarded its service marks.

In 1966, another company opened a series of trailer parks under the name *Holiday Out* and *Holiday Out in America.* Holiday Out registered its trademark on January 23, 1967, describing its business as "maintaining and operating campground facilities for campsite owners." When Holiday Inn learned of this, it filed suit in July of that year.

The court found that there was no likelihood of the consumer being confused by the two trademarks. They were totally different markets, and no proof was shown to validate Holiday Inn's claim of infringement. The court felt that allowing both trademarks to be used "is not reasonably calculated to cause confusion or mistake or to deceive." Holiday Out was allowed to retain its trademark.

DECEPTIVE FORMS OF TRADEMARKS

In addition to the Trademark Office's regulations, the FTC can become involved if the trademark or trade name used is deceptive. The FTC's concern is any form of deception of the consumer, whether in an ad or a name. Having a trademark registered does not protect it against causing other violations of the law. In cases where the name does fall into the deceptive or false advertising arena, the FTC can force the company to stop using the name.

A rental car company using the trade name *Dollar-A-Day Car Rental* was brought into court by the FTC in *Resort Car Rental System, Inc.* v. *F.T.C.,* 518 F.2d 962 (9th Cir. 1975). It was shown that the name created an obvious impression to the public. The court said: "The 'Dollar-A-Day' slogan carries strong psychological appeal. Its connotations are obvious." The consumer could expect to be charged $1 per day for a rental car. This was certainly not true, however.

This case turned on the issue of deceptive advertising. The point here is that trademark registration did not create a shield to protect what was essentially a deceptive claim in the guise of a trade name. Dollar-A-Day was required to change its name.

FOREIGN WORDS AS TRADEMARKS

Another area to consider is the use of foreign words in trademarks. Some companies try to register marks using foreign words in place of the English version that they could not ordinarily register in English. If the words are descriptive of the product in that foreign language, then the United States will also consider them not qualified to be protected under trademark law. The guide should be that if the mark would not qualify in English, for whatever reason, it wouldn't qualify using another language either.

On another point, if a company desires to market its product in other countries, it must consider the trademark laws of those governments. They all vary and may have a large impact on the choice of a trademark. A specialist should be consulted in this case, since the requirements of foreign countries far exceed the scope of this book.

RESTRICTIONS IMPOSED BY STATE LAW

While the Trademark Act grants protection of trademarks on a federal level, the separate states can also grant trademark registration. However, only trademarks for professional services may be registered by the state. This applies only to businesses that the state categorizes as professional (medical, legal, architectural, etc.). These firms—which are prohibited from using fictitious names—may trademark their firm name even though they are using surnames. The regulations of the respective state should be considered in these situations.

CHAPTER 8

COMPARATIVE ADVERTISING

One man's ceiling is another man's floor.
—*Paul Simon*

The year was 1949, June to be exact. At 350 Madison Avenue in New York, Ned Doyle, Maxwell Dane, and William Bernbach, along with 13 employees, started an ad agency with a simple philosophy of Bernbach's: "Don't be slick. Tell the truth." Bernbach had a clear and deliberate approach to advertising. He felt that most advertising was dull and failed to motivate the consumer. "Business is spending money for advertising," he would say, "and is achieving boredom with typical American efficiency."

Doyle Dane Bernbach has produced its share of memorable ad campaigns over the years since its inception. In the beginning, the agency took on clients like Ohrbach's, Levy's Rye Bread, Polaroid, El Al Airlines and in 1959, Volkswagen. Doyle Dane Bernbach created the Volkswagen campaign that stands as one of the industry's best.

Then, in the fall of 1962, Avis moved its $1.5 million account from McCann-Erickson to Doyle Dane Bernbach. At that time Hertz was the car-rental leader and pulling way ahead of Avis. So, Doyle Dane Bernbach gathered art director Helmut Krone and copywriter Paula Green together. They came away with the first of a new series of Avis ads.

The first ad headline read:

Avis is only No. 2
in rent-a-cars.
So why go with us?

The copy continued:

"We try harder. (When you're not the biggest, you have to.)
We can't afford dirty ashtrays. Or half-empty gas tanks.
Or worn wipers. Or unwashed cars. Or low tires.
Or anything less than seat-adjusters that adjust.
Heaters that heat. Defrosters that defrost.
Obviously, the thing we try hardest for is just to be nice.
To start you out right with a new car, like a lively
super-torque Ford, and a pleasant smile.
To let you know, say, where you can get a good, hot
pastrami sandwich in Duluth.
Why?
Because we can't afford to take you for granted.
Go with us the next time.
The line at our counter is shorter.

Before the client was shown the new ad, Bernbach commissioned a consumer survey to pretest the ad. It scored very poorly. Nonetheless, Bernbach sold the client on the ad. Two years later Avis had increased its market share by 28 percent.

While Avis never mentioned who it tried harder than, everyone knew. Hertz was the number one car rental company at the time. Because of this, the Avis ads have become acknowledged as the first major comparative advertising campaign.

While the Avis campaign might have been the first comparative ad campaign, many more have followed, and they have run the gamut. My personal favorite started life in the late 1970s. The commercial depicted a small, bulbous store owner standing in his electric light bulb store. On the phone he proclaims: "If those bulbs aren't here tomorrow morning, I am out of business!" In the next scene, Dingbat Air Freight pulls up in front of the store, two days late. The courier scurries around frantically looking at the front door. A sign across the front of the store reads, "OUT OF BUSINESS."

Federal Express took on the giants of air freight, Emery, United Parcel, and even the United States Postal Service. Its slogan "Twice as good as the best in the business" became fighting words for Federal Express. The company started in 1971, and promptly fell $30 million into debt. But by 1983, Federal Express had broken the $1 billion mark in annual revenue. The Federal Express ads, created by Ally and Gargano, were classics of comparative advertising. They did the job, and did it very well.

When a company compares its product to another, both are identified—either by name, implication, or reputation. The use of another company's identity involves the use of its image trademark, or trade name. If this use is truthful, honest, and accurate the law allows products to compare themselves. On the other hand, if Bunko Company compares its product as being superior to Binko's product and a deception results, the image—and therefore value—of Binko's trademark can suffer. As we saw in Chapter 7, a company's trademark is of great value and can be protected by its owner under the law.

Therefore, comparative advertising is based on trademark law. In fact, comparative advertising is controlled by a section of the Trademark Act, which we discuss later. Under this law there is nothing illegal about comparing a product to a competitor's—unless a deception is created.

When this happens, there are basically two avenues of court action for victims. One is under federal law: Section 43(a) of the Lanham Act. The other is under state law: Antidilution statutes. We examine the advantages and disadvantages to both in this chapter.

THE DEVELOPMENT OF COMPARATIVE ADVERTISING

Today, comparative advertising bombards the consumer. But this hasn't always been the case. For the most part, comparative ads were not used prior to the 1970s. One main reason was that mentioning a competitor's name gave recognition to it and, in effect, free publicity. For this reason major companies rarely had any interest in comparative ads. These companies felt that nothing was to be gained from mentioning competitors.

Many companies also felt that showing a competitor in a bad light would create consumer sympathy for the competitor, thereby causing consumers to buy its products. As a result, companies did not want to be pictured as a "big bully picking on the little kid."

Taking part in comparative advertising was also considered by many advertising agencies to be unethical, hitting below the belt so to speak. Also, many advertisers and their agencies shied away from this practice for moral reasons. The main deterrent, however, was the FTC and the television networks—they would not allow comparative ads.

There was a concern over the use of advertisements that compared products. Until 1972 two of the television networks and some major print publications banned comparative ads altogether. But in 1972 the FTC came out in favor of comparative ads, and the media changed its stance. The media finally accepted comparative advertisements. The FTC proclaimed that by having the ability to compare the features of various products, the consumer could make a more informed and intelligent purchasing decision, as long as the comparison was fair and accurate.

The FTC Policy Statement established the commission's position on comparative advertising.

> The commission has supported the use of brand comparisons where the bases of comparison are clearly identified. Comparative advertising, when truthful and nondeceptive, is a source of important information to consumers and assists them in making rational purchase decisions. Comparative advertising encourages product improvement and innovation, and can lead to lower prices in the marketplace.[1]

Suave Shampoo's comparative advertising is a good example of the FTC's position. The ads for Suave compared it to other leading brands and claimed that Suave performed as well, but at half the price. The consumer benefited because that person could purchase a product that would do the same job at a lower cost. Because of its campaign, Suave Shampoo increased its sales from $10 million to $50 million in just four years.

---

[1]S. Kanwit, *Regulatory Manual Series, Federal Trade Commission,* Section 22.17 n. 13 (1985).

Comparative advertising also contributed to a 20 percent increase in sales in one month for Wendy's Restaurants. Wendy's superb "Where's the Beef?" campaign compared its single to McDonald's Big Mac and Burger King's Whopper.

Comparative advertising can have positive benefits for both the consumer and the advertiser. But it must be fair, truthful, and accurate. Otherwise it can be a dangerous instrument. This is why the FTC and the courts keep a very watchful eye on comparative ads.

The television networks, to help assure truthful comparative advertising, have established guidelines for advertisers to follow. I've included the National Broadcasting Company's (NBC) guidelines as an example in Exhibit 8–1 below.

EXHIBIT 8–1

NATIONAL BROADCASTING COMPANY
DEPARTMENT OF BROADCAST STANDARDS

Comparative Advertising Guidelines

NBC will accept comparative advertising which identifies, directly or by implication, a competing product or service. As with all other advertising, each substantive claim, direct or implied, must be substantiated to NBC's satisfaction and the commercial must satisfy the following guidelines and standards for comparative advertising established by NBC:

1. Competitors shall be fairly and properly identified.

2. Advertisers shall refrain from disparaging or unfairly attacking competitors, competing products, services or other industries through the use of representation or claims, direct or implied, that are false, deceptive, misleading or have the tendency to mislead.

3. The identification must be for comparison purposes and not simply to upgrade by association.

4. The advertising should compare related or similar properties or ingredients of the product, dimension to dimension, feature to feature, or wherever possible be a side-by-side demonstration.

EXHIBIT 8–1—*Continued*

5. The property being compared must be significant in terms of value or usefulness of the product or service to the consumer.

6. The difference in the properties being compared must be measurable and significant.

7. Pricing comparisons may raise special problems that could mislead, rather than enlighten, viewers. For certain classifications of products, retail prices may be extremely volatile, may be fixed by the retailer rather than the product advertiser, and may not only differ from outlet to outlet but from week to week within the same outlet. Where these circumstances might apply, NBC will accept commercials containing price comparisons only on a clear showing that the comparative claims accurately, fairly and substantially reflect the actual price differentials at retail outlets throughout the broadcast area, and that these price differentials are not likely to change during the period the commercial is broadcast.

8. When a commercial claim involves market relationships, other than price, which are also subject to fluctuation (such as but not limited to sales position or exclusivity), the substantiation for the claim will be considered valid only as long as the market conditions on which the claim is based continue to prevail.

9. As with all other advertising, whenever necessary, NBC may require substantiation to be updated from time to time, and may re-examine substantiation, where the need to do so is indicated as the result of a challenge or other developments.

Challenge Procedure

Where appropriate, NBC will implement the following procedures in the event a commercial is challenged by another advertiser.

1. If an advertiser elects to challenge the advertising of another advertiser, he shall present his challenge and supporting data to NBC in a form available for transmittal to the challenged advertiser.

2. The challenged advertiser will then have an opportunity to respond directly to the challenger. NBC will maintain the confidentiality of the advertiser's original supporting data which was submitted for substantiation of the claims made in the commercial. However, NBC will ask the challenged advertiser to provide it with a copy of its response to the challenger and, where the response is

EXHIBIT 8–1—*Concluded*

submitted directly to NBC, the challenged advertiser will be requested to forward a copy of its response to the challenger.

3. Where NBC personnel do not have the expertise to make a judgment on technical issues raised by a challenge, NBC will take appropriate measures in its discretion to assist the advertiser and challenger to resolve their differences, including encouraging them to obtain a determination from an acceptable third party.

4. NBC will not withdraw a challenged advertisement from the broadcast schedule unless:

   a. it is directed to do so by the incumbent advertiser;
   b. the incumbent advertiser refuses to submit the controversy for review by some appropriate agency when deemed necessary by NBC.
   c. a decision is rendered by NBC against the incumbent advertiser;
   d. the challenged advertiser, when requested, refuses to cooperate in some other substantive area; or
   e. NBC, prior to final disposition of the challenge, determines that the substantiation for the advertising has been so seriously brought into question that the advertising can no longer be considered substantiated to NBC's satisfaction.

5. NBC may take additional measures in its discretion to resolve questions raised by advertising claims.

TYPES OF COMPARATIVE ADVERTISEMENTS

There are basically three types of comparative ads. The most obvious category includes ads that specifically name the competitor and the product. One form of this can be seen in Suave's advertising claim that it's as good as five other (named) shampoos at half the price. Another form includes ads that attack the other product. Here are some examples: Scope mouthwash

ads claim that Listerine gives "medicine breath," and Minute
Maid lemonade ads label Country Time as being the "no lemon
lemonade."

The second type of comparative ad is more subtle. It does
not name the competitor, but rather implies it. The Avis ad
campaign that we discussed earlier falls into this area because
Avis does not name the competitor, but the implication is
understood by everyone. There's no doubt that it is Hertz.

The last area involves ads that do not identify the competitors. Comparisons between "our product" and "Brand X" are
good examples. This type of comparative ad was very popular
in years past, probably because it was safer.

THE LANHAM ACT

The federal government has developed a policing resource
through private court action that can overcome the inherent
drawbacks to an FTC action for deception. If you recall, we discussed in Chapters 2 and 3 that Section 5 of the FTC Act
allows the government to sue companies for deceptive advertising. But what about the company that was the victim of the
deception?

The Lanham Act allows one company to sue directly another company for damages due to deception and also serves as
a way of avoiding the red tape, time, and expense of an FTC
action. However, to qualify under the Lanham Act, the deceptive claim must also be a comparative claim. The Lanham Act
provides for private litigation for "all actions . . . without regard to the amount in controversy or to . . . the citizenship of
the parties."[2]

Congress passed Section 43(a) of the Lanham Act in 1946.
The section provides:

> Any person who shall . . . use in connection with any goods . . .
> any false description or representation, including words or other
> symbols tending falsely to describe or represent the same, and
> shall cause such goods or services to enter into commerce . . .

---

[2]Section 39 of the Lanham Act, 15 U.S.C. Section 1125(a).

shall be liable to a civil action by . . . *any person who believes that he is or is likely to be damaged* by the use of any such false description or representation. (Emphasis added)

The real power here is in the phrase, "believes that he is or is likely to be damaged." The important word is *likely*. Unlike many other areas of law that we've seen, the Lanham Act does not require that proof of actual damage be shown, only that damage is likely. This is a very broad concept, which gives the Act a tremendous amount of strength.

Another benefit to the Lanham Act is expressed in the phrase *any person*. What this means is that Section 43(a) actions are available not only to companies who are in competition, but individual consumers as well. For this reason the Lanham Act is a law that advertisers must be very aware of. The reasons that a company may decide not to sue a competitor, even if it is the victim of a deceptive comparison, usually won't apply to the consumer. A deceived consumer, now, is someone to be concerned with.

Originally the courts placed severe limitations on actions brought under Section 43(a) of the Lanham Act with its inception in 1946. As we have seen before, it takes time for courts to adjust to new legislation. Just as water seeks its own level, laws also need a period of adjustment to find their level in society. For example, initially the courts refused to act unless 30 or more cases were reported against an advertiser. However, this all changed in 1954 when the Lanham Act found its level as a result of the following case.

L'Aiglon Apparel manufactured and sold through an ad campaign a distinctively styled ladies dress for $17.95. In its advertisements, L'Aiglon pictured its dress along with the price. This combination of picture and price became very identifiable with the public at the time.

Lana Lobel, a retailer, sold a different dress of much lower quality. Lobel advertised its dress in a national magazine for the price of $6.95, available through mail order. The Lobel ad showed an actual photographic reproduction of the L'Aiglon dress. This fraudulently represented to the buying public that the L'Aiglon dress was being sold at $6.95, a representation that was not true.

Lobel's ads provoked L'Aiglon to sue in *L'Aiglon Apparel, Inc.* v. *Lana Lobel Inc.*, 214 F.2d 649 (3rd Cir. 1954). L'Aiglon alleged that two forms of damage existed. First, Lobel's misrepresentation "caused some trade to be diverted" from L'Aiglon to Lobel. And, second, other trade was lost by L'Aiglon because of the inaccurate impression given to the public that L'Aiglon had been selling a dress worth only $6.95 for $17.95.

The resulting lawsuit was filed under Section 43(a) of the Lanham Act. Here, the court gave a new and clear interpretation for Lanham Act cases to follow. The court said:

> It seems to us that Congress has defined a statutory civil wrong of false representation of goods in commerce and has given a broad class of suitors injured or likely to be injured by such wrong the right to relief in the federal courts.

This case interpreted the Lanham Act to mean that a single individual or company could bring suit. Abolished was the earlier rule requiring a minimum of 30 victims before a suit could be started. L'Aiglon won its case against Lobel and helped establish the Lanham Act as a versatile tool against deceptive comparative advertising. The decision established the way the Lanham Act would be interpreted from then on—the way it is today.

GROUPS THAT CAN SUE UNDER THE LANHAM ACT

As I mentioned earlier, under the Lanham Act any "person" may bring a civil suit "who believes that he is or is likely to be damaged by the use of any such false description or representation." This broad definition creates a huge group of people who could become potential litigants. The term *people* covers businesses, groups, or individuals. Now, let's look at each of these various groups separately.

The Consumer's Standing to Sue

As I've mentioned, an individual consumer may bring suit under the Lanham Act. Although, in practice, this is not very common, mainly because of the high cost of a court battle.

Also, some but not all courts feel that individual consumers must show a "commercial interest" in order to bring suit. In the case that follows we see how the court dealt with both issues.

Arneson, an inventor, brought suit against the Raymond Lee Organization, a patent service. The suit claimed that Raymond Lee had lured clients through misleading advertisements. The case was *Arneson* v. *Raymond Lee Organization, Inc.,* 333 F. Supp. 116 (C.D. Cal. 1971).

The court felt that the wording in the act should be taken literally. That is "any person" could bring an action under the Lanham Act. Arneson was "any person" and was allowed to sue Raymond Lee. That is what the act says, and that is what it means. After all, consumers can be injured by deceptive comparative advertising. An ad can clearly compare two products, pointing out the flaws in one. But, if this is done through incorrect, misleading, or deceptive statements, the consumer will be damaged if the claim is relied on to make the purchase. As a result, the consumer will purchase the product based on incorrect information and a commercial interest will become involved.

A Company's Standing to Sue

The most common Lanham Act case involves direct competitors in business, companies having a commercial interest that is directly threatened by deceptive comparative advertising. Situations that are most likely to create court actions involve companies or products who compete directly for the same market. We see this in most of the cases illustrated throughout the rest of this chapter.

However, a company may have a commercial interest even though it does not compete directly with the other company. As an example, two companies may be in totally different industries, selling to completely separate markets. Yet, one company may create a deception that affects the other company's name or image.

The best example I can recall to illustrate this point occurred in 1978. This is also one of the more unique cases we discuss in this book. In November of that year Pussycat Cinemas began showing an X-rated movie called *Debbie Does Dallas*. The film was described by the court as "a gross and revolting sex film whose plot, to the extent that there is one, involves a cheerleader at a fictional high school, Debbie, who has been selected to become a Texas Cowgirl." (Courts sometimes make editorial opinions.)

The movie ends with a scene showing Debbie in a cheerleader's uniform bearing a striking resemblance to the outfit worn by the Dallas Cowboys Cheerleaders. In fact, 12 minutes of the film shows Debbie engaging in various sexual acts while wearing all, or part, of the uniform.

The movie was promoted with a poster showing Debbie wearing the same outfit. That is, she wore a combination of white boots, white shorts, blue blouse, white star-studded vest and belt, all of the same style and cut as that used by the Dallas Cowboys Cheerleaders.

As soon as the Dallas Cowboys Football Club learned of the movie, they filed suit under the Lanham Act in *Dallas Cowboys Cheerleaders, Inc.* v. *Pussycat Cinema, Ltd.*, 604 F.2d 200 (1979). The Dallas Cowboys organization sought an injunction prohibiting the distribution and showing of *Debbie Does Dallas* because of the movie's use of the Dallas Cowboy image and trademark.

The actual Dallas Cowboys Football Club employs 36 women who perform as the Dallas Cowboys Cheerleaders. *The Dallas Cowboys Cheerleaders, Dallas Cowgirls,* and *Texas Cowgirls* are all registered trademarks. The group has gained world-wide exposure (excuse the pun) and has made many public appearances outside of the football stadium. As a result, the Dallas Cowboys organization has earned substantial revenue from its commercial ventures involving the Cheerleaders.

The Dallas Cowboys wanted the movie banned because it felt that the public was likely to be deceived by the representations in the movie and promotional poster. Pussycat claimed, as a defense, that the public would not be confused about the origin of the film. Such confusion is a requirement the courts look for in Section 43(a) actions. Yet, the court said about the existence of consumer confusion, "the public's belief that the [trademark's] owner sponsored or otherwise approved the use of the trademark satisfies the confusion requirement."

Simply put, the issue here was the association between *Debbie Does Dallas* and the Dallas Cowboys Football Club— or, more accurately, the assumed association between the two. In fact, a commercial interest existed even though the two "products" did not directly compete. The movie did create a confusion in the consumer's mind and injured the Dallas Cowboys' business, name, and reputation. The Dallas Cowboys Cheerleaders won their case.

REQUIRED ELEMENTS OF A LANHAM ACT VIOLATION

The concept of the Lanham Act is very simple. When an ad claims a superiority over another product, a comparison is used. This occurs many times in today's advertising— Mitsubishi compares itself against Toyota, Hebrew National against Oscar Mayer, Chrysler against Ford, and on and on.

However, if that comparison is deceptive or misleading, a lawsuit may be brought by the victim. But certain specific conditions must exist in order to create a violation of the act. In fact, there are five elements that must exist.

One case, where all of these requirements developed, involved two power tool manufacturers, Skil and Rockwell. The two companies manufacture portable electric drills and jigsaws for sale to the consumer. In 1973, Rockwell began a major national advertising campaign using television, magazine, and newspaper. It was estimated that the campaign reached approximately 80 million people.

The Rockwell campaign revolved around a comparison of product testing, which had been done by an independent testing lab. Under "supposedly normal-use situations," Skil, Rockwell, and other manufacturers' tools were tested. The results of this independent testing was used in Rockwell's ad campaign. In the ads, Skil products were clearly shown and were identifiable by their labels.

The Lanham Act was violated because Rockwell's ads were not factually accurate regarding the performance of the Skil product line. Mainly, the test results used to compare product performance were biased. The testing was not conducted under normal-use conditions. The Skil products were put through much more demanding test conditions than would have been encountered in normal use and this was not disclosed in the advertising.

As a result, Rockwell used false, misleading, deceptive, and incomplete claims in its ads about Skil. When Skil realized the content of Rockwell's ads, it filed suit in *Skil Corp.* v. *Rockwell International Corp.*, 375 F. Supp 777 (N.D. Ill. 1974).

Skil not only sought an injunction against the Rockwell campaign, it also wanted damages for its loss of profits and damage to its name (which would affect future earning power). This one case developed the guidelines for the elements required to bring a lawsuit under the Lanham Act. Now let's look at each of those requirements.

Making False Statements about a Product

The first requirement to bring a lawsuit under the Lanham Act is that the ad makes false or partially correct claims, or fails to disclose material facts about its product. In other words, the ad must create a deception in one form or another.

Going back to our case, Rockwell made false statements about the performance qualities of Skil tools. The facts used in its ads were supposedly the result of testing the tools under normal-use conditions. This was not the case, however, so the results used in the ads were clearly false, misleading, and deceptive.

Advertising Actually Deceived or Has a Tendency to Deceive

The next element required to bring a lawsuit under this act is that the advertisement actually deceived consumers or had a tendency to deceive a substantial portion of the intended audience. This also refers to the confusion requirement we saw in the *Dallas* v. *Pussycat* case. Confusion is another way of saying "tendency to deceive."

Consumers who buy power tools base their decision on many factors. One of these is price, another is features of the tool, and still another is performance and durability. If a consumer buys a Rockwell power tool over a Skil tool, it would be for one or more of these reasons. If, as in this case, the consumer buys Rockwell based on performance features, which it claims to have over Skil, the consumer has been clearly deceived. Since the Rockwell ads gave factually incorrect information in the comparison of Skil products, actual deception occurred.

The Deception Must Be Material

Another requirement necessary to bring suit is that any deception created must be a material one. That is, it must have been likely to have influenced the purchasing decision. We also saw this earlier in Chapters 2 and 3 in our discussion of deception and the FTC Act. The same reasoning applies here.

In the Rockwell case, its false and misleading claims involved the performance of Skil products. This is a primary criterion for purchasing a power tool, as we discussed in the previous section. Statistics about the durability and performance of a power tool would weigh heavily in the consumer's decision to purchase or not to purchase a specific brand of product. Rockwell's deceptive statements were without question material.

The Advertised Product Must Have Entered Interstate Commerce

Another requirement under the Lanham Act is that the goods advertised were involved in interstate commerce. Simply, the product must have been involved in commerce between two or more states. At first glance this may seem to disqualify many products. However, the courts feel that if any portion of the product—during any stage of its manufacture—crossed state lines, then the product is considered to have entered interstate commerce.

It is not just the end product that can meet the interstate requirement. If a part of the tool, say the power cord, is purchased out of state, then interstate commerce is involved. What this means is that many more products qualify under the interstate commerce requirement than would first appear to.

In the case of Rockwell, both its and Skil's finished products were sold in every state and therefore were clearly involved in interstate commerce. There was no need to look into the manufacturing of either product to see if a more subtle form of interstate commerce was involved.

Injury or Likelihood of Injury Must Exist

The final requirement that must be present in order to sue under this act is that the advertisement has injured, or is likely to injure. Actual injury can result either from a diversion of sales or by a weakening of goodwill of the product or service.

In the Rockwell case actual injury occurred in both forms. For Skil, the injury involved sales (lost profits) that were lost to Rockwell due to the deception. Skil also suffered potential future injury because, in the consumer's eye, Skil products were of a lesser quality based on Rockwell's deceptive advertising. In essence, the future selling power of Skil's long-developed name and reputation had been diminished. By the way, Skil won its case. It received an injunction and was awarded damages.

TYPES OF CLAIMS THAT VIOLATE THE LANHAM ACT

As the use of comparison advertisements grew, certain types of claims began to appear. Of those, a certain group has emerged that can violate the Lanham Act—claims that a product does something that others don't do. If the product claims are true and accurate and can be supported, then this is legal.

However, claims that unjustifiably attack another product's qualities or performance are another matter.

There are a few different forms that this can take. The claim may be implied or it may be created through the use of a survey, disclaimer, trademark, or in other ways.

Implied Claims

Certain claims are literally true but create a misleading impression. We saw this in the FTC's interpretation of deceptive advertising. From a comparative advertising standpoint this can also occur. We can see a good example in a situation between Avis Rent-A-Car and Hertz.

Hertz ran a series of ads in early 1984 that contained the following copy:

> Hertz
> has more new cars
> than Avis has cars.
> * * * *
> If you'd like to drive some of the newest
> cars on the road, rent from Hertz.
> Because we have more new 1984 cars than Avis
> or anyone else has cars—new or old.
> * * * *
> Hertz. The #1 way to rent a car.

The ad above was produced by Hertz's ad agency—Scali, McCabe & Sloves. Obviously, the objective of the ad was to lure renters to Hertz and away from Avis. The lure was based on the claim that Hertz had more cars to choose from. Therefore, Hertz implied that it had an advantage over Avis—an advantage that consumers should exploit. The reality though was quite different. While the statements were literally accurate, they painted an inaccurate picture for the consumer.

Here's the problem. As of the time the ad ran, Hertz had a total of 97,000 (1984 model) cars. Avis, on the other hand, had a total of 95,224 (1984 model) cars. So, literally, the claim that Hertz had more 1984 model cars than Avis was true. However, of the 97,000 Hertz cars, only 91,000 were available for rental. The others were part of Hertz's licensee fleet. Although Hertz did own them, these cars were not part of the cars available to rent.

When you make an "apples-to-apples" comparison (that is, cars available for rental), Hertz had only 91,000 as opposed to Avis's 95,224. That is why the claim was misleading. The ad claimed that Hertz "has more new cars." But the impression on the potential car renter—to whom the ad was directed—was that Hertz "has more rental cars" than Avis. Because of this ad campaign Avis sued Hertz for violation of the Lanham Act in *Avis Rent-A-Car* v. *Hertz Corp.,* 782 F.2d 381 (2nd Cir. 1986). Avis won.

One of the difficulties in succeeding in a Lanham Act case involves proving that a comparative ad is deceptive, or is likely to deceive. The best method is to show market research or consumer surveys as evidence to prove that the consumer was deceived or is likely to be deceived. Consumer surveys are widely used in Lanham Act cases for this reason.

A good case in point involved Coca-Cola. In early 1984 Tropicana Products began airing a television commercial for its orange juice product. Olympic athlete Bruce Jenner was shown squeezing an orange and claimed: "It's pure, pasteurized juice as it comes from the orange." In the next scene, Jenner poured the fresh-squeezed juice into a Tropicana carton while continuing: "It's the only leading brand not made with concentrate and water."

When the ad came to the attention of the makers of Minute Maid orange juice, a Coca-Cola Company, a lawsuit was filed in *The Coca-Cola Company* v. *Tropicana Products, Inc.,* 690 F.2d 312 (1982). In this case, Tropicana's claim was blatantly false. The ad claimed that Tropicana contained unprocessed, fresh-squeezed juice. The truth was that it was pasteurized (heated to 200 degrees) and then frozen prior to being packaged. In the commercial, Jenner claims that Tropicana is "pasteurized juice as it comes from the orange." Well, pasteurized juice doesn't come from oranges. The representations in the commercial were clearly untrue.

Tropicana and Minute Maid, at the time, were the top selling ready-to-serve orange juices on the market. If Tropicana's advertising were allowed to mislead consumers into believing that its juice was better because it was fresh-squeezed and unprocessed, then Minute Maid would lose a significant share of the market.

Prior to the trial, Coca-Cola commissioned a consumer reaction test to be conducted by ASI Market Research, Inc. to measure recall of the spot. At the trial, Coca-Cola produced this evidence showing that a "significant number of consumers would be likely to be misled" by the Tropicana ad. The court ruled in favor of Coca-Cola.

Understand, though, that this does not mean that any survey can be used effectively in court. On the contrary, the courts are very critical about the credibility and thoroughness of any survey that is brought into court as evidence. Their intent is to make certain that damages are awarded accurately. Surveys are acceptable as evidence only if they reflect the consumers' true impressions.

Using Consumer Surveys as Comparison

Until now we've looked at surveys as a way of showing the existence of deception. However, surveys can also be used in an ad as a way of comparing products. Here's another area to be concerned with. Using consumer-survey information as part of a comparative advertisement may create a deception. This can occur if the results or the methodology are misrepresented.

Two of the leading cigarette manufacturers in the United States are Phillip Morris and Lorillard (which is owned by Loew's Theatres). In 1972 Phillip Morris introduced Marlboro Lights, and in 1975 it introduced Merit. Merit was supported by an intensive ad campaign pushing a claim of good taste in a low-tar cigarette. In 1979, Lorillard began marketing its low-tar brand Triumph.

In April of 1980, Lorillard hired SE Surveys to conduct "A National Taste Test: Triumph Menthol versus Winston Lights,

Marlboro Lights, Vantage and Merit Non-Menthols." The results of that test were used in Triumph's advertising. Lorillard's ads for Triumph claimed:

> "Triumph. National Taste Test Winner.
> Triumph tastes as good or better than
> Merit, or . . . Marlboro Lights.
> In rating overall product preference,
> more smokers independently chose Triumph over Merit,
> or . . . over Marlboro Lights."

As a result of these ads, Phillip Morris filed suit to stop the ads. The case was *Phillip Morris, Inc.* v. *Loew's Theatres, Inc.,* 511 F. Supp. 855 (S.D.N.Y. 1980). At the time of the trial, Merit was the largest selling low-tar cigarette in the United States generating over $350 million in revenue. About $80 million was spent on advertising that one brand alone.

The actual issue in this case revolved around the use of a taste test. Lorillard claimed that its brand Triumph was the "National Taste Test Winner." Yet, when the actual test results are investigated it revealed that for taste: 36 percent preferred Triumph over Merit; 24 percent considered the two brands to be equal; 40 percent preferred Merit.

Obviously, from the test results, Merit was preferred for taste, not Triumph as claimed in the ads. Although the body copy in the ads also claim that "an amazing 60 percent said 3 mg. Triumph tastes as good or better than 8 mg. Merit." The claim is statistically accurate. However, the ad failed to inform the consumer that, based on the same criteria, 64 percent stated that Merit tastes as good or better than Triumph. In other words, Triumph stated a statistic, which was true, and implied that the figure made it the winner. In reality, the other brand scored higher, which the ad failed to report.

Obviously, the results of the taste test were not used accurately in the Triumph advertisements. Phillip Morris submitted evidence at the trial that consumers believed that credible tests had proven that Triumph tasted better than Merit. As a result, the court stated: "there is convincing evidence that consumers are being deceived by Triumph's false claim of taste superiority."

Using Disclaimers in a Comparative Advertisement

There are situations in which an advertiser adds a disclaimer to an ad to offset what would otherwise be a deceptive claim. In 1984 the FDA authorized the sale of the drug ibuprofen in over-the-counter 200 mg. tablet form. American Home Products marketed the aspirin substitute under the brand name *Advil*. A competitor, Upjohn, markets the drug under the brand name *Nuprin*. Prior to the over-the-counter release of ibuprofen, Upjohn had manufactured and sold ibuprofen only on a prescription basis under the trademark of *Motrin*. Now, who's on first?

American Home Products produced an ad campaign for Advil through its ad agency, Young & Rubicam. The campaign included magazine ads and television commercials. In the ads, an Advil tablet was shown. The tablet was orange in color and the same size and shape as the prescription drug Motrin. Copy in the ads exclaimed: "ADVIL contains ibuprofen, the same medicine as the prescription drug MOTRIN now in nonprescription strength."

When Upjohn learned of the ads, it contacted American Home Products requesting that it change them to avoid any confusion for the consumer. American Home Products changed the color of its Advil tablets to brown. It also changed the disclaimer used in its ads to read: "ADVIL contains a nonprescription strength of ibuprofen, the medicine found in the prescription brand, MOTRIN." American Home Products also added a super to the television commercial that stated that Advil is from Whitehall (a division of American Home Products) and that Motrin is manufactured by another company.

The revised print ads read:

ADVIL IS ADVANCED MEDICINE FOR PAIN
ADVIL isn't Tylenol and it isn't aspirin.
Advil contains ibuprofen—the medicine in the prescription brand
Motrin, the product of another company.
Now ibuprofen is available in nonprescription strength
in Advil. Ibuprofen has been proven so effective in relieving
many types of pain that doctors have already
prescribed it over 130 million times.

However, after American Home Products made these changes and added the disclaimers, Upjohn went to court requesting an injunction in *Upjohn Co. v. American Home Products Corp.*, 598 F. Supp. 550 (S.D.N.Y. 1984). Upjohn felt that the consuming public would still be misled and confused by American Home Product's ads for Advil. Upjohn wanted to stop any implication that Advil tablets were the same color as Motrin, that Advil was manufactured by Upjohn, that Advil was the equivalent of Motrin, or that the ingredient in Advil was Motrin.

The court examined these issues and determined that the new changes and disclaimers used in the Advil ads were sufficient. For the trial, consumer reaction surveys were instituted to determine the effect of the revised ads on the public. The surveys found that a higher percentage of consumers polled recalled the disclaimers as opposed to those who felt that Advil and Motrin were made by the same manufacturer. The court said: "[s]uch disclaimers are preferred to an absolute prohibition of the potentially misleading reference as a means of alleviating consumer confusion . . . "

The important point to remember is that consumer confusion can be alleviated through the use of disclaimers or qualifying language. However, if this is challenged in court by the competitor, consumer surveys will be relied on. The survey will be used to determine if the disclaimer alleviates the majority of consumer confusion.

Fair Use of Trademarks in Comparative Advertising

There is nothing illegal in making a reference to another company's trademark. But this is true only if the use is informational and not likely to cause confusion about the source of the product or its qualities. We see many instances where an ad will make reference to, or show, another company's product. In most cases this is done fairly and to compare qualities or features that one product has that makes it distinctive over the other. These comparisons must be true and accurate. Comparisons must not be deceptive or mislead the consumer, and proof to support the claim must exist prior to making the claim.

Here is another example of deceptive comparisons. Johnson & Johnson Company is a major manufacturer of Johnson's Baby Oil, Johnson's Baby Powder, and Johnson's Baby Shampoo. Quality Pure also manufacturers skin oil, skin powder, and shampoo. Its products are packaged in containers that exhibit an amazing resemblance to the J & J products. At a quick glance, the competing product packages look the same. Such similarity can be an infringement of trademark. This close similarity, known as "palming off" involves the use of another company's trademark because of a likely confusion as to the origin of the product.

As an example, let's look at the shampoo products. The Johnson & Johnson Baby Shampoo bottle is elongated and made of clear plastic. The clear, yellow shampoo can be seen through the container. The Quality Pure shampoo package was almost identical to J & J's, down to the style and color of label. The J & J label contained a tear drop with the slogan, "No More Tears," while the Quality Pure label used three tear drops on the label with the words *Tear Free.*

The packaging of all of the Johnson & Johnson products was distinctive and unique. Suffice it to say that Quality Pure was in competition with Johnson & Johnson. But the competitor is not allowed to package its product so as to ride on the coattails of the image, reputation, and goodwill built over many years by Johnson & Johnson.

Quality Pure produced and aired a 30-second commercial to promote its new line of products. In its commercial an actress, Jane Paley, claimed that Quality Pure Shampoo "gave me the same lather" as Johnson & Johnson Baby Shampoo. The commercial also claimed that "both were extremely mild." The gist of the commercial was that while the products gave the same results and had the same qualities, Quality Pure was cheaper than Johnson & Johnson.

As a result Johnson & Johnson brought suit in *Johnson & Johnson* v. *Quality Pure Mfg., Inc.,* 484 F. Supp. 975 (D.N.J. 1979). Two items were at issue in this case—first, the similarity of the packaging and, second, the advertising claim of equal performance and lower price. The court expressed its feelings that competing on a price level is perfectly acceptable. Yet it is not acceptable to "sell a competing product on the basis of a lower price and at the same time use [packaging] designed and calculated to fool the customer into the belief that he is getting someone else's product."

Quality Pure also had no basis for the claims that it used in its commercial. Quality Pure conducted a "survey" by handing out samples of competing shampoos to shoppers at shopping centers. The competing shampoos were unidentified except for a mark on each bottle—either X or Y. Then Jane Paley was also given the samples, and after using them she scored each to be equal. This result is what appeared on the television commercial.

The problem rests on the credibility of the "survey." There was no way of determining which brand of shampoo was in which bottle, or if they were even different. The test was rigged and without any substantiation, and in the court's eye "had far too much resemblance to three-card monte to be accepted . . ."

REMEDIES AVAILABLE UNDER THE LANHAM ACT

There are essentially three remedies available under the Lanham Act. These include an injunction against the deceptive ad, corrective advertising by the company that ran the deceptive ad, and monetary damages. In order to recover damages or corrective advertising, however, it must be shown that the buying audience was actually deceived. If only a likelihood of deception can be shown, then only an injunction will be allowed.

Injunction as a Remedy

This is the most common (and quickest) remedy under the Lanham Act. Essentially, an injunction bans the ad from running. The most important function of an injunction is that it stops the publication of the abusive ad.

Most people have the view that the legal system moves very slowly. It may be refreshing to learn that a preliminary injunction can be obtained within months or even weeks of filing a complaint. This can be a major consideration to a company who is the victim of an advertisement that shows its product in a misleading way.

As I said earlier, one of the features of an injunction is that it stops further damage. The negative side, though, is that it does not remove the deception already created. An injuction also does not compensate the victim for injury.

In order to be granted an injunction, the person or company requesting one must show the court two things. The first is that the company will suffer irreparable damage if the injunction is not issued. The company doesn't need to show actual lost sales, but it must establish that there is more than a belief of injury. If the advertising claim is explicitly false, no other proof is required. However, if the advertisement is less than explicit, some other evidence must be shown that establishes that the claim is likely to deceive the consumer.

The Toro Company and Jacobsen Manufacturing (a division of Textron) are manufacturers of various labor-saving machines for consumer use. A few years ago a controversy arose when Jacobsen produced an ad directed toward dealers. The ad showed a performance comparison between its Sno-Burst snow thrower and Toro's Snow Master. In the ad Jacobsen's Sno-Burst appeared to come out ahead in the categories rated.

When Toro learned of this, it filed suit seeking an injunction against the ad. Toro obviously felt the ad was deceptive. The case, *Toro Co.* v. *Textron, Inc.*, 499 F. Supp. 241 (D. Del. 1980), discussed whether the ad misled dealers about the features of both machines. The ad headline claimed: "The New Jacobsen. You Get More To Sell." The ad then proceeded to compare categories such as reserve power, engine size, starter priming, gas/oil ratio, wheel size, snow-throwing distance, fuel capacity, auger housing, handle adjustment, and warranty.

The basis for Jacobsen's comparison, however, proved to be insignificant and arbitrary. Here are some examples. Regarding the category under "starter," Jacobsen claimed that its machine didn't need to be primed to start, while the Toro did. The court found that, in fact, the Jacobsen required pulling the starter cord a number of times before the machine would start.

This was just the same as the Toro model. This, the court reasoned, constituted priming. The comparison was considered false.

Some of the other claims by Jacobsen were literally true, but they were insignificant as a valid comparison. Jacobsen claimed that its handle was adjustable and Toro's was not. A true statement. However, on closer examination, the Jacobsen handle was only adjustable one inch. Truly, the claim that the handle on the Jacobsen was adjustable was very misleading.

As you can see, a number of the compared features between the two machines were found to be false or so insignificant that there was a likelihood of confusion of the buyer. While Toro could not show that purchasers were actually deceived (a requirement for damages), it could show that the ads had a tendency to deceive. In order to obtain an injunction, "[Toro] need only show that the misrepresentations of which it complains 'have a tendency to deceive' . . . the three claims found to be false do have a tendency to mislead consumers into purchasing a Jacobsen rather than a Toro, and injunctive relief is, therefore, appropriate." Toro was granted an injunction against Jacobsen for making the deceptive claims.

Corrective Advertising

This type of remedy is essentially an award of money. Yet, in the case of corrective advertising damage awards, the company who created the deception is ordered by the court to use its own money to produce advertising that will offset the originally deceptive ads. The intent of corrective advertising is for the new ads to correct the confusion created by the deceptive ad. The company must produce its own ads with a message that effectively counters the previous, deceptive message—much like a public apology.

Durbin Brass Works is a manufacturer of brass lamps. Durbin sells its lamps through, among other outlets, The Sharper Image stores and catalog. In the early 1980s, Richard Schuler also sold lamps of the same style and design as Durbin's. The Schuler lamps were sold through, among other outlets, the American Express Company catalog. Schuler's lamps were manufactured in Taiwan as opposed to Durbin's lamps, which were manufactured in the United States.

Durbin filed suit in *Durbin Brass Works, Inc.* v. *Schuler*, 532 F. Supp. 41 (E.D. Mo. 1982), claiming that Schuler's lamps caused a decline in sales of its lamps because of consumer confusion between the two manufacturers. In other words, due to the identical appearance of the two brands of lamp, consumers were drawn to buy the cheaper version while believing that they were buying the original Durbin lamp.

Schuler sold over $60,000 worth of imitation lamps before Durbin brought suit. The court felt that these sales were a result of the public's confusion. Durbin testified at the trial that it would cost his company $10,000 in advertising to offset the deception created by the Schuler ads. The court concluded that Schuler's actions created actual consumer confusion, and therefore an award of corrective advertising was appropriate. Durbin was awarded $10,000 as damages plus court costs. It was ordered, by the court, that the $10,000 be spent by Schuler on corrective advertising to offset the deception that it had originally created.

Monetary Damages as a Remedy

Until the early 1980s no courts had awarded monetary damages to a plaintiff under Section 43(a) of the Lanham Act. All of the prior awards were either injunctions or corrective advertising. This, however, was to change when a case came to court that was able to prove a direct loss of sales or potential sales. In seeking damages, two things must be shown: actual consumer deception and consumer reliance on the false claim.

Another section of the Lanham Act, Section 35, has been utilized in comparative advertising cases. This has given even more punch to an already strong law by expanding the damages allowed. Under Section 35, the other company's profits, actual damages, and the cost of the lawsuit may be recovered. Treble damages and attorney's fees may also be recovered in certain extreme cases. The biggest such case occurred in 1984.

Ryder System was in the car and truck rental business. In the mid-1970s, James A. Ryder began to lose control of the company that he had begun. New internal management had largely ignored him for a few years.

Even though Ryder was over 60 years old, he decided to leave Ryder System and start a new company to compete with Ryder. The new car and truck rental company was originally named *Jarpool,* but was later renamed *Jartran.* Originally Jartran, with only mediocre results, leased large truck and trailer units to businesses. Seeing the potential in consumer rentals, Mr. Ryder wanted to expand into the self-move rental field. This would bring the new company directly into competition with the leader, U-Haul.

In order to put his plan into motion, Mr. Ryder went heavily into debt to acquire the vehicles that he needed. Once Jartran obtained its vehicles, it needed to get them on the road fast. And that meant competing head-to-head with U-Haul for customers. As anyone in advertising knows, it is extremely difficult to dislodge the number one company in any field. But Jartran was determined to do it.

So, Jartran, through its ad agency Sandra C. Tinsley Advertising, created an ad campaign to generate consumer rentals. The campaign was designed to compete on a price advantage over U-Haul. Did the campaign work? Jartran's gross revenues in 1979 (its first year) were $3 million. In 1980 however, gross revenue rose to $58 million, and in 1981 to $95 million. Yes, I'd say it worked. Within months Jartran had taken over more than 10 percent of the market.

The campaign worked so well that it won the Gold Effie award from the American Marketing Association, for "its overall marketing effectiveness." In Mr. Ryder's opinion the campaign "knocked the competition (U-Haul) on their ass."

How did this affect U-Haul? In 1979 U-Haul had almost all of the self-move rental business in the United States. Others had entered the field over the years but with very little effect. U-Haul's largest competition came, coincidentally, from Ryder System in 1979. However, U-Haul's revenue began to decrease after Jartran's campaign broke. In 1981 U-Haul saw, for the first time, its revenue decrease with a loss of $49 million. To stem the tide, U-Haul tried to counteract Jartran's efforts with $13.6 million spent on advertising between 1981 and 1982.

Without its concentrated and comparative ad campaign, directed at U-Haul, Jartran would not have gained the market share that it did. The ads were simple. The headlines claimed:

U-Haul It to Dallas for $0000
. . . Jartran It to Dallas for $000.
Save big money . . . to almost any city.

The price stated for Jartran was always less than the stated U-Haul price. In the ads, a picture of each company's rental truck was shown. However, the size of the U-Haul truck used in the ad was smaller to make it look less attractive.

In June 1980, U-Haul filed suit to stop Jartran's campaign. *U-Haul International. Inc.* v. *Jartran, Inc.*, 601 F. Supp. 1140 (D. Az. 1984), was the case. U-Haul claimed that Jartran's price comparison ads were false and that Jartran knew it. The court agreed.

The Jartran rental prices shown in the ads were "special promotion prices," although this very important point was never mentioned. The intent, which worked, was to convey that the advertised price was Jartran's regular price. Actually, the rates advertised were considerably lower than those stated on Jartran's one-way price sheet. On the other side, the price Jartran quoted for U-Haul rentals was its regular price plus a distribution fee. Again this was not disclosed in the ad. In fact, a distribution fee is charged in only certain unique rental cases.

The price claims that Jartran made were blatantly false and were intended to mislead the consumer into renting from Jartran instead of U-Haul. A series of consumer surveys were used as evidence to substantiate that: "The false and deceptive statements contained in the Jartran ads were material in influencing rental decisions of a substantial segment of the public interested in renting self-move equipment."

The claims in the Jartran ads were published deliberately. They were known by Jartran to be false, and they were intended to damage U-Haul by taking business away through deception. Under the Lanham Act, "a court may award additional damages, up to three times the amount awarded for actual damages according to the circumstances of the case."

In this case, the court awarded actual damages of $20 million to U-Haul. In addition, the court felt that Jartran's advertising was "willful, malicious or in reckless disregard of the rights of [U-Haul]," and an additional $20 million was awarded—$40 million in all. Also, U-Haul was awarded court costs and attorney fees.

ANTIDILUTION STATUTES:
STATE ACTION AND COMPARATIVE ADVERTISING

What we've seen up to now is federal control over comparative advertising. But many states have also gotten involved on their own by enacting what are termed *antidilution statutes*. See Exhibit 8–2 for a complete list. In practice these statutes give each state control over deceptive comparative advertising. Since these are state laws, the necessity for interstate commerce is not a requirement.

Dilution is defined basically as any whittling away or general eroding of the trademark's selling power. In other words, any nonowner use of a trademark or trade name that diminishes the selling power of that mark violates the statute. As we saw with the Lanham Act, a comparative ad, if untrue, can diminish the selling power of the competitor's trademark.

Antidilution actions can take place under three situations: generic usage, unrelated usage, and comparative advertising. The first is generic usage. This situation exists when a competitor uses another trademark to denote a class of product, in other words, using another company's mark as if it were the generic type of product.

The second area, unrelated usage, covers use of a trademark on products that do not compete and have no connection. Here again this type of use erodes the value of the mark. We saw this earlier in *Dallas Cowboys Cheerleaders, Inc.* v. *Pussycat Cinema, Ltd.* Although that case was brought under the Lanham Act (federal law), the principle is the same.

EXHIBIT 8–2
State Antidilution Statutes

Alabama	Alabama Code, section 8–12–17 (1975)
Arkansas	Arkansas Statutes Annotated, section 70–550 (1979)
California	California Business & Professions Code, section 14330 (West Supp 1980)
Connecticut	Connecticut General Statutes, section 35–11i (1979)
Delaware	Delaware Code Annotated iti., section 3313 (Supp 1978)
Florida	Florida Statutes Annotated, section 495.151 (West 1972)
Georgia	Georgia Code, section 106–115 (1978)
Idaho	Idaho Code, section 48–512 (1977)
Illinois	Illinois Revised Statutes Chapter 140, section 22 (1975)
Iowa	Iowa Code, section 548.11(2) (1979)
Maine	Maine Revised Statutes Annotated, Title 10, section 1530 (1964)
Massachusetts	Massachusetts General Laws Annotated Chapter 110B, section 12 (West Supp 1980)
Montana	Montana Annotated Statutes, section 417.061 (Vernon 1979)
Nebraska	Nebraska Revised Statutes, section 87–122 (1976)
New Hampshire	New Hampshire Revised Statutes Annotated, section 350–A:12 (Supp 1979)
New Mexico	New Mexico Statutes Annotated, section 57–3–10 (1978)
New York	New York General Business Law, section 368–d (McKinney 1968)
Oregon	Oregon Revised Statutes, section 647.107 (1971)
Rhode Island	Rhode Island General Laws, section 6–2–12 (Supp 1980)
Tennessee	Tennessee Code Annotated, section 47–25–512 (1984)

The final area involves literal comparative advertising. As we saw in federal cases, comparative advertising can injure a product's selling ability by re-routing the trademark's image to another company's product. This violates antidilution statutes because consumers no longer associate the reputation of the trademark exclusively. In other words, a dilution of the mark has occurred.

CELEBRITY LOOK-ALIKES AND
THE LANHAM ACT

In Chapter 5 we discussed how look-alikes can violate a celebrity's right of publicity or privacy. However, in 1985 the issue of look-alikes was taken one step further. It crossed over into the comparative advertising realm.

Early in 1984, a man named Phil Boroff appeared in an ad for National Video, a video rental service. Boroff was hired through his agency, Ron Smith's Celebrity Look-Alikes in Los Angeles, California, because he bore a striking resemblance to Woody Allen.

In the National ads, Boroff appeared behind the counter where two of Woody Allen's films were displayed. The headlines for two of the ads claimed:

> We'll Make You Feel Like A Star.
> * * * *
> You Don't Need A Famous Face
> To Be Treated To Some Famous Service.

These ads ran in national magazines including National Video's own publication and *Video Review* magazine. In the *Video Review* issues the ad carried the disclaimer: "Celebrity double provided by Ron Smith's Celebrity Look-Alikes, Los Angeles, Calif."

Allen was not amused by this. He filed suit in *Allen* v. *National Video, Inc.*, 610 F. Supp. 612 (S.D.N.Y. 1985). What made that case unique was that it was the first time that a suit of its type succeeded under the Lanham Act. Allen claimed a violation of Section 43(a). He argued that a likelihood of confusion existed between Boroff and himself.

Even if some consumers realized that the person in the ad was not Allen himself but a look-alike, these same people most probably will assume another possibility. That is, the public "may be led to believe by the intentional reference to [Allen] that he is somehow involved in, or approves of their product."

You might say that there was a disclaimer in the ad stating that the person was a double for Allen. Yet, a small disclaimer at the bottom of an ad was not sufficient to offset an overall deceptive ad.

The result of this case was that an injunction was issued, stopping the use of any of the ads with Boroff as Woody Allen. National Video paid Allen $425,000, and Boroff was barred from appearing as a look-alike for Allen in any advertising that "creates the likelihood that a reasonable person might believe that he was really [Allen] or that [Allen] had approved of the appearance." However, Boroff could appear in advertising only if a "clear and bold" disclaimer or clarifying body copy was used.

While this case is very recent, not to mention revolutionary, it shows a trend. Other courts may follow; they may not. Only time will tell. Yet, the Lanham Act was effectively used to stop the use of a look-alike who in essence created a false impression by comparing Boroff to Allen. And after all, that's what the Lanham Act was created for. The moral of this story is that the deceptive comparison can be that of people as well as of products.

CHAPTER 9

CONTESTS AND LOTTERIES

This is essentially a people's contest . . .—to afford all an unfettered start, and a fair chance, in the race of life.
—*Abraham Lincoln*

The summer of 1955 brought the era of the game show. All across America people tuned in to watch an immigrant welder win a fortune through his knowledge of art or a file clerk dazzle the audience with her grasp of opera trivia—the common citizen getting the chance to become richer than his or her wildest hopes. The things dreams are made of—to win a fortune on such shows as "Twenty-One," "The $64,000 Question," "Tic-Tac-Dough," "Name That Tune," "Dotto," and "The Big Surprise." That moment of glory. As Andy Warhol said, " . . . everyone will be world famous for fifteen minutes."

To assure honesty, the questions were guarded so that no one could discover them, or their answers. The audience was sure that contestants could not possibly have known what they would be asked. On many shows isolation booths were used so that the contestants could not get help from the audience. Some shows went so far as to use bank officials accompanied by armed guards to hand deliver the questions to the host. The questions had been locked in a bank vault until that time.

The tension would build with each question, and the audience would sigh with relief after each correct answer. The appeal of the game show was, what appeared to be, the unrehearsed spontaneity of the shows, and the fact that the contestants were masters of certain areas of knowledge, memory, and intelligence. These game shows were a spectacle to behold. The audiences became engrossed in the show. But it came to be that they were just that—all show.

In July 1958, the Federal Communications Commission (FCC) was drawn into the scene when a contestant of "Dotto" complained that the show was deceptive. Not much resulted from this investigation. The station denied any wrong-doing, and the case was dropped. But news had leaked out, and the game show scandal began to draw public attention. In late 1959, a subcommittee of the House Committee on Interstate and Foreign Commerce opened hearings on the matter.

Witnesses (who were previous contestants) who were called before the subcommittee testified that they were given the questions and in many cases the answers as well. Some were given scripts to memorize. Even the theatrics of their responses were coached. Despair, agony, exuberance, elation were all prerehearsed to create the desired effect for the audience.

Good-looking contestants were promoted to increase the television audience; unattractive ones were routinely eliminated (or so the producers would try). Dr. Joyce Brothers, the (now well-known) psychologist, was one such contestant. The producers of the game show tried to get her to lose the game, but her knowledge of boxing was so extensive that she answered every question they threw at her.

Quite obviously the game shows were fixed, and the advertising community was also involved. The advertisers and their agencies were the ones who were truly in control of the purse-strings. At that time it was common for a single advertiser to sponsor an entire show, therefore wielding a tremendous amount of control over the show and its content to the point where the advertiser actually directed the contestant briefing.

The television game show scandal caused the networks to re-think their priorities and their motives. As a result of the bad press, television began to move away from game shows and in their place came the era of the Western. "Gunsmoke," "Wagon Train," "Have Gun, Will Travel," "Bonanza," "Wanted Dead or Alive," and many others saw the sun set on the era of the game show.

Since then, contests of every kind have drawn acute attention from the networks and the courts alike. That is why it is very important for advertisers and their agencies to understand the laws that apply to contests. Sometimes they are called games, sweepstakes, games-of-chance, or just contests. Regardless of the name, the intention is obvious. The advertiser expects that the consumer will enter the contest and be drawn to its product.

In other words, contests generate interest because they get the consumer involved. They appeal to a basic human trait— the desire to get something for nothing. The real intent, then, is to transfer this desire to the product and with that increase sales.

Somewhere, right now, people are filling out entry forms and dreaming of what they'll do with the money if they win. Winning a fortune in a contest is a dream of many Americans, an easy reward for very little effort. Yet, the odds of winning a contest are extremely low. For example, the odds to win first prize in the January 1969 *Reader's Digest* sweepstakes were about 1 in 480,000.[1]

But what does the advertiser need to be concerned with when creating and promoting a contest? Actually, the answer is very simple. There are guidelines that must be followed to run a contest and to prevent it from becoming a lottery. We will look at these in this chapter. If the contest is structured according to the guidelines, these games are legal. However, if the game falls outside the guidelines, it will be considered a lottery—which is gambling and is illegal (unless state sponsored). To prevent an illegal lottery, there are specific and stringent laws that control contests. This heavy regulation evolved because of how closely contests resemble lotteries. In the states that permit this form of gambling, it is very heavily regulated. For the advertiser, a contest must not be allowed to cross over the line and become a lottery.

WHAT CONSTITUTES A LOTTERY

Recently, many of the states have sponsored lotteries to raise funds for various government institutions. In California, for example, the lotteries were intended to benefit public educa-

---

[1]*In the matter of Reader's Digest Assn.*, 79 FTC 696 (1971).

tion. With the growth and popularity of these lotteries, many companies have jumped on the contest band-wagon. Companies that had not been involved with contests in the past have begun promoting their products through contests and sweepstakes of every kind.

In order to remain within the boundaries of a legal contest, it is important to understand what is considered an illegal lottery. The generally accepted definition of a lottery is "a chance or chances taken, for a consideration, in the hope or expectation that something would be obtained of greater value than that which was given up, but with the full knowledge that nothing at all might be obtained . . . "[2]

As I said earlier, contests are legal, but lotteries are not. The difference between a contest and a lottery is quite simple, and advertisers must understand the difference. Let's take a look at the three basic conditions that create a lottery.

1. A prize must be offered.
2. The entrant must give up something (consideration) in order to participate.
3. Winning must involve an element of chance rather than skill.

If one, or more, of these elements is missing, a lottery does not exist. All three are required for a lottery. Two elements occur in most all games of chance: a prize and chance. The tricky element, as you'll see, is consideration. We'll look into each of these areas in more detail.

In the late 1930s the government confiscated 83 cases of merchandise marked *Honest John, Wonder Store,* and *Diamond Store.* Each of these boxes contained smaller boxes with a number on each. On the main display case were small pull-tabs, which a consumer would remove to reveal a number underneath.

The consumer purchased a chance to remove one pull-tab for 1, 2, or 5 cents. After the pull-tab was removed to reveal a number, the consumer got the prize in the small box that had

---

[2]*United States* v. *83 Cases of Merchandise Labeled "Honest John,"* 29 F. Supp. 912, 915 (D.C. Md., 1939).

the same number on it. Each box contained a small amount of inexpensive candy and some other trinket. The value of the items in the prize boxes was only a few cents, and each box contained a prize of equal value.

Now the question is, was that a legal contest or an illegal lottery? That question is what the court answered in *U.S.* v. *83 Cases of Merchandise Labeled "Honest John,"* 29 F. Supp. 912 (D.C. Md., 1939). The court examined the three elements that needed to exist in order for this to be a lottery: a prize, consideration, and chance. In this case, "there is no single prize, no group of prizes, but a prize given for every chance that is taken."

In a lottery, the consumer takes a chance on winning a prize that is much greater than the price paid to participate. In this case there was no substantial difference between the amount of money that the participant paid and the value of what would be received. In essence there was no "prize" involved.

No chance was involved either, because all participants received an item for their participation in the game. This game then was a legal contest because it did not meet all three of the elements required of a lottery.

Prize as an Element

Most games of chance end with a winner, or a couple of winners, who receive a prize. A prize is a special item given to the winner. It is also what is used to induce the consumer to enter the game.

Prizes can range from cash, to cars, vacations, merchandise, to just about anything. A few years ago Zerex antifreeze, made by DuPont Corporation, offered as first prize in its contest a radiator filled with Zerex antifreeze. What made this prize worth winning was the fact that the radiator was installed in a new Rolls-Royce.

If every entrant receives a gift of equal value, and in the same way, then no "prize" is awarded. We saw this in the case just discussed. If the gifts have different values, the game would be considered a lottery (if the other two elements also existed).

In the early 1900s, a company in Georgia named Purvis Investments offered a plan to customers. The plan involved offering a loan on very favorable terms to the first few people who mailed in an investment of a specific amount. However, the investment return was not as good as other savings institutions at the time. The main feature of the scheme was the possibility of obtaining a loan at better than average rates. That was the incentive for entering the "contest" and paying the investment amount. The fact that the customer paid the investment constituted consideration.

When the entries were received at the company, they were opened and numbered. But if a batch of entries were received in the same day's mail, it would be pure chance which envelope was opened first. So, we have the element of chance. When this scheme made its way to the courts in *United States* v. *Purvis,* 195 F. 618 (N.D. Ga. 1912), the court said, "it was of course a mere matter of chance as to which the . . . clerk . . . should take up first, as he opened and entered them."

The final element necessary for this to be a lottery was the existence of a prize. In this case the prize was an opportunity to obtain a loan on favorable terms. "It was the desire to obtain loans on the very attractive terms proposed . . . which made these contracts so much favored and which induced the purchase of these loan contracts." The investment return itself was not particularly attractive. Better returns could have been achieved at other savings institutions. But the chance to obtain one of the loans was a thing of value. It also made this qualify as the element of a prize. The scheme was held to be a lottery.

Consideration as an Element

The next element of a lottery is consideration. If the other two elements exist but there is no consideration, then there is no lottery. But what is the definition of consideration? The most obvious form of consideration is money. There are others, and we look at those here.

It is extremely important to understand that what we are discussing are general rules under federal law. Each state has specific laws concerning what it feels qualifies as consideration in relation to a lottery. The advertiser should, therefore, check into the laws of any state in which it intends to operate a contest.

As I just explained, the exact definition of consideration varies from state to state. But generally, consideration can be money or anything of value. It can also be an act such as exerting substantial time and effort in some way. In Wisconsin, which is unique in this respect, consideration is defined by statute as "anything which is a commercial or financial advantage to the promoter or a disadvantage to any participant."[3] What this means is that some states feel that any burden put on the participant constitutes consideration. But, generally, the requirement that a consumer visit the store to obtain game pieces is not interpreted as consideration.

Around 1950 George Wagner was the Postmaster of Garden City, New York. Mr. Wagner wanted to ban the mailing of a card that he felt constituted a lottery. Here's how the game worked. The consumer who received the card in the mail would remove the coupon portion which contained a number. Then the consumer kept the coupon and mailed the other portion of the card to the Garden City Chamber of Commerce.

Later, the consumer visited the stores that participated in the game. If the consumer saw an article in the store window that had the same number as the person's coupon, the store would give the item as a prize. In essence, this was a treasure hunt.

The question is, does the act of visiting stores create a consideration which would make this a lottery? That question was answered in *Garden City Chamber of Commerce v. Wagner,* 100 F. Supp. 769 (E.D.N.Y. 1951). The Postmaster (who brought the suit) felt that "consideration is present in the substantial amount of time and effort involved in examining the various prizes to ascertain whether one holds a winning ticket."

As we saw earlier, consideration can take the form of a payment of money, purchase of a ticket, or the expenditure of substantial time or effort. The basis of the controversy in this case is whether the act of visiting a store "actually involves an

---

[3]Wisconsin Statutes Annotated, section 945.01(2)(b)(1)(1981).

expenditure of substantial effort and time." The court ruled that it did not, saying: "[We] have found no case in which the element of consideration has resided in walking or driving to look in a window."

Generally, situations that are not classified as consideration include requiring participants to:

- Visit a store to enter.
- Return to store to learn of winners.
- Visit different stores.
- Witness a demonstration or take a demonstration ride.
- Pay postage.

Once again, it is important to consult specific state statutes for exact regulations.

Now let's look at typical situations where consideration does exist.

Use of Consumer's Name or Likeness. Requiring the authorization to use the name or likeness of a participant or winner could be held to mean that consideration was given. This is because there is a consent to do something in the future. It is consideration nonetheless.

The Gift Enterprise. In many cases the consumer must purchase the advertiser's product to qualify for the contest. This is known as a "gift enterprise." Then usually a proof of purchase in the form of a box top, wrapper, facsimile, or the like is sent in to register for the contest.

Even though the price of the product remains the same, there is consideration because the consumer is required to do something. The consumer is required to make a purchase. Therefore, a gift enterprise scheme involves the element of consideration. This explains the common "No purchase required" disclaimer used in many contests.

There is another situation that is very closely related to a pure gift enterprise. That involves games where a lottery is created when a customer is required to promise to buy a product to enter a game. A good example of this situation occurred in 1976, with a radio promotion called *Dial-a-Discount.*

Don J. Plumridge Advertising in Washington, D.C. developed a radio campaign for one of its clients, Allyn's Pants Ranch. A typical commercial read:

> Dial your own discount on a pair of pants.
> This is our Pants Ranch Wheel of Fortune.
> On it are various dollar amounts.
> Two dollars, three dollars, four, five, and ten dollars.
> After you purchase any pair of pants—and the Pants Ranch
> has over 40,000 to choose from—
> you get to dial your own discount.
> What you spin on the wheel is what you save
> on the purchase of your first pair of pants.
> If the wheel stops on "freebie," lucky you!
> Cause there's no charge.
> The pants are on us!

The concept of the game was pretty straightforward. The customer took a pair of pants to the counter where the Wheel of Fortune was spun. Wherever the wheel stopped was the amount of the discount off the purchase price of the pants.

When the Federal Communications Commission found out about the game, a complaint was initiated *In the matter of Metromedia Inc.,* 60 F.C.C.2d 1075 (1976). The Commission discussed "whether a 'Dial-a-Discount' participant's commitment to purchase a pair of pants alone [constituted] the requisite element of consideration, since if money has not yet changed hands, any participant may refuse to pay after spinning the discount wheel and return the pants to the shelf."

However, the game rules required this agreement to pay in order to participate, and therefore, consideration existed because there was an *agreement* to pay at least the regular price of a pair of pants in order to participate. This game was an illegal lottery because it required that the consumer purchase the pants without knowing, in advance, the amount of the discount. Metromedia lost the case and was required to pay a $16,000 fine for promoting an illegal lottery.

Presence at the Drawing.   Here again there is a difference of opinion. But most courts feel that requiring participants to be present in order to win a drawing is consideration.

Obstacles in Obtaining Entry Blanks.   If free entry
blanks for a game are offered but the company has irregular
office hours, a problem can result. Also, if the participant
must, let's say, purchase a newspaper to obtain entry forms,
an illegal lottery exists. The purchase of the newspaper is consideration. In other words, entry forms must be made readily
available, and a purchase must not be required in order to obtain an entry form. Otherwise, consideration is given.

The following case provides a good example of obstacles for
participants. Dreem Arts, Incorporated published a newspaper
in Chicago called *Nightmoves*. The paper cost $2 and contained
a game called *Pick and Play*. The idea of the game was for the
reader to pick the winners of upcoming professional and college
football games. All of the upcoming games were listed along
with the point spread. Participants mailed in their entry blank
listing the teams they picked to win. If an entrant picked 10
winning teams, the prize was $1,000 in cash. Other prizes
were available if a person picked at least four winning teams.
The advertised contest rules were the following:

> Free contest entry forms are available at office of publisher.
> Please send stamped self-addressed envelope and free entry
> form will be mailed to you; a reasonable hand-drawn facsimile
> can be used—in addition to stores and news stands, copies of
> *Nightmoves* are available at Chicago public libraries for your in-
> spection (no limit to number of contest entries.) . . . No purchase
> necessary—tax liabilities for all prizes are the sole responsibil-
> ity of winners.

Late in 1985 the Chicago Police Department confiscated newspapers from various locations, and *Dreem Arts, Inc.* v. *City of
Chicago,* 637 F. Supp. 53 (N.D. Ill. 1986), was the result. A detective investigated the case and found that the *Nightmoves*
offices had no sign displayed. The office was closed, and there
were no employees present. He was unable to obtain the "free

entry form." The detective also tried to obtain an entry blank by mail, but none was ever received. Another detective visited over 24 Chicago libraries, none of which had ever subscribed to the newspaper.

If the consumer is allowed to submit a reasonable facsimile for an entry, no consideration exists. There is a problem, though, when the consumer can't get a copy from which to make a facsimile without buying something. That was the case here.

Obviously the publisher devised the rules to "purposely [make] it more difficult to obtain free entry forms than to pay the $2 newsstand price of *Nightmoves*." The court found that the obstacles in obtaining free entry blanks made this option inordinately difficult. Because the only realistic way to enter the game was to pay the $2 price of the newspaper, this was consideration, and that made the game a lottery.

Chance as an Element

Chance is another element that must exist in order to qualify as a lottery. If chance dominates the game, rather than skill or judgment, it becomes a lottery. Chance is usually involved in games in which the participant must guess something to win— from guessing the number of beans in a jar to guessing the number of people that will attend a grand opening event. (There are other ways chance can create problems, and we look at those later.)

Chance is an interesting element. Pure chance is not the issue in most of the cases that have gone through the courts. Rather, the courts look to whether chance is the controlling factor in awarding prizes. For example, a dice game involves pure chance. On the other hand, a chess game involves pure skill. Then, in the middle are card games, which are games of chance. They do not stop being games of chance simply because some element of skill is involved. Card games are still predominantly controlled by the luck of the draw.

One of my favorite examples of a game of chance involved a trade newspaper, the *United States Tobacco Journal*. The case occurred about 1900 and involved an advertisement for a game advertised in the newspaper. The ad read as follows:

The *United States Tobacco Journal*

SAVE OUR BANDS
Another free Distribution of
$142,500.00
Will be made in December, 1903
Based on the Month of November, 1903
TO SMOKERS OF
[Here follow the names of 30 brands of cigars.]
How many cigars (of all brands, no matter by whom manufactured) will the United States collect taxes on during the month of November, 1903?
(Cigars bearing $3.00 tax per thousand)
The persons who estimate nearest to the number of cigars on which $3.00 tax per thousand is paid during the month of November, 1903, as shown by the total sales of stamps made by the United States Internal Revenue Department during November, 1903, will be awarded as follows:
To the person estimating the closest . . . . $5,000 in cash.

The list continued for the number of people who guessed next closest in descending order. At the end of the list were people who won $5 or a box of free cigars. In theory, over 35,000 people could win something. Obviously, because of the newspaper's audience, the game was directed to retail sellers of cigars and other tobacco products. These retailers would get to make four estimates for every 100 cigar bands sent in.

The game was sponsored by a cigar manufacturer, the Florodora Company. As part of the rules, the company allowed each Florodora cigar band to count as two for the purpose of entering the game. Suffice it to say that the purpose of Florodora was to increase sales of its brand of cigar. There is nothing wrong or illegal in this.

Yet, the State of New York felt that the game was an illegal lottery, so they arrested the magazine publisher, Ismar Ellison. In many states, operating a lottery is a criminal offense; in this case it was a misdemeanor. The case was *People ex rel. Ellison* v. *Lavin,* 179 N.Y. 164 (1904).

According to the elements of a lottery, this game provided for awarding prizes. It also possessed the element of consideration by requiring the dealer to purchase cigars from which to get the bands required to enter the game. "Therefore," said the court, "the only question presented by the case is whether the distribution is made by chance or not."

This game was a lottery because the outcome was based primarily on chance. That is not to say that there is no skill or judgment involved, but it is slight compared to the chance involved. "A lottery," said the court, "does not cease to be such . . . because its result may be affected, to some slight extent, by the exercise of judgment." In this case, the controlling factor in receiving a prize was chance, not skill or judgment.

Earlier in this chapter we looked at a case that involved picking the winners of upcoming football games. Surely chance is involved in that game, you may think. Not so. Let's look at a situation to explain why that is.

Charles Rich and Frank Camarrata ran a game for which they were essentially bookmakers. The two men solicited bets or wagers on the outcome of sporting events from horse racing to baseball. They also took bets on elections. A complaint was filed against these two men charging that they were operating an illegal lottery in *United States* v. *Rich,* 90 F. Supp. 624 (E.D. Ill. 1950).

The participant wagered an amount by placing a bet. The requirement of consideration was met. The participant also stood to win a large return if the right team won. That meant that the requirement of a prize was also present. What was left to be determined was whether the game involved chance. That was the issue that the court was left to ponder.

The court said about *chance* that, " . . . the word has reference to the attempt to attain certain ends, not by skill or any known or fixed rules, but by the happening of a subsequent event, incapable of ascertainment or accomplishment by means of human foresight or ingenuity." Obviously, a blindfolded man pulling a winning ticket from a jar involves pure chance. Here, though, it's a different story.

The government argued that choosing the winner of a horse race or baseball game offered extremely narrow odds. Because of the huge amount of uncertainty, the winner could attribute the win to nothing more than a guess.

The court, however, felt that "there is always something more than a mere guess" involved. "The odds may often be long," the court said, "and the chance of winning small so as to tempt the ignorant and the greedy to risk amounts small or large on the chance of getting a much larger return, and yet in every case there is a race or a game of skill or an election or something in which natural forces are involved and upon which knowledge, skill and judgment are brought into play."

In the case of a horse race, bets are placed on races that may be run quite some time in the future. Yet, the bets are placed based on information that can be obtained about the horses in advance. The stable that the horse comes from, the owner, the jockey, and the track are all conditions on which knowledge, skill, and judgment can be used to make a selection. There is no pure chance here as applied to lotteries. The government lost its case.

But chance in determining the winner is not the only way this element can be involved to turn a contest into a lottery. Chance is also created when the amount of the ultimate prize is unknown or undetermined, when the amount of the prize is to be determined by some event yet to happen, like the dollar sales of a particular store on a certain day in the future. Another situation could exist when the prize depends on the number of people who ultimately enter the contest.

In 1963 Boris Zebelman was a car dealer in Gardner, Kansas. He developed a game to promote his dealership, which he advertised through the mail. He claimed that anyone who bought a car from him would become an "automobile owner representative." This rep would then submit names and addresses of others who would be potential buyers. For each person whose name was submitted and who purchased a car (and also became a rep), the original rep would receive $100 in cash. Also, the original rep would receive $50 for each person whose name was submitted by the new participant, if that person bought a car and participated as a rep.

In other words, let's say Mr. Smith bought a car from Zebelman and became a rep. He would submit names of others including Ms. Jones. Now Ms. Jones buys a car and becomes a rep, and Mr. Smith receives $100. Then Ms. Jones submits the name of Mr. Adams, who buys a car and becomes a rep. In that case, Ms. Jones would receive $100, and Mr. Smith would receive $50. If this sounds like a pyramid scheme, it is.

Zebelman was caught and charged with 15 counts of running a lottery. The case was *Zebelman* v. *United States,* 339 F.2d 484 (10th Cir. 1964). The question here is tricky. Is chance involved? In the case of the original purchaser rep, the answer is no. In this phase of the game, chance is not the controlling factor. The person has control over this part of the game.

The chance element enters into the picture because "the original purchaser has no control over the payment or receipt of the $50 since it is the person whose name he submits that must locate another buyer." This situation requires, in large part, the element of chance, and this makes the scheme a lottery.

Use of Skill. If skill or judgment is dominant, then the game is not a lottery. In games that ask for the *best letter, best essay,* or *best name,* no chance is present. Also, as we saw in the *Rich* case involving sports games, skill or judgment is required because picking the winner is determined in part by the skill of the entrant.

As long as the winners are determined on the basis of a comparison of the skill of the entries, it is legal. In these games if a tie exists, both winners must receive prizes of equal value; otherwise chance enters into the picture again.

In 1912 the Armstrong-Byrd Music company in Oklahoma City, Oklahoma, ran a promotion for a give-away of one of its pianos. The company ran ads promoting the contest. The object of the game was to complete a puzzle by filling in spaces with numbers to make a total of 15. The puzzle was quite simple, but the challenge was to submit an entry that was the neatest or most unique design.

On May 10, 1912, a group of judges gathered together to pick the winner from the 6,500 entries. Most were simply filled in puzzles from the entry blank supplied in the newspaper ad. But a few were very original. One was actually made out of burnt wood, and another was embroidered on a pillow. The five most unique and original were awarded the promised prizes.

When the winners were notified of their prizes by mail, the Postmaster, H. G. Eastman, filed suit to stop what he considered an illegal lottery. The case was *Eastman* v. *Armstrong-Byrd Music Co.*, 212 F. 662 (8th Cir. 1914). The court determined that the contest winners were picked based on a use of their skill and judgment. As the court said, "There was no element of chance in this scheme or plan." This contest was not a lottery and was legal.

REGULATION OVER CONTESTS

There are basically three agencies that have control over contests and how they are promoted. The Post Office has control over any contest that uses the mail in any way. The Federal Trade Commission has control over any activity which is deceptive or unfair, including contests. The Federal Communications Commission controls any contest advertised over radio, television, or cable. And, finally, each state has specific statutes that govern the use of contests.

Post Office

The first form of regulation over gambling activities took place in 1868 in the form of postal regulations.[4] These laws were created in an attempt to curb the fraud and abuse in state sponsored lotteries after the Civil War.

Under current law, it is a crime to mail any advertisement of any lottery, gift enterprise, or similar scheme where prizes are awarded based on chance. Violation of this law carries a fine of $1,000 or two years in prison, or both.[5] In addition, the

---

[4]15 Stat. 194 (1868).
[5]18 U.S.C., section 1302 (1982).

Post Office is authorized to issue a cease-and-desist order and refuse to mail any such advertisement.[6] Violation of a cease-and-desist order carries a civil fine of up to $10,000 per day.

Contests that use the mail in any way must be approved by the General Counsel, Mailability Division, U.S. Postal Service, Washington, D.C. 20006. When I say "contests that use the mail," I mean anything from mailing entry forms to mailing notices to winners after the contest.

We've seen cases earlier where the Post Office brought suit because the mail was used in the scheme. *United States* v. *Purvis, Garden City Chamber of Commerce* v. *Wagner, Dreem Arts, Inc.* v. *City of Chicago, People ex rel. Ellison* v. *Lavin* and *Eastman* v. *Armstrong-Byrd Music Co.*, are good examples of cases where the Post Office became involved.

Federal Trade Commission

The FTC has established certain rules that apply to contests. It requires the following:

1. Disclosure of the exact number of prizes to be awarded.
2. Disclosure of the odds of winning.
3. Disclosure of the area within which the game will exist.
4. Disclosure of the length of the contest.
5. That all game pieces must be distributed to stores on a totally random basis.
6. That the game cannot be ended until all game pieces are handed out.

Also, any game that continues beyond 30 days must disclose the number of unredeemed prizes and revised odds on a weekly basis. Successive games must be separated by 30 days or the length of the previous game (whichever is shorter).

These rules do not apply to broadcast media; however, the information must be made available to consumers. The company must disclose where the consumer can go, or write, to get complete contest information.

---

[6]39 U.S.C., section 3001, 3005 (1984 Supp.).

R. F. Keppel & Brothers operated a business which manufactured and placed in retail stores a candy game known as Break and Take. In the early 1930s, Keppel promoted its game in stores that were located near schools. It displayed the game in a way that would be attractive to children. The company earned about $234,000 a year from the game.

The game involved an assortment of wrapped candy. The participant would pay one cent and pick a piece of candy from the 120 in the display. The candy would be opened to discover if it contained a penny as a prize, or a slip of paper with a purchase price of 1, 2, or 3 cents. In reality, only four pieces contained a penny. The other pieces of candy contained prices of 1 to 3 cents each. If the candy contained a ticket, that was the price that the participant had to pay. There was a possibility that the person could win back the initial penny investment and get the candy free. But the odds were very low.

Obviously, this game qualified as a lottery. All three essential elements were present: consideration, prize, and chance. Yet, the Federal Trade Commission brought suit in *Federal Trade Commission* v. *R. F. Keppel & Bros. Inc.*, 291 U.S. 304 (1934), because of the game's effect on children. They were the audience that the game was directed toward.

The Supreme Court, in upholding the FTC's decision, felt that "the method of competition adopted . . . induces children, too young to be capable of exercising an intelligent judgment of the transaction, to purchase an article less desirable in point of quality or quantity than that offered at a comparable price."

That is why the FTC became involved with the lottery. The method exploited children who were unable to protect themselves. The FTC, as we saw in Chapters 2 and 3, concerns itself with deception and unfairness. As the court said, "It would seem a gross perversion . . . to hold that the method is not 'unfair.' " Keppel lost its case.

In many cases, the FTC may issue a cease-and-desist order over games that are not deemed to be literally illegal lotteries. Remember that the FTC has the authority to stop any activity which is unfair or deceptive, even if it does not violate lottery regulations.

A good example of this involved the *Reader's Digest* Sweepstakes. Entry forms were mailed to members of the public. The entry forms contained a number and a ticket with the same number printed on it. The participant was to return the ticket to *Reader's Digest* where it would be compared against preselected winning numbers. If the number on the ticket matched a winning number, that prize would be awarded.

The intent of the sweepstakes was to build sales in its products. To promote its sweepstakes, *Reader's Digest* made claims about the contest, including:

- Participants only needed to mail in their ticket to receive their prize if they were winners.
- Participants had a reasonable chance of winning.
- All advertised prizes had been purchased by *Reader's Digest* prior to the contest.
- Consumers who received entry forms were "selected," "chosen," or were "one of the few people to be invited."
- Entry forms were mailed on a limited basis.
- In January 1969 (a typical contest), 101,751 prizes were offered worth $999,000.

This well-known sweepstakes ran into trouble with the FTC in 1971. The FTC stepped in and filed suit *In the matter of Reader's Digest Assn.*, 79 FTC 696 (1971). The FTC took action, not because this was an illegal lottery, but because the sweepstakes was deceptive.

In reality, the claims that *Reader's Digest* made in its advertisements and promotion were not accurate. Participants were not "one of the few to be invited." In fact, millions of copies of the *Reader's Digest* Sweepstakes entry forms were mailed to consumers. In the January 1969 contest, there were not 101,751 prizes worth $999,000. In reality there were 40,517 prizes worth $441,789. Also, winners were required to do more than send in their ticket to receive a prize. They were required to do other undisclosed things—for example, submit to interviews by a private detective before being allowed to obtain their prize.

In addition, there was no "reasonable opportunity to win" in *Reader's Digest* Sweepstakes. As I said at the beginning of this chapter, the odds of winning first prize were about 1 in 480,000. The *Reader's Digest* Sweepstakes was simply not what it was promoted to be. Because of the deception, the FTC issued a cease-and-desist order.

Generally, there are specific situations that the FTC does not allow regarding contests. The following list represents a general outline of practices that are prohibited by the FTC as they apply to contests:

1. Making false representations of the value of a prize.
2. Promising cash and awarding merchandise instead.
3. Failing to follow contest rules as established.
4. Offering a number of prizes that differ from those advertised.

Federal Communications Commission

The Congress first attempted to regulate the airwaves under the Radio Act of 1927.[7] However, the issue of lotteries was not regulated in broadcast until the Federal Communications Act of 1934.[8] Then later these regulations were made a part of the criminal code as Section 1304.[9]

Under the current law, Section 1304, it is a criminal offense to broadcast (by radio, cable, or television) any advertisement for a lottery, gift enterprise, or similar scheme. Specifically, the statute prohibits "any advertisement of or information concerning any lottery, gift enterprise, or similar scheme, offering prizes dependent in whole or in part upon lot or chance, or any list of the prizes drawn or awarded by means of any such lottery, gift enterprise, or scheme, whether said list contains any part or all of such prizes . . ."[10]

A good example of this occurred in 1973. The University of Florida radio station WRUF in Gainesville, Florida, broadcast a radio commercial for its client, Shaw and Keeter Fordtown. Any person who purchased an automobile from the dealership received a prize. Here's the radio copy:

---

[7]44 Stat. 1162 (1927).
[8]H. R. Rep. No. 72-2106, 72 Cong. 2d Sess. (1933).
[9]18 U.S.C., section 312 (1982).
[10]18 U.S.C., section 1304.

> Shaw and Keeter has an extra bonus for you . . .
> A U.S. Savings Bond with every new car or truck delivered!
> At least a $25 bond . . . it might be a $50 bond . . .
> it could be a $500 bond!
> After purchase, check the sealed envelope in the glove box
> with the sealed envelope in the office.
> It will be a $25 bond . . .
> it might be a $50 bond . . . it could be a $500 bond!
> Offer ends March 31st!
> Hurry to Shaw and Keeter Fordtown,
> downtown at 238 West University Avenue!

When the FCC learned of the commercial, it filed a complaint against the school. The FCC held that a violation of lottery restrictions was created *In the matter of University of Florida,* 40 F.C.C.2d 188 (1973).

All three elements of a lottery existed in this case. A prize was offered in the form of a savings bond. While every purchaser received a bond, their values varied considerably. Consideration existed since the consumer was required to purchase a car or truck before being eligible to win a savings bond. Finally, chance was present as to which bond would be won. Since the University of Florida created, produced, and aired the spot, it was required to pay a fine of $2,000.

In any case, where broadcast media is involved, the advertisement should include information on the following:

- Who may participate.
- Type of entries required.
- Where, when, and how the entry is to be submitted.
- Number and nature of prizes.
- The existence of duplicate prizes in the case of ties.
- The closing date.
- Where complete contest details can be obtained.

At the end of the book in Appendix B is a copy of the National Broadcasting Company (NBC) Broadcast Standards for Television. These contain guidelines that NBC follows in reviewing proposed commercials. Refer to the section on contests and lotteries. They are fairly typical of other networks. Each of the networks has compiled its own set of guidelines, and these should be consulted when developing contests that will use broadcast media.

State Regulation

Each of the states is in agreement as to what constitutes an illegal lottery, as we've discussed in the previous part of this chapter. They agree with the federal guidelines in most all cases. The difference shows up in how the states interpret the requirements. What constitutes *chance,* a *prize,* and especially *consideration* is where the states vary in some ways.

Each state has legislated specific requirements for contests. The specific state regulation should be consulted before creating a contest advertisement. Exhibit 9-1 includes a list of current state statutes.

EXHIBIT 9–1

STATE STATUTES REGULATING CONTESTS

Alabama	Alabama Constitution article IV, section 65
Alaska	Alaska Statutes, section 11.66.280 (1985)
Arizona	Arizona Revised Statutes Annotated, section 13-3304 (1985 Supp)
Arkansas	Arkansas Constitution Article 19, section 15
California	California Constitution Article 4, section 19
Colorado	Colorado Constitution Article XVIII, section 2 Colorado Revised Statutes, sections 18-10-101, 102 (1980)
Connecticut	Connecticut General Statutes Annotated, sections 53-278a & b (West 1985)
Delaware	Delaware Constitution article 11, sections 17, 17B
Florida	Florida Constitution article 10, section 7 Florida Statutes Annotated, section 849.09 (West 1985 Supp)
Georgia	Georgia Constitution, section 2-208 Georgia Code Annotated, section 26-2701 (1983)
Hawaii	Hawaii Revised Statutes, section 712-1220 (1976)
Idaho	Idaho Constitution article 3, section 20 Idaho Code, sections 18-4901, 4903 (1977)

EXHIBIT 9–1—*Continued*

Illinois	Illinois Revised Statutes, chapter 38, paragraphs 28-1(a), 28-2(h) (1972)
Indiana	Indiana Constitution article 15, section 8 Indiana Code Annotated, sections 35-45-5-1, -2 (1985)
Iowa	Iowa Code Annotated, section 725.12 (1979)
Kansas	Kansas Constitution, article 15, section 3 Kansas Statutes Annotated, section 21-4305 (1985)
Kentucky	Kentucky Constitution, section 226 Kentucky Revised Statutes Annotated, section 528.010 (1985)
Louisiana	Louisiana Constitution, article 12, section 6 Louisiana Revised Statutes Annotated, chapter 14, section 90 (1986 Supp)
Maine	Maine Revised Statutes Annotated, title 17a, section 952 (1983)
Maryland	Maryland Annotated Code, article 27, sections 356, 363 (1982)
Massachusetts	Massachusetts General Laws Annotated, chapter 271, sections 7, 11, 6c (1985 Supp)
Michigan	Michigan Comprehensive Laws, sections 750.372, .375 (1968)
Minnesota	Minnesota Constitution, article 13, section 5. Minnesota Statutes Annotated, section 609.75 (1986 Supp)
Mississippi	Mississippi Constitution, article 99 Mississippi Code Annotated, sections 97-33-1, -33, -39 (1973)
Montana	Montana Code Annotated, sections 23-5-201, -202 (1983)
Nebraska	Nebraska Constitution, article 111, section 24
Nevada	Nevada Constitution, article 4, section 24 Nevada Revised Statutes, sections 462.010, 598.070, 598.080 (1985)
New Hampshire	New Hampshire Revised Statutes Annotated, section 647.1 (1977)
New Jersey	New Jersey Statutes Annotated, sections 2C: 37-1 (1982), 5: 12-1, 5: 12-70 (1985 Supp)
New Mexico	New Mexico Statutes Annotated, sections 30-19-1, 30-19-2 (1984)
New York	New York Constitution, article 1, section 9 New York Penal Code, section 225.00 (McKinney 1980)
North Carolina	North Carolina General Statutes, sections 14-289, 14-290, 14-291 (1985 Supp)

EXHIBIT 9–1—*Concluded*

North Dakota	North Dakota Constitution, article XI, section 23 North Dakota Cent. Code, section 12.1-28-01 (1985)
Ohio	Ohio Constitution, article XV, section 6 Ohio Revised Codes Annotated, section 2915.01 (Page 1982)
Oklahoma	Oklahoma Statutes, title 21, section 1, sub-sections 1052, 1053, 1054, 1056 (1983)
Oregon	Oregon Constitution, article XV, section 4 Oregon Ev. Statutes Annotated, section 167.117 (1983)
Pennsylvania	18 Pennsylvania Cons. Statutes Annotated, section 5512 (Purdon 1983)
Rhode Island	Rhode Island Constitution Amended XLI, section 1 Rhode Island General Laws, section 11-19-1 (supp 1985)
South Carolina	South Carolina Constitution, article XVII, section 7 South Carolina Code Annotated, section 16-19-10 (1985)
South Dakota	South Dakota Constitution, article III, section 25 South Dakota Codified Laws Annotated, section 22-25-24 (1979)
Tennessee	Tennessee Constitution, article II, section 5 Tennessee Code Annotated, sections 39-6-609, 39-6-624 (1982)
Texas	Texas Constitution, article 3, section 47 Texas Penal Code Annotated, sections 47.03, 47.01 (Vernon 1974)
Utah	Utah Constitution, article VI, section 27 Utah Code Annotated, sections 76-10-1101, 76-10-1102 (1978)
Vermont	Vermont Statutes Annotated, title 13, sections 2101, 2102 (1974)
Virginia	Virginia Code, section 18.2-325 (1982)
Washington	Washington Constitution, article II, section 24 Washington Rev. Code Annotated, section 9.46.020 (1977)
West Virginia	West Virginia constitution, article 6, section 36 West Virginia Code, section 61-10-11 (1984)
Wisconsin	Wisconsin Constitution, article 4, section 24 Wisconsin Statutes Annotated, section 945.01 (9185 Supp)
Wyoming	Wyoming Statutes, section 6-7-101 (1983)
Washington, D.C.	District of Columbia Code Annotated, sections 22-1501, 22-1517 (1981)
Puerto Rico	Puerto Rico Laws Annotated, title 33, sections 1211, 1212, 1213, 1214 (1983) title 15, section 17-84 (1983)

CHAPTER 10

GUARANTEES AND WARRANTIES

Guarantees . . . are not worth the paper they are written on.
—*Johann Bernhard*

When someone mentions the word *guarantee,* most people think of a piece of paper that comes with their new car, dishwasher, or compact disk player. In that case, the guarantee explains what the manufacturer will do if certain parts of the product fail within a certain time. This type of product guarantee is very common in today's market economy.

But there are other guarantees. Probably the most important and powerful one ever created was devised by a group of 55 men who met at a convention in Philadelphia. The first to show up for the meeting was a 36-year-old educator from Virginia named Jim Madison. The others, who joined the meeting later, were people from business, government, shipping, farming, education, and law. In fact, more than half of them were lawyers.

The group had the task of creating a guarantee for a new product. It was a different, rather revolutionary product. So they had to consider new situations that might arise and what would happen if they came about. This group continued their meeting for almost 17 weeks before they had ironed out the conditions of their guarantee. Finally, they were satisfied. And, then as with all good guarantees, they put it in writing so that anyone who needed to could rely on it should a claim become necessary.

The guarantee that I have been discussing was written sometime ago—in 1791 to be exact. And it's still in effect today. It's called the *Bill of Rights*—the first 10 amendments to the Constitution of the United States. It's a guarantee for the people, a guarantee of personal freedom. It is probably the most powerful (the Magna Carta being the only other that comes close) and yet misunderstood guarantee ever written.

Although most people don't consider the Bill of Rights to be a guarantee, it surely is one. It guarantees the people of the United States certain "inalienable rights" that cannot be taken away or overlooked. Of all the cases that the Supreme Court hears, involving constitutional liberties, most of them are breaches of the Bill of Rights.

Since this chapter deals with guarantees, I thought it appropriate to start with the first ever written in this country. The Ninth and Tenth Amendments essentially say, "we mean what we said." Specifically, the Tenth specifies that powers not delegated are reserved. The Ninth guarantees, "The enumeration in the Constitution, of certain rights, shall not be construed to deny or disparage others retained by the people." For over 200 years this guarantee was ignored until the Supreme Court used it to announce that the privacy of the bedroom involved an "unenumerated" right. Specifically, the issue was contraception.

The Eighth Amendment disallows cruel and unusual punishment, and excessive bail and fines. The Seventh guarantees the right to a jury trial in civil cases "where the value in controversy exceeds twenty dollars." The Sixth begins, "The accused shall enjoy the right to a speedy and public trial." That word *enjoy* still bothers me.

The Fifth Amendment declares two guarantees. The first specifies that no person "be subject for the same offense to be twice put in jeopardy of life and limb." Today we call this *double jeopardy*. The other guarantee is that no person "shall be compelled in any criminal case to be a witness against himself." We call this *self-incrimination*. This Amendment has probably caused the greatest amount of activity in the courts, from the "Communists-are-everywhere" era of Joe McCarthy and Richard Nixon, to the "read-him-his-rights" era of the *Miranda* rule[1] in 1966.

---

[1]*Miranda v. Arizona,* 384 U.S. 436 (1966).

The Fourth Amendment guarantees "the people" protection ". . . against unreasonable search and seizures." The Third touches on a person's right of privacy in his or her home. The Second Amendment specifies a guarantee that a "well regulated Militia being necessary to the security of a free State, the right of the people to keep and bear Arms shall not be infringed." (This originally applied to the right of a militia to keep and bear arms, not the individual citizen.)

The First Amendment, although it lay dormant for over 130 years, guarantees freedom of speech, freedom of the press, the right of people to peacefully assemble, and the right to practice one's religion.

So there you have it. The first guarantee written in this country. And yet it wasn't unanimously adopted by every state until 1939. Massachusetts, Georgia, and Connecticut were the hold-outs.

All guarantees have the same purpose. They are intended as a protection. They give confidence to people who must rely on a claim. But the guarantees we are concerned with here are simpler. They are guarantees that involve the state of the marketplace, rather than the state of the Union.

In the fall of 1986, American Express started an ad campaign promoting its "Buyers Assurance Plan." American Express would automatically extend the manufacturer's warranty on any purchases made on its charge card. In some cases the manufacturer's warranty was extended for up to a year. The campaign was intended to run for only four months, but it was so successful that it was continued through 1987. The plan was instituted because American Express was used mostly for such business and travel purchases as air fare, hotels, and meals. But the company wanted to increase sales of retail merchandise with its charge card. As a result of the extended warranty, consumer use of the card increased considerably.

In the spring of 1987, Lufthansa German Airlines began a program for first class and business class passengers. It guaranteed to pay $200 for any missed connecting flights or late baggage due to the airline's fault. Passenger ticket sales increased, as a consequence, with only minimal claims being filed.

These examples show just how dominant the use of guarantees has become. Entire ad campaigns are built around them. Today, an increasing number of companies are turning to guarantees and warranties to increase sales. Companies recognize the value of customer satisfaction and tie that into their products with stronger guarantees. Airlines, appliances, banks, cars, computers, hotels, and many others are developing strong guarantees for products and services and are advertising the fact heavily. Warranties and guarantees have become a part of comparative advertising and are major elements that one company can use to position itself against the competition.

Most of the car manufacturers now offer 6-year or 60,000-mile power-train warranties. Ford even offers a lifetime service guarantee covering major repairs for as long as the customer owns the car. Advertisements that exclaim "money-back guarantee," "quality assurance," "customer satisfaction," or "extended warranty," have become strong selling tools. Suffice it to say, the advertiser must understand the legalities of promoting guarantees and warranties in its ads.

DIFFERENCE BETWEEN A GUARANTEE AND A WARRANTY

The terms *warranty* and *guarantee* are often used interchangeably. In reality there is very little difference between the two, but there is some. To be technical, a warranty is an assumption by the seller of the quality, suitability, character, and performance of the product. On the other hand, a guarantee is the agreement that comes with the purchase of the merchandise that, if the product fails to live up to the claims, the seller will remedy the situation in some way.

A warranty is, simply put, a promise that becomes a contract between the manufacturer and the buyer. The contract goes into effect at the moment that the consumer makes a purchase. A guarantee is a promise that if something goes wrong with the product, the manufacturer will do certain things.

Let's say a roll of photographic film claims that it is "free from defects in workmanship and materials." That's a warranty. If the film turns out to be defective, the guarantee states that "if defective it will be replaced with a new roll of equivalent film free of charge." The warranty states what the product is claimed to be able to do. The guarantee states what the manufacturer will do if the product fails to live up to the warranty.

THE SCOPE OF WARRANTIES AND GUARANTEES

As we saw in Chapter 4 on advertising's role in products liability actions, there are different forms of warranties. Warranties can be expressed, that is clearly stated, or they can be implied. I would recommend a review of that chapter to re-examine the ways in which warranties can have an impact on advertising.

Here, however, we will deal mainly with how guarantees should be advertised. It is not my intent to discuss the legalities of developing guarantees, only how they should be advertised. The balance of this chapter will be devoted to considerations about using guarantees in advertising.

REPRESENTATIONS MADE IN ADS ABOUT GUARANTEES

When advertisements discuss guarantees about a product, the advertiser must be concerned with making certain representations. When claims are made in an ad about the quality, results, or effects of guaranteed merchandise, the advertiser must do certain things—identify the guarantor and state the characteristics, performance, duration, conditions, and charges involved.

Identifying the Guarantor

In Maryland in the early 1960s, World Wide Television Corporation sold television sets and appliances to the public. As part of its promotion the company advertised in newspapers and on radio, focusing on a guarantee for its products.

The company had a unique way of selling its products. World Wide's giant screen Olympic console televisions were controlled by a coin meter, called the *Metermatic Plan*. Instead of making monthly payments for the appliance, the purchaser would insert coins in a box to turn on the unit, similar to a coin-operated laundry. The purchaser couldn't use the appliance unless money was put in. A typical ad stated that the products were guaranteed. Here's what was claimed:

BRAND NEW GIANT SCREEN OLYMPIC
CONSOLE TELEVISION
WITH ONE FULL-YEAR GUARANTEE including picture tube.
Service is fully guaranteed!
Service guarantee included!
The Metermatic Plan is better because service is guaranteed.

In truth, the Olympic televisions were guaranteed by Siegler Corporation, the makers of the television, and not World Wide. Yet this was not stated anywhere in the ads, but only in the instruction booklet included with the television set. The implication in the ad was that World Wide was guaranteeing the television sets. The consumer could not have known the true identity of the guarantor until after the television was delivered. This was deceptive.

There's another unique thing about World Wide's service guarantee. The reason that service was guaranteed was because if the company didn't fix a broken set, it couldn't be used by the consumer—and the company wouldn't get paid. That's the only reason service was fully guaranteed. The FTC, learning of the situation, filed a complaint *In the Matter of World Wide Television Corp.*, 66 F.T.C. 961 (1964).

In that case the commissioner exclaimed: "[World Wide's] products are not unconditionally guaranteed for one year. Said guarantee is subject to numerous requirements, limitations, and restrictions. The advertised guarantee fails to set forth the nature, conditions and extent of the guarantee, the manner in which the guarantor will perform . . . and the identity of the guarantor." The commissioner ordered that World Wide could not claim that its products were guaranteed unless the nature, extent, and duration were clearly stated. Also, World Wide had to clearly state the name and address of the guarantor.

Stating the Characteristics or Attributes to Be Guaranteed

An advertiser can build whatever guarantee it wants into a product. In other words, an advertiser may create the limits of any guarantee on its products. However, it must state the characteristics, attributes, and limitations in its guarantee. But simply using the word *guaranteed,* alone without clarification must be avoided.

One of the earliest situations to establish this involved the Parker Pen Company. Parker manufactured fountain pens and sold them to the public. In 1946 Parker ran advertisements for its pens that contained a statement "Guaranteed for Life by Parker's." The specific terms of the guarantee were spelled out elsewhere in the ad: "Pens marked with a Blue Diamond are guaranteed for the life of the owner against everything except loss or intentional damage, subject only to a charge of 35 cents for postage, insurance and handling, provided complete pen is returned for service."

The Federal Trade Commission filed a complaint against Parker because it felt that by charging 35 cents a deception was created as to the "Lifetime Guarantee." The FTC claimed that the 35 cent charge limited the guarantee. The case was appealed to the Federal Circuit Court of Appeals in *Parker Pen Co.* v. *F.T.C.,* 153 F.2d 509 (C.C.A. 1946).

There the court voiced its opinion. "Ordinarily the word, *guarantee,* is incomplete unless it is used in connection with other explanatory words." To say a pen or other object is guaranteed is meaningless. What is the guarantee? Is it a limited guarantee? Is it an unlimited guarantee? The answer to these questions gives meaning to the word *guaranteed.* The same is true of the words *Guaranteed for Life* or *Life Guarantee.*

In this case, Parker advertised its guarantee, claiming that it would make needed repairs during the life of the original buyer, if that person paid 35 cents per repair. There is nothing wrong with that. It clearly spelled out the terms of its guarantee. Parker won its case.

Specifying How the Guarantee
Is to Be Performed

Another element of the claim that a product is guaranteed involves how the guarantee will be performed. In other words, what will be done.

Capitol Manufacturing Company in New York offered watches that were represented to be manufactured by Hamilton and Gruen Watch Companies. In reality, Capitol did not sell Hamilton or Gruen watches, but rather cheap imitations. In its ads, Capitol made statements about its watches, including:

ELECTRA TWO-YEAR SERVICE GUARANTEE

We guarantee this watch for two years from date of purchase against defects in material and workmanship.

This guarantee appears to name a company called *Electra* as the guarantor. It claims that any obligations that the company has under the guarantee will be performed fully, satisfactorily, and promptly. The ad also states that the watch will operate properly for at least two years.

Capitol's guarantee came to the attention of the Federal Trade Commission. Since the guarantee did not specify how the guarantor would fulfill the guarantee, it filed a complaint *In the Matter of Capitol Mfg. Corp.*, 73 F.T.C. 872 (1968). The FTC felt that the guarantee was deceptive. The watches that Capitol sold were so cheaply made that "[f]ew, if any, . . . will operate for at least the two year period represented in the guarantee."

The problem with this guarantee was that it failed to state what Capitol would do if the watch broke within the two-year period. Would it repair the watch? Would it replace the watch? Would it refund the purchase price? None of this was stated. In truth, it wasn't going to do anything. This is probably how the FTC learned about the situation in the first place.

When any guarantee is claimed, the "manner in which the guarantor will perform . . . [must be] clearly and conspicuously set forth in immediate connection therewith." Since Capitol failed to provide this information with its guarantee the FTC issued a cease-and-desist order.

Duration of the Guarantee

All guarantees should specify a limit as to the length of time that it will be honored by the manufacturer. Advertisers can get into trouble with guarantees that are described as "for a season of use," or "for the year." The guarantee should specify when the time of the guarantee starts. For example, a statement such as, "guaranteed for one year from the date of retail purchase," leaves little interpretation.

Another way to list the duration of a guarantee is to state its termination date. Let's go back to our example of photographic film, which is commonly guaranteed in this way. Film generally lists an expiration date for the "guaranteed" use of the product such as "not good after . . . "

A common way to start the clock running on a guarantee is through a mail-back registration card. Many products are guaranteed only after a registration card is filled out and returned to the manufacturer. Many home appliances, stereos, cameras, and watches are commonly guaranteed in this way.

In the late 1950s, a sewing machine manufacturer placed ads in national consumer magazines including *McCall's* magazine. The manufacturer, International Stitch-O-Matic in Chicago, promoted its guarantee in these ads. The guarantee stated that the product was backed by a "money-back" guarantee on the entire machine for 25 years. When it turned out that this was false, *In the Matter of International Stitch-O-Matic Corp.*, 54 F.T.C. 1308 (1959; consent), resulted. The guarantee claimed that the entire machine was covered for 25 years. In fact, only the motor was guaranteed, and for just one year. The Stitch-O-Matic guarantee had limitations, including time, which were blatantly misstated in its ads.

Stating Conditions of Guarantee

In the late 1960s Universe Chemicals, Incorporated, manufactured and sold a water-repellent paint by the name of *Kleer-Kote* and *Kolor-Kote*. The sales demonstration of the product was quite impressive. Various items were shown to the prospective buyers, and they were told that the items were coated with Kleer-Kote or Kolor-Kote.

A piece of sheet metal, coated with Kolor-Kote, was shown, and the prospect was told that the paint would not crack, peel, or break even if the metal was bent. In another example, a treated brick showed the repellent quality of the coating when water was poured over it. The coating was heated with an infrared bulb to demonstrate its heat resistance. A sieve was coated with Kleer-Kote and was shown to hold water without leaking.

The product appeared to be truly amazing, and the demonstrations were convincing. Kleer-Kote and Kolor-Kote even came with a "10-year, unconditional guarantee." Unfortunately, the product failed to live up to its claims, and the guarantee turned out to be not much of a solution. The Federal Trade Commission became involved *In the Matter of Universe Chemicals, Inc.,* 77 F.T.C. 598 (1970).

While the wording in the Kleer-Kote brochure stated that the product was "unconditionally guaranteed for 10 years," this was not the case. When a guarantee is claimed to be unconditional, it means just that: no conditions. If there are any conditions, the guarantee is not unconditional. In that case, it should be stated as a "limited guarantee," and then the limits must be specified.

Actually, in Universe Chemicals's case the company would only replace the product if defective. In certain cases the product was replaced, but in many cases the company refused. "The guarantee," said the commissioner, "was clearly not unconditional, and the conditions were not stated in the advertising."

Stating Charges Involved in a Guarantee

Western Radio Corporation manufactured pocket-sized radio transmitters and advertised them in such magazines as *Popular Science* and others in the mid 1960s. Its Radi-Vox transmitter was advertised with a "Money-back guarantee." However, the company failed to inform the consumer that a service charge applied to the guarantee.

The case went to court in *Western Radio Corp.* v. *FTC*, 339 F.2d 937 (7th Cir. 1964). There, the court said that the advertising had the capacity and tendency to mislead the public, "by failure to disclose a service charge in connection with the advertised unconditional guarantee."

When a guarantee is advertised as a *money-back* guarantee, it means just that. Any guarantee must state "the terms and conditions of such guarantee . . . clearly and conspicously . . . including the amount of any service or other charge which is imposed."

PROBLEMS WITH ADVERTISING GUARANTEES

The most obvious problem encountered in advertising a guarantee is whether the ad creates a deception about the actual guarantee. When there is a difference between the guarantee and the way it is advertised or it is a blatant falsehood, the Federal Trade Commission can step in.

Variations between Advertised Guarantee and Actual Guarantee

Montgomery Ward offered rebuilt car engines through its chain of retail department stores in the 1960s. In its advertisements the engines were promoted as having an unconditional guarantee. The customer would read the ad, go to the store, and purchase the engine only to learn later that the guarantee had quite a few restrictions.

The Montgomery Ward guarantee was not unconditional. It actually covered only a period of 90 days or 4,000 miles.

FOR A PERIOD OF NINETY DAYS
from the date installed or four thousand miles
(whichever comes first) we warrant this
rebuilt assembly for passenger car service
against defects in material and factory workmanship
provided our installation and
operating instructions are followed.

The guarantee also contained other restrictions. For instance, the guarantee only provided for the following:

- Replacement of parts, no labor.
- A claim for engines installed by Wards.
- A claim if required checkups are made.
- A claim if damage was not caused by misuse or accident.
- A claim if a valid certificate was on file.

Eventually, the FTC learned of Montgomery Ward's guarantee and a complaint was filed. *Montgomery Ward & Co.* v. *FTC*, 379 F.2d 666 (7th Cir. 1967), was the case. Montgomery Ward argued that it had a policy of honoring claims for defective merchandise even though its guarantee stated many restrictions. In fact, the court acknowledged that there was no evidence "that any customer had any claim under any guarantee . . . or that [Wards] failed to satisfy any claim under its guarantees."

The point, however, was that Ward's actual guarantee placed many restrictions, which were not revealed in its advertising. Plain and simple, this is deceptive. If you'll recall from Chapters 2 and 3, the FTC does not require a showing that actual deception occurred, only that the ad has the capacity to deceive.

"The capacity to deceive," said the court, "involved in Ward's advertisements lies in the inducement to buy created by the unlimited, advertised guarantee." It is clear from this case that an advertiser must specify the terms of its guarantee in an ad unless it truly offers an *unconditional* guarantee. The advertising of a guarantee must clearly express the actual guarantee that the consumer will get with the purchase.

False Statements Regarding a Guarantee

Certain industries place specific restrictions and requirements on guarantees of quality, origin, and authenticity of merchandise. Industries such as alcohol, tobacco, medicines, textiles, and others have such regulations. An advertiser should consult the regulations of these industries before preparing ads. Refer to Appendix A at the end of this book for a list of reference sources for specific industries.

M. Reiner & Sons was a fur dealer in New York. In 1969 the company advertised and sold furs with the guarantee that the furs were authentic and in compliance with specific laws governing the fur trade.[2] The company claimed that the proper guarantee (as required by the Fur Products Labeling Act) was on file with the Federal Trade Commission.

It was learned later that this was not the case; therefore, a complaint was filed by the FTC *In the Matter of M. Reiner & Sons,* 77 F.T.C. 862 (1970). The commission discovered that Reiner had no certificate of guarantee on file and therefore violated the law and created a deception about its guarantee.

The commission stated that Reiner "falsely represented in writing that [it] had a continuing [guarantee] on file with the Federal Trade Commission when [it] in furnishing such guarantees had reason to believe that the fur products so falsely guaranteed would be introduced, sold, transported, and distributed in commerce." Reiner was ordered to cease and desist from such practices.

TYPES OF GUARANTEES

There are many different types of guarantees. Among the most common are money-back, satisfaction, lifetime, repair, limited, and refund or replacement guarantees. The type of guarantee offered is dependent on the manufacturer. Now let's take a look at each of these.

---

[2]Fur Products Labeling Act, section 10(b), (CX 1, 5, 33).

Money-Back Guarantees

This is one of the most common. A *money-back* guarantee means just that. If the consumer is not satisfied, a full refund must be given. This type of guarantee must be honored in a timely manner. If a customer asks for a refund he or she must not be made to make numerous attempts to collect the refund.

This guarantee can be offered in a number of situations, and it should be clearly stated in any ads and on the packaging of the product. Typical money-back guarantees cover these situations: the consumer is not satisfied with the product; it can be purchased elsewhere for less; it fails to perform a specific job; or it does not do its job better than its competition. The specifics should be clearly stated in any case.

Satisfaction Guaranteed

If an ad claims "satisfaction guaranteed," without any clarification, then the consumer is entitled to determine if the product satisfies or not.

In cases where the claim is "satisfactory-fit guaranteed" the consumer is still able to determine if satisfaction resulted from the purchase of the product. Satisfaction is a subjective judgment call, and the purchaser is allowed to use his or her judgment as to whether satisfaction exists.

Lifetime Guarantees

Lifetime guarantees are legal, but the terms of the guarantee should be spelled out. The guarantee must be stated as *conditional* if charges are applied for service or replacement parts. A full disclosure of any conditions or service charges must accompany the guarantee. Terms such as *guaranteed forever* should not be used unless the manufacturer intends to live up to the claim, literally. The Sears Craftsman tool guarantee is a good example of a valid lifetime guarantee.

Specific claims that should not be made include the following:

- Guaranteed to last through the ages.
- Guaranteed to give a lifetime of service.
- Guarantee of a lifetime.
- Guaranteed for a lifetime.
- Guaranteed forever.

Repair Guarantees

Certain guarantees involve service repairs. These guarantees, usually found with appliances or automobiles, should be carefully explained. The following elements should be included in any repair guarantee:

- Time restrictions.
- Service charges.
- Cost of repairs.
- Who is responsible for repairs.
- Types of defects that are covered.

Limited Guarantees

As we saw earlier, any guarantee that is not unlimited is limited. If a guarantee is claimed in an ad and it is not unlimited, then it must be called a *limited* guarantee.

A good example of a limited guarantee can be found in our earlier example of film. Typically the manufacturer provides that if the film is defective the original roll of film will be replaced. But no other obligations exist; the company cannot be made to pay for loss of the photographic images or the costs to reshoot.

Refund or Replacement Guarantees

Some guarantees may specify whether the manufacturer will refund the purchase price (sometimes pro-rated) or replace the item. The manufacturer may make this decision, but it must specify this in the guarantee.

GUARANTEES THAT APPLY TO
SPECIFIC INDUSTRIES

As I mentioned earlier, there are many specific industries that control the form and content of the guarantees related to them. While a comprehensive list of these regulations is far too complex to list here, those industries that are heavily regulated are listed in Appendix A at the end of this book.

Advertisers should check the Appendix for reference sources listed by industry. These sources provide areas in which specific regulation may be found.

CHAPTER 11

THE CLIENT/AGENCY RELATIONSHIP

The client is, of course, god. And so it has been ever since the days of the first great ad man—Jesus Christ.
—*Robert C. Pritikin*

If you'll allow me, I have a short story to tell you. A very long time ago, let's say somewhere around 10 million B.C., there lived a man we'll call *Urr.* He lived a simple life, mainly concerned with providing for his family. Back in those days, life could be pretty rigorous. Even cutting firewood could be a major ordeal. So, in order to make the job easier, Urr designed a crude but effective device, which he called for lack of a better name, a *tree cutter.* With it, the first tool was invented.

Everything went along fine until one day a fellow named Ogg happened by and saw Urr working with his tree cutter. Realizing that he could make excellent use of this device for his own daily chores, and being quite a bit larger in stature than Urr, Ogg used this advantage to negotiate for the cutter. As you'd expect, he took possession of it, thereby carrying out the first business transaction in history.

Thoroughly frustrated, Urr thought that there had to be a better way to do business. He soon realized that since he had built something that Ogg wanted, perhaps others would also want his invention. Urr reasoned that rather than letting others steal his device, he could make more and offer them in exchange for items other people possessed that he needed. Setting his plan into motion, he soon found to his pleasure that it worked.

Yet, it was only a matter of time before Urr became aware of a growing problem, competition. As expected, other people began making and selling their own brand of tree cutter. With salespeople cropping up (excuse the pun) everywhere, Urr knew that he had to do something. So he called on his cousin Aad.

Being a good salesman, Aad got the word out that Urr's tree cutters were better than any of the other cheap imitations on the market. Finding out that he had a real skill at this sort of thing, Aad decided to go into business promoting other products. He called his company The Aad Agency, and a new industry was born.

If you don't believe my version of how the first agency came about, here is another that can be better documented.

A common practice in Italy around 1250 was to sell wine by the flask. Many unscrupulous wine merchants filled the bottom of their bottles with wax, thereby reducing the amount of wine in the bottle and improving the profit margin substantially. When the public found out about this deception, wine sales dropped rapidly. So the legitimate wine merchants began sending agents out into the streets promoting wine with placards saying *Sine Cere,* which means *without wax.* From this phrase comes our word *sincere,* and from this practice comes one of the earliest examples of an organized advertising agency.

THE ADVERTISING AGENCY

A professional agency is a business that acts on behalf of others. Attorneys, accountants, brokers, factors, auctioneers, and, yes, advertising agencies may fall into this category. Any profession—if it qualifies as an agent—is regulated by the same laws. As a result, some of the cases we examine in this chapter do not involve advertising agencies, but the principles are binding on any agency relationship.

First, there are a couple of terms that need to be clarified. An *agent* can be an individual alone, a group of people, a large corporation, or a full-time employee. A *principal* can be the client or the employer. But for purposes of clarity, we refer to the *principal* as the *client* throughout this chapter.

Advertising agencies that want the legal benefits of being an agency must abide by the duties that go along with the title. Simply calling a company an *advertising agency* does not mean that it is one legally. The legal relationship is what exists, not what is claimed. It must act like a true agency to be treated as one. We will examine this idea more closely in the balance of this chapter.

Now you may ask why ad agencies are called *agencies* if they are not. It's more out of tradition than for any other reason. The title creates a trade name more than an establishment of legal status. It is actually a misnomer, a throwback from the early space-broker days.

The alternative to being an agency is being an independent contractor. Here's an example for illustration. A person owns a Chevrolet dealership in Los Angeles. This dealer sells Chevrolet cars and trucks, and the business is referred to as a Chevrolet agency. However, this dealer is not an agent. The person simply sells Chevrolet products as an independent contractor. He or she does not work on the behalf of others.

The distinguishing feature between *agent* or *independent contractor* is the amount of control retained by the client over the physical conduct of the person performing the service. The independent contractor obligates herself or himself to produce a result and is free to pursue her or his own methods in the performance of the work.

For example, if Acme Company wants a new machine, it can use its own employees to build it. Or, it can contract with Bosco Corporation to build the machine according to Acme's specifications and at an agreed-on price. If Acme hires Bosco to build the machine, Bosco is an independent contractor. Bosco has been hired to produce a result: a specific machine at a specific price. Acme has no physical control over how Bosco produces the machine.

However, in most cases advertising agencies are true agencies in the legal sense. They don't have the independent contractor's freedom of control. The ad agency is subject to direct control by the client. In the advertising business, most clients reserve the right to select, approve, confer, and be advised of the work of their advertising agencies during every stage of the process. Anyone who has ever worked in an agency can vouch for that. So most courts have maintained that agencies have, in fact, acted as agents for their clients.

DUTIES OF THE ADVERTISING AGENCY

An advertising agency is able to commit the client to contracts, and at the same time it owes a duty of confidence and trust (fiduciary) to the client. Duties that the agency owes to the client fall into one of two areas: specific duties that are spelled out in a written contract, and duties that are imposed by law. Specific duties can be anything that does not violate a law that the client and agency want to make a part of the contract.

Even if no written contract exists between the client and agency, the agency's duties imposed by law still exist. These include the following:

- Higher level of skill required of agency.
- Full disclosure to client.
- Obligations regarding competitive accounts.
- Trustee of client, and handling of funds.
- Accountability to client.
- Duty to cooperate with client.
- Obligation to preserve trade secrets.
- No undisclosed interest in suppliers.

Now let's look at each of these duties in more detail.

Higher Level of Skill Required of Agency

An advertising agency represents itself as being an expert in its field. When an ad agency makes a presentation to a prospective client, it goes out of its way to impress upon the client that it possesses a tremendous degree of skill in a specialized area—both the area of advertising and that of the client's product. Once stated, the agency is then obligated to deliver. It must not merely show a general level of skill, but it must demonstrate the level of a highly skilled professional.

It is not enough that an advertising (or any other) agency apply the usual degree of care to the business entrusted it by its client. It must put forth its best efforts using its skill, experience, and knowledge to the best of its professional ability. When an agency fails to deliver on this, breach of contract may exist. The breach may be cause for the client to terminate the contract, or in some cases, bring suit for damages.

On the other hand, it is true that an agency is not required to guarantee the success of the advertising that it produces, only to put forth all of its best efforts toward the success of it. That means not doing anything that would diminish its chance for success.

Full Disclosure to Client

An agency owes its clients complete loyalty. This may seem simple to accomplish, but it can affect an agency in many ways. Part of this loyalty includes a responsibility to inform the client of any fact or occurrence that affects the client in any way. For instance, if the agency has been late in paying a supplier, who in turn threatens to cut off services, the agency is under a duty to inform its client. As unpleasant as this may be, the client is legally entitled to be informed quickly and thoroughly on all such matters.

Let me give you a good example. The disclosure required of an agent was discussed in *Crocker* v. *United States,* 240 U.S. 74 (1916). Frank Crocker owned a company, which had a contract to furnish mail-carrier satchels to the U.S. Post Office. His company did so, but something happened to cause the Postmaster General to rescind the contract and refuse to pay for the satchels.

Two employees of Crocker, Mr. Lorenz and Mr. Crawford, made a secret agreement with Mr. Machen, who was superintendent of the division that needed the satchels. Machen arranged for the contract to go to Crocker's company in exchange for half of the profits. The arrangement was made, and Crocker got the government contract, with Machen getting half the profits from the sales. The company furnished over 10,000 satchels before the Postmaster General learned of the collusion.

Lorenz and Crawford were agents of Crocker and were acquiring the contract at the company's request. They were trying to secure the government contract by working out a fraudulent deal with Machen. By virtue of the agency relationship, Crocker in essence sanctioned what they did. Because the contract was obtained fraudulently, Crocker lost his claim for payment.

Obligations as to Competitive Clients

A problem arises when an agency tries to serve two clients who are in competition with each other. The agency can't serve both unless it has the consent of the two parties in advance. This became the issue in *Joyce Beverages of New York, Inc.,* v. *Royal Crown Cola,* 555 F.Supp. 271 (1983).

Joyce Beverages was a licensee—and as such an agent—of several soft drink manufacturers including Royal Crown Cola, 7-Up, Diet 7-Up, A&W Root Beer, Sugar-Free A&W, Perrier, Nestea, Hawaiian Punch, and Nehi drinks. Royal Crown's licensing agreement with Joyce stated that Joyce must use its best efforts to build, maintain, and expand the sales of the Royal Crown drinks that it handles—to Royal Crown's satisfaction.

The contract between the parties would not allow Joyce to distribute any soft drinks that were "substantially or reasonably similar" to Royal Crown products. The contract further provided that: "any cola shall be deemed substantially or reasonably similar to any . . . cola [and] any diet cola to any . . . diet cola."

One of the ways Joyce could breach this agreement was to take on a competing drink. That's exactly what it did. In 1982, Joyce began marketing LIKE, a decaffeinated cola drink manufactured by the 7-Up Company.

By handling another competitive cola in its market area, Joyce created "inevitable and corrosive divided loyalty and effort and made impossible a continued relationship . . . of confidence and cooperation." In essence, Joyce would be selling a new product to old customers, with advertising and promotion practices that it established for the old product. This breaches the duty of an agent not to handle competing clients without consent.

Joyce argued, in its defense, that Royal Crown would not be put in a position to "sink or swim" by itself. Joyce also claimed that Royal Crown wouldn't "go down the drain." This points up a common misconception. That is, Joyce's duty to its client is to vigorously promote the product—to expand its market share, not simply to keep it alive. The court agreed and allowed Royal Crown to rescind the contract.

Sometimes it is not easy to determine whether two clients compete with each other. Clients compete, basically, when their products are similar or interchangeable or where one product may replace the need of the other. Such products that could replace the other might be toothpaste and dental cleaning powder, floor wax and a product that eliminates the need to wax, and bandages and a cut spray that replaces a bandage.

Another area of competition that needs to be looked at is situations in which products are advertised and sold in different geographic areas. In these cases there may be no direct competition of products, yet clients may not be pleased. Clients may claim that information obtained from one is being used to benefit the other. While this may not violate any duty, the agency could have some very irritated clients on its hands. The best practice is to inform the agency's existing client and get its approval beforehand.

However, many agencies do represent different clients who compete for the same market. These agencies promote the fact that they specialize in a certain area: banking, real estate, medical, and so forth. In many fields, this agency specialty is preferred by clients. In these cases, clients who know of this are considered to have consented to the agency's representing other competitors. If the client is told about representing other competitors in the same field before it becomes a client, it will have very little to complain about later. The point is that the client must be made aware of, and give its consent to, this multiple representation. It is not something that the agency can take on itself.

Trustee of Client and Handling of Funds

Handling of Funds. The financial relationship of an agency can be a major source of aggravation for both agency and client, especially in the area of commingling of funds. That is, mixing the money that belongs to the agency with that which belongs to the client. The agency is the trustee of the funds taken in on behalf of the client and must treat that money accordingly.

Basic agency law requires that an agent must keep money belonging to its client separate from its own. The only time that this does not need to happen legally is when the client has knowledge and has consented in advance.

The common practice, however, is to the contrary for a number of reasons. Rarely, when a client sends money to the agency, does it identify what it should be applied to. It is very uncommon that a client will send a separate check for each type of payment. However, payments that are intended to cover the agency's fees and costs need not be kept separately. But, money that merely flows through the agency on the way to suppliers or media—less commissions—should not be mixed with the agency's money. To avoid problems later, this subject should be specifically addressed in the client/agency contract.

The best way to protect the agency is to have separate bank accounts: one as a trust account for the client's money, which can be drawn on as needed, and another account for the agency's money, which is not subject to accountability to the client.

Trustee of Rights and Materials. Everything that the agency creates for its client belongs to the client. The agency holds these items in trust for the client. This could include such materials as photographs, artwork, videotapes, or rights such as copyright, trademark rights, rights of publicity, and so on.

The agent does not own these items or rights, but it has a duty to guard them for its client. Here's an example which occurred between The Molle Company and its agency, Stack-Goble Advertising, in 1933.

Molle manufactured shaving cream and through Stack-Goble wanted to develop radio advertising. Stack-Goble hired Sedley Brown to produce and direct a program with Molle as the sponsor. We must remember that years ago it was common for advertisers to sponsor shows by themselves, and it was the job of the advertising agency to put the shows together. For example, "Amos 'n Andy" sold Pepsodent, "The Story of Mary Marlowe" sold Kleenex, "Fibber McGee and Molly" for Johnson's Glo-Coat floor wax, "The Rhythm Boys" (featuring a youngster named Harry Lillis Crosby, later to be known as Bing) for M. J. B. Coffee, and the list went on and on.

But back to Molle. As part of producing the show, Brown created a jingle out of Molle advertising slogans and set the words to the music of E. L. Gruber's "West Point Caisson Song." The jingle went:

> Mo-lle, Mo-lle,
> The way to start your day,
> As your razor goes sliding along,
> Over cheek, over chin,
> You don't have to rub it in,
> As your razor goes sliding along.
> Then it's sing, boys, sing,
> Good-bye to pull and sting,
> Your whisker troubles quickly fade away,
> You can shave close and clean with this
>   brushless shaving cream,
> So remember the name Molle, Molle.

Brown produced the first radio show on September 25, 1933, and continued to do so until late December, when he left the show. The show, along with the theme song, continued to air without any protest from Brown. In April 1934, Brown filed a copyright for the words to the song and gave notice to Molle in September of that year of his claimed ownership.

When Molle refused to acknowledge his claim, Brown brought suit for copyright infringement in *Brown* v. *Molle Co.*,

20 F.Supp 135 (1937). He claimed that he owned the rights to the jingle. While it was true that the words were written by Brown, they belonged to Stack-Goble, who held them as trustee for Molle. Brown was employed by Stack-Goble to produce the program, including the theme song. Brown was an employee of Stack-Goble, and as such, anything he created as part of his duties became the property of Molle. When an agent creates work for, and at the direction of the client, it gives up, along with the work, any right to the work. Brown lost his case. We delve deeper into the subject of copyright in Chapter 6.

Accountability to Client

An agency is under a strict duty to account for all funds passing through the agency, or controlled by it, on behalf of its client. The client has the right to inspect books, records, papers, invoices, orders, receipts, and any other items that apply to its account with the agency. These must be made available to the client, at any time, for its inspection. Along these lines, the client can demand an accounting of all commissions, discounts, and so on received from or credited by third parties (suppliers, media, etc.) to the agency on the client's account.

One major problem area regarding accountability involves hidden profits. This constitutes a serious breach of the agency's duty. Legally, this is called *fraudulent concealment.* I have known of a few agencies that made a practice of stating in their contracts that they charged a 17.65 percent markup on third-party bills. Yet, the estimates and invoices given to clients actually included an undisclosed but considerable markup in excess of 30 percent.

If an agency makes a purchase for a client based on an estimate, and the actual billing comes in lower, the agency must pass this savings on to the client. It cannot legally keep the difference. At some agencies, the policy is to estimate a job and get the client to sign the estimate. Then the agency prebills the client for that amount before beginning the project, often receiving payment before the project is completed. Sometimes the final cost of the project comes out lower than the estimate. If the ultimate costs are lower than the estimate, and the difference is not returned to the client, the agency is breaching its duty.

If pre-billing must be done, the best practice is to provide a recap of the project showing any amounts billed in excess of the estimate and credit them back to the client. At least this will avoid liability for concealing hidden profits.

Purchase Orders. One other important item is that the agency should document all of its purchases for its client with a written purchase order. The purchase order must establish what has been ordered and what will be paid. It should also establish that the order is being placed on behalf of the client. Exhibit 11–1 shows a sample purchase order from my agency for reference.

Duty to Cooperate with the Client

Rarely do we hear mentioned the duty of obedience when discussing the relationship between agency and client. This may be due to the fact that advertisers are usually inclined to bow to the expertise of the agency. Or it may be attributable to good business sense on the part of the agency. Whatever the reason, this is an area that we need to discuss, nonetheless.

An advertising agency has a duty to do its best to cooperate with the client. Sometimes this can be difficult when an agency is determined to sell a campaign to its client. Let's say that the agency submits a campaign plan to its client. The client has the right to disapprove of the campaign plans—media, copy, art, or any other proposals of the agency—simply because it does not like them. An agency cannot force the client to produce advertising that it does not like or has not approved of. The client cannot be deprived of the right to disapprove of the agency's creative work, in a campaign or in an individual ad.

Such a situation became the subject of *Medivox Productions Inc.* v. *Hoffman-LaRoche Inc.*, 107 NJ Super 47, 256 A.2d

EXHIBIT 11–1
Sample Agency Purchase Order

north & fueroghne
advertising · marketing · public relations
a professional corporation

PURCHASE ORDER
410893

TO:

DATE:

CLIENT:

JOB NO:

Please provide the following for: ☐ AGENCY DIRECT ☐ This order is placed for and in behalf of the client named herein as principal;

SPECIAL PRINTING INSTRUCTIONS

QUANTITY:
INK COLOR:
SIZE:
FOLD TO:
PUNCH:

SCREEN:
STOCK:

TRIM TO:
PERF: PAD:

Agency must approve proof before run is authorized

	PROOF DUE DATE
☐ BROWNLINE	
☐ COLOR KEY	
☐ PRESS PROOF	

DELIVERY DATE FINAL ◊ [   ]

SHIP TO: ☐ AGENCY ☐ CLIENT
☐ OR

PRICE QUOTED $

PLEASE READ CAREFULLY – For account of client, if named, please supply the above and bill as directed in DUPLICATE. Billing must include P.O. and (if applicable) JOB number. Because this agency quotes firm prices to clients, based upon advance quotes from vendor, we must be advised immediately when circumstances will result in extra costs. Charges for changes and alterations due to vendor errors, omissions or over-run will not be accepted. Proof due dates and final delivery dates are vital to this purchase order and vendor's failure to deliver on time may result in cancellation of this order. Acceptance of this order binds the vendor to all the terms and conditions noted or printed hereon. All artwork, negatives, separations and all other materials produced pertaining to this job shall become and remain the property of the agency.

FOR RESALE: Agency resale number:
○ SR AS
BILL AGENCY ○
BILL CLIENT DIRECT ○

By: _____

803 (1969). Hoffman-LaRoche, a well-known pharmaceutical manufacturer, entered into a contract with Medivox Productions to be its agent in the production of a series of radio programs entitled "Milestones of Medicine." The contract called for 260 programs to be created and produced during one year at a total cost of $140,000. These programs were to be dramatic episodes depicting important medical events in history. Hoffman-LaRoche was to have a credit line in each episode. The intent was that of enhancing the public's image of those connected with medicine and health and at the same time promoting the importance of drugs.

The contract stated that before being produced and broadcast, scripts would be submitted to Hoffman-LaRoche for their review and approval. Even without a contract this would be required. By the time Medivox had produced 135 of the programs (which the client had approved), Hoffman-LaRoche terminated the contract, having paid only $63,000. Medivox sued for breach of contract and sought the completion of the shows and the balance due on the contract. Hoffman-LaRoche claimed that they were entitled to terminate the contract because Medivox produced poor quality scripts.

Hoffman-LaRoche was dissatisfied with the scripts because they were inaccurate factually, and many of them discussed events that were not in keeping with the "Milestones of Medicine" theme. Medivox failed to satisfy its client, and as a result, Hoffman-LaRoche terminated the relationship. The court ruled that Medivox could not force the continuation of the relationship (legally called *specific performance*) or collect on the balance due on the contract. However, Hoffman-LaRoche could not recover the money that it had paid Medivox because it had accepted, used, and received the benefits of the 135 programs.

The client has the right, in an agency relationship, to approve and disapprove of the work of its agency. Termination of the relationship, then, is based on the genuineness of its dissatisfaction, not necessarily on the reasonableness of it. Generally, the client makes this determination. Keep in mind, when the client expects satisfaction, the agency must allow the client to be the sole judge of its satisfaction.

The agency also has a duty to obey the instructions of its client in all but extreme situations. The agent has the right to refuse under certain extreme conditions and not be liable for damages. However, the client also has the right to terminate the contract if the agent does refuse to perform. The four situations when the agent can legally refuse to obey its client are listed below.

1. The instructions are unlawful. The agency has the right to refuse to produce advertising that is illegal—that is, advertising that violates any rights of others (including such things as publicity rights, copyrights, and trademarks), or when it would be engaging in unfair methods of competition, deception, and so on.

2. The instructions conflict with other duties of the agency. The agency may refuse to perform any instruction, such as the client's demanding that the agency hold off paying certain media bills. Yet this would only be valid if it would be a conflict of an agency duty. Also, the agency may refuse if the client demands that the agency take on a new product made by the existing client, which competes with another existing client of the agency.

3. The instructions defeat the agency's right to protect its own interests. A good example would be demanding the agency accept work on a speculative basis, with payment contingent on the client's sales or profits.

4. The instructions are unreasonable. This fourth area may cause some problems as we saw in the aforementioned Medivox case. What is considered unreasonable becomes the question. In many situations agencies feel that creating an ad that it knows to be ineffective is unreasonable. An agency is hired for its expertise in a certain area, and it should be allowed to use its judgment. Logically, this may be true; legally, it may not.

Basic agency law states that, barring one of the above exceptions, an agent must obey the instructions of its client. Failure to abide by the instructions of the client could result in agency liability for damages. On the other hand, the agency may terminate the relationship, at any time—with proper notice given—if it does not want to abide by the instructions.

The Obligation to Preserve Trade Secrets

Frequently it is necessary for a client to familiarize its agency with many matters that it desires to keep secret. An advertising agency is under an obligation, both during and after its employment, to preserve those trade secrets—that is, secrets that were disclosed or learned during the relationship.

Originally the issue was discussed in *Du Pont de Nemours Powder Co.* v. *Masland*, 244 US 100 (1917). A former employee, Mr. Masland (an agent), was sued to prevent him from disclosing or using secret trade processes learned while in the employ of Du Pont.

Masland intended to open a company to manufacture artificial leather. He admitted that he was going to use processes related to those learned while employed with Du Pont. Masland's former employer did not want any of its secret trade processes divulged, and it had the right to enforce this. Masland learned the facts about Du Pont's processes through a confidential relationship.

It is difficult to define what a trade secret is. However, some examples would be a specialized manufacturing process as we just saw, or special ingredients in a product such as Coca-Cola or Dr. Pepper. It seems that courts are more interested in the unfair use of the information than by the nature of the information itself.

The best story that I can recall about trade secrets occurred a number of years ago. I was working for an agency that handled the Mitsubishi Electronics account. One day we got the news that two Mitsubishi executives had been arrested by the FBI. Evidently, Mitsubishi had paid $26,000 to undercover FBI agents, who posed as grey-market electronics dealers. The money was paid in exchange for confidential trade secrets about IBM's newest computing products. This event was dubbed *Japanscam* by the press.

On the other hand, any information that is easily accessible through other sources cannot be a trade secret. Lists of customers would be a good example. As a general rule these are not considered trade secrets because they are readily obtainable through such other public sources as trade publications.

There's another area to consider. A few years ago, Chiat/Day Advertising was in the running for the Godfather Pizza Parlor account. In order to prepare a speculative presentation to Godfather, the agency was given access to confidential information by the restaurant chain. A number of Chiat/Day employees were given this information, which contained many trade secrets.

Before the presentation was made to Godfather, Chiat/Day declined the account in favor of the Pizza Hut account. At that point, Godfather went to court to stop the use of the confidential information that Chiat/Day had obtained. The California Superior Court judge granted an injunction against Chiat/Day. The injunction stated that Chiat/Day could not use any of the confidential information it obtained from Godfather. In addition to that, the injunction banned the Chiat/Day employees who were involved in the Godfather presentation from being involved in any way with the Pizza Hut account. The point here is that, even at the presentation stage, the duty to preserve trade secrets is in force, and the courts are backing this up by issuing injunctions.

Lastly, the agency has a continuing duty, even after termination, not to disclose or use trade secrets or other confidential information that it obtained during the course of its employment.

No Undisclosed Interest in Suppliers

Another area of concern involves suppliers, vendors, or media that provide work for the agency's clients. The agency cannot have an undisclosed financial interest (part ownership, kickback arrangement, etc.) in them. Let's say that Acme Advertising produces brochures for its client, ABC Company. Bogus Photography Studio photographs ABC's products for the brochure. However, Acme Advertising owns 33 percent of Bogus Photography, and ABC doesn't know it. This would breach Acme's duty as an agency and make it impossible for the agency to make decisions in the client's best interests. The agent cannot perform as a true, impartial, and unbiased agent for its clients. Or at least it couldn't convince a court that it could.

Two other areas of this type of conflict of interest need to be discussed. First, the agency must not contract with suppliers who use them as their agency. To go back to our earlier example, if Bogus Photography uses Acme Advertising as its agency, Acme cannot let ABC Company's brochure be photographed by Bogus. Second, the agency must not perform work itself that it has been instructed to contract out. Again, let's say Acme is told by ABC Company to have Bogus photograph its brochure. Acme Advertising cannot photograph ABC's brochure itself, in-house.

Although these types of situations do exist, it is usually without the client's knowledge. If the agency has the client's consent, in writing, then it is not a breach of the agency's duty since no trust has been violated.

DUTIES OWED BY CLIENTS TO THEIR AGENCIES

The most important duty that the client has to its agency is to make the payments that it owes to the agency. There are other duties, however, such as furnishing information to the agency and approving or disapproving programs or ads. The client must perform its duties within a reasonable time so as not to cause the agency additional delay and expense. Also, it should make its decisions based on reason and good faith, not on a whim. Further, as we saw earlier, the client does not have a right to demand the agency produce any advertising that violates any laws. Finally, the client is bound by any contracts made by the agency for it, again, provided the agency acted within the scope of its authority.

In 1869 the advertising agency was beginning to gain respect as a true agent of the client instead of a common space-broker. In that year in Philadelphia, a man named Francis Wayland Ayer took $250 and opened an agency named after his father, N. W. Ayer & Son.

One of Ayer's clients, Devlen, manufactured Dent's Toothache Gum. In 1905 Devlen instructed Ayer to place an advertisement in daily newspapers. He also informed Ayer that he wanted "full position" (only editorial around the ad) for his small-space ad. Ayer informed its client that it was impossible to guarantee full position for a very small ad, and in some papers only at an increased rate.

As the ad began to run, Devlen noticed that he was not getting full position in all newspapers. He complained to Ayer about this, but the ads continued to run for many months. Devlen also continued to make payments for the ads that ran.

In October 1907, Ayer terminated the contract with Devlen and in *Ayer* v. *Devlen,* 179 Mich. 81 (1914), asked the court for damages of $3,801.22 for the balance of the media charges. Devlen wanted his ads to receive a certain position in newspapers and was told that this was not possible in most cases. He authorized the placement of the ads for some time, while still demanding full position. The main issue here was whether Devlen had a contract for his ads to be placed in full position only. The court decided that Devlen did not, and he was ordered to pay the back media charges.

BREACH OF CONTRACT SITUATIONS

In the most simplistic terms, a contract is based on a promise, or promises. When the promise is broken, a breach of contract can exist and a lawsuit can result. The client/agency contract can be breached when either party fails to perform in some area. For the agency, this can occur when it fails to comply with a duty, written in the contract or required by law. Placing an ad that the client had not approved, or taking more than the amount of commission stated in the contract are examples. The client can also breach the contract if it fails to live up to its duties. Failure to pay the agency's bills is the most obvious example.

Generally, remedies for a breach of contract claim are recision (canceling the contract), damages, specific performance (forcing the other to fulfill the contract), or termination. Specific performance does not apply to personal service situations; that is called slavery, and there are laws against that now. The two main remedies left are recision and damages. A party may find that recision is more realistic than seeking damages. And termination is always a remedy available to both parties.

In breach of contract cases the most common problem is not whether the contract has been breached, but rather determination of the amount of damages. Here's a good example of a breach of contract situation. An ad agency, William B. Tanner Company, bought space from Action Transit Ads. Action sold space on buses and subways in New Jersey. Tanner, at the request of its client Tanya Hawaiian Tanning Oil, entered into a contract for the three years, 1969 through 1971. The contract provided for three things: the advertising was for Tanya, the agency would receive a 15 percent commission, and the contract could be canceled at the end of each year.

In mid-1971, another contract was entered into between Tanner and Action for Tanya for the years 1972 through 1974. As with the previous contract, Action was to be paid $22,500 per year. However, the difference here was that Tanner did not have the permission of its client to enter into this new contract. At the end of 1972, Tanner notified Action that it was terminating the contract when Tanya refused to pay the bills. As a result, Action sued in *Action Ads Inc.* v. *William B. Tanner Co.,* 592 S.W.2d 572 (1979).

William Tanner was authorized by Tanya to purchase the transit ads for the first three years, 1969 through 1971. However, it was not authorized by Tanya to make the second three-year contract. Because of that, Tanner was acting on its own in entering into the 1972 through 1974 contract. Tanner had breached its contract with its client Tanya and was itself liable for the $22,500 for the 1972 contract with Action.

DURATION OF CONTRACTS

In all written contracts the length of time that the agreement is to run must be stated. If it is indefinite, that should be stated as well. All contracts between advertising agencies and clients should be made in writing. Oral contracts are not a good idea for a variety of legal reasons—mainly because they can be found to be unenforceable in many situations.

TERMINATION OF CONTRACTS

Notice of Termination

When a contract is terminated, the first thing to consider is the amount of time that must be given to the other party as notice. This "grace period" is built into client/agency contracts to allow the agency time to restructure for the change and for the client to settle its business with the agency. In other words, no undue hardship should be placed on either party.

The length of the notice period, according to industry trade custom, is usually 60 to 90 days, although it can be any period of time that both parties agree to. (A trade custom is law because of the length of time that the practice has been accepted and used.) To be on the safe side, the notice period should be stated in the contract. On this subject, Doyle Dane Bernbach tried to recover $126,729 for advertising from a former client, Avis Flowers, in *Doyle Dane Bernbach, Inc.* v. *Warren E. Avis,* 526 F.Supp. 117 (1981).

Doyle Dane also handled the Avis Rent-A-Car account, which was started by the owner of Avis Flowers, Warren Avis, and later sold to a conglomerate. Avis Rent-A-Car put the agency on notice that it had to choose between the two clients due to the similarity in names and identity. Obviously, Doyle Dane opted to keep the Avis car account.

When Doyle Dane terminated the agreement with Avis Flowers in November 1977, it gave 90 days notice. During the notice period, Doyle Dane contacted the flower company to arrange for the transfer of the account to another agency. Even though it had given a notice of termination, Doyle Dane continued to handle the Avis Flowers account through the end of 1977, placing ads in *People* magazine that had been approved prior to when notice was given.

Avis claimed that Doyle Dane placed the ads after termination (breach of contract) and, therefore, was liable for any media charges incurred after the agency gave notice for those insertions. In fact, there was no written contract, so there was no stated notice period. However, the 90-day notice period is standard in the advertising industry and is accepted as a trade custom—one that Avis should have been well aware of. Doyle Dane gave Avis a sufficient amount of notice—the standard amount in the industry—and continued to perform through the notice period. As a result, Avis was required to pay the media fees incurred during the 90-day period.

Commissions Due after Termination

As we just saw, certain postcontractual liabilities and duties are imposed on both parties. If the agency had entered into contracts with third parties, on behalf of the advertiser, and the relationship was terminated, the agency is entitled to the commissions that it would have received.

In 1952 Hansman-Joslyn Advertising entered into a contract with Uddo & Tormina Company, makers of Progresso Italian foods. Hansman, as its agent, entered into a contract with WBOK radio. The one-year radio contract with Progresso was canceled after only a few months, causing the radio station to charge a "short rate" amount for the time because the full contract period was not used. The short rate policy is a trade custom in the advertising business.

In *Hansman* v. *Uddo and Tormina Co.*, 76 So.2d 753 (Lous. App. 1955), the court said: "Contracts made with any kind of advertising media . . . provided therein a short rate cancellation, that is to say, the advertiser contracts to use the media for a stated length of time at a certain rate . . ." However, the court felt that ". . . if the advertiser sees fit to cancel the contract prematurely, then he is obligated to pay the rate which would be applicable had the contract . . . been for the number of advertisements actually used." Uddo was ordered to pay the amount due the media.

Now, for the case of media contracts that were entered into by the previous agency. If the client takes its business to a new agency, the client is liable to the old agency for the media commissions unless a contract agreement covers this occurrence.

To illustrate, let's go back to our hypothetical situation from earlier. Acme Advertising had placed media for an ad for its client, ABC Company, in *American Widget Monthly* magazine. A week later ABC notifies Acme that it is moving its account to a new agency, Dinkum Advertising, in 30 days. Even though Dinkum produces the ad and coordinates with the magazine, ABC must still pay Acme the amount of commission that it would have received.

What if the client uses material from the former agency in preparation for another advertising campaign, after the termination of the relationship? If that material was never used or paid for, the client must compensate the original agency for its efforts. It cannot use the fruit of the agency's labor for future advertising without paying for it. In legal terms this principle is known as *quantum meruit.*

When ABC Company transferred its account over to Dinkum Advertising, it also gave them campaign concepts and layouts that were developed by Acme Advertising. Acme had prepared the campaign on a speculative basis, but it was never approved by ABC. Since ABC never paid for the concepts and layouts, if it produces the campaign through Dinkum, it must compensate Acme for the work. On the other hand, if ABC had paid for the campaign to be created, the company would be free to produce it without further compensating Acme.

Soliciting New Accounts after Notice of Termination

When notice of termination has been given, can the agency service a competing account? It is certainly free to do so after termination. What is doubtful, though, is whether the agency is free to associate with prospective new clients who are in competition with the current advertiser before termination becomes effective. The best advice would be that the agency still should not jeopardize itself by creating a potential liability.

Limit to Use of Information Gained

In the natural course of the advertising business an agency becomes familiar with the workings of its clients. It obtains a certain expertise in each client's line of business. There can be no doubt, however, that intimate knowledge of a client's trend of thought and method of doing business can become part of the agency's general knowledge and expertise. Therefore, the postcontractual duty not to divulge or use details of the client must be restricted to actual trade secrets and the kind of confidential information that is separate from the general knowledge about a trade or business.

Here's a strong case in point. Murray Salit and other employees of Irving Serwer Advertising were sued by Serwer in *Irving Serwer Inc. Advertising* v. *Salit,* 17A.D.2d 918 (1963). This occurred after they left the agency to open their own shop, Salit & Garlanda Advertising. Serwer claimed that Salit and the others had taken accounts over to the new agency by obtaining confidential information while in its employ and that they "entered into a course of conduct and conspiracy to destroy [Serwer's] business." However, the court felt that simply gaining information about clients while working for an agency does not, in and of itself, constitute trade secrets or confidential information. As a result, Serwer lost his case.

While the situation we just saw involves employees of an agency, this reasoning applies to agencies who use knowledge gained from other clients. If the information does not constitute a trade secret or is confidential (as we discussed earlier), the agency cannot be stopped from making use of the knowledge.

LIABILITY TO MEDIA

Is a client liable for media commitments by the agency? There is a conflict here, but the general feeling is that the ultimate liability is on the advertiser. In essence, if the media knew who the client was and knew that the agency was acting in its behalf, any claims would be against the client. The agency would not be liable on the contract as long as it entered into the agreement with the client's knowledge and consent. One exception to this is a sole liability clause, which we'll discuss later in this chapter.

American Manufacturers Mutual Insurance contracted, through its agency Clinton E. Frank Advertising, to sponsor a news broadcast entitled "ABC Evening Report." At the end of one broadcast on November 9, 1962, a promotional announcement was run that displeased American Manufacturers. The announcement promoted a show called "The Political Obituary of Richard M. Nixon." American Manufacturers terminated its sponsorship of the "ABC Evening Report" and refused to pay the media fees.

American Broadcasting Company filed suit for the amount due for media charges: *American Broadcasting-Paramount Theatres* v. *American Manufacturers Mutual,* 42 Misc.2d 939, 249 N.Y.S.2d 481 (Sup.Ct. 1963), aff'd 251 N.Y.S.2d 906, aff'd 17 N.Y. 2d 849 (1966). In this case, Clinton E. Frank Advertising was named as one of the defendants, but was held not to be liable for the media fees. This case points up the fact that even though Clinton Frank was the agency and placed the order, it was not liable for any damages because ABC knew Frank was acting as the agency for American Manufacturers. ABC also knew that the agency had entered into the contract on behalf of its client. ABC won the suit for breach of contract, and American was liable for the media.

The client/agency relationship exists only with the knowledge and consent of both parties. The client who hires an agency voluntarily empowers it to bind the client to contracts with others. Simply put, the fact that someone hires an agency creates an implied acknowledgment that the client intends to be bound by any contract or transaction that the agent must enter into to fulfill his agency duties. Further, parties who deal with a known agent generally assume that the client intends to be bound by the agency's commitments.

In 1971 Lennon & Newell was the ad agency for Stokely-Van Camp foods company, as it had been for the previous 17 years. Lennon & Newell had purchased media space for Stokely on CBS. In 1967 the agency began to suffer substantial losses and by 1970 was in severe trouble. It had been paid by Stokely for media billings but had not, in turn, paid the media. By the end of 1971 Lennon owed CBS $714,000 out of total payables of $3 million, and could not make its payments. About that time, Lennon & Newell filed for bankruptcy.

Because of the situation, CBS filed suit: *Columbia Broadcasting System, Inc.* v. *Stokely-Van Camp, Inc.,* 522 F.2d 369

(1975), directly against the client. This was a case of who is liable when an agent goes bankrupt owing money to media. Does the media have a claim against the client? In this case, it did—even though the client had paid the agency for the media.

In 1978 Sander Rodkin/Hechtman/Glantz Advertising purchased television time for its client Climate Control, an air conditioning distributor. At the time, Sander was having financial problems. When the agency received money from Climate Control for media, it did not pay the media. Climate Control, however, had paid its total bill and documented each payment. The final payment for $15,000 was designated as "final payment for WLS-TV air time."

WLS-TV was the local ABC affiliate in Chicago. It sued for the amount due in *American Broadcasting Companies, Inc.* v. *Climate Control Corporation,* 524 F.Supp. 1014 (1981). It was not until December 1979 that ABC contacted Climate Control and told them that it was liable for the unpaid balance. Right after that, this lawsuit was initiated.

In this case, Sander was the agency for Climate Control, and as such, bound Climate Control to any contracts it had made for the client. Climate Control was liable for the unpaid balance to ABC. Sander Rodkin went out of business.

For reference, I've included a sample media insertion order form (Exhibit 11–2) that I used at my agency. This should serve as a general format for others.

Sole Liability Clauses

The advertising agency is directly liable to the media under certain conditions. One is when the agency voluntarily agrees to be directly liable for media bills. The other is when the media contract contains a "sole liability" clause, to which the agency has committed. In both cases the agency accepts full liability for media costs.

The sole liability clause, which is included in many media contracts, says that the agency is solely liable for the debts incurred on behalf of the client. As a consequence of the sole liability clause, the agency can impose on the client a duty to pay the media charges to the agency prior to the media's due

EXHIBIT 11–2
Sample Media Insertion Order

☐ INSERTION
☐ CHANGE
☐ CANCELLATION

ORDER

north & fueroghne
advertising - marketing - public relations
a professional corporation

IMPORTANT !

Send invoice in duplicate by 1st of month following insertion

NEWSPAPERS:

Send 3 tear sheets of ad within seven days of insertion

MAGAZINES:

Send 1 complete copy and 2 tear pages of magazine with invoice.

Advertisers:

Division:

Date of Order:

Order No.:

Change No.:

Job No.:

Caption:

Key No.:

Space:

Position Requested:

Schedule Dates:

Rate:

Mechanicals:

☐ Plate
☐ Mat   ☐ Enclosed
☐ Camera Ready ☐ To Come
☐ Layout/Copy ☐ You Have
☐ Film

CHECKING DEPARTMENT		
ISSUE	TEAR PAGES REC'D	INV. REC'D

Media

dates. Failure to make these payments on time can easily lead to cancellation of the media space as well as substantial damage claims by the agency against the client.

AGENCY LIABILITY FOR ADVERTISING

As we saw in other chapters, the agency can be liable along with the client for the advertising it produces. If the advertising makes deceptive or unfair claims, the agency can be held liable for those claims, along with the client. This has been proven many times in court. Claiming, as many agencies do, that they only did what the client told them to do does not relieve the agency's liability. The courts generally consider that an advertising agency should know what its clients are doing.

Other areas where the agency can be liable involve defamation (libel and slander), copyright and trademark infringement, violation of privacy and publicity rights, and many others. In general, advertising agencies must realize that the courts look on them as the professionals. This idea goes back to the "higher degree of skill" concept discussed earlier. More and more, agencies are being held liable for the joint actions of the client/agency relationship. It is very important that agencies understand this idea.

ELEMENTS OF THE CLIENT/AGENCY CONTRACT

While it is not imperative that a written contract be created, it is the much wiser option. When the rights, duties, and intentions of both parties are fixed in writing, there is less interpretation and guesswork involved if a problem arises.

There are certain considerations that should be addressed when the contract provisions are drawn up. The following list includes the most important ones:

1. Appointment as the agency.
2. Nature and extent of services to be provided.
3. Compensation (commission, fees, etc.)
4. How supplier contracts are to be handled.
5. Rights on termination of contract.
6. Indemnity against claims.
7. Handling of competitive clients.
8. Liability to media.

I have included a sample contract (Exhibit 11–3) and a project proposal (Exhibit 11–4) used at my own agency. The contract and project proposal work together and make reference to each other. The contract covers the general provisions of the relationship. The project proposal is used as an estimate for each specific project. While every agency should consult an attorney to have its specific contract drawn up, Exhibits 11–3 and 11–4 will serve as general formats to follow.

EMPLOYEE RELATIONS WITHIN
THE AGENCY

One of the areas that agencies need to be aware of involves situations when an employee leaves and takes accounts. Account piracy is a growing internal problem for ad agencies. Many agencies are dealing with the problem by adopting restrictive covenants in employment contracts to prevent this.

Let's say that you own Acme Advertising agency and your employees become increasingly dissatisfied with you and the way you run the agency. Some of the key people get together and decide that they will give you an ultimatum: sell them the agency and get out, or they will leave and take some of the accounts with them. Is this legal?

Let's take a look at just that type of situation to find the answer. The Duane Jones Company was an ad agency founded in 1942 by Duane Jones, who was the president and operating head of the agency until August 1951. But what happened that August threw a wrench into the machinery of the agency. At

EXHIBIT 11–3
Sample Agency Contract

north & fueroghne

advertising · marketing · public relations
a professional corporation

THIS AGREEMENT, entered into this _____ day of _____, 19____ , by and between NORTH & FUEROGHNE INCORPORATED, a California corporation, ("Agency") and _____, ("Client").

ARTICLE I
ADVERTISING REPRESENTATION AND SERVICES

1.01 Term of Agreement. This Agreement shall become effective as of the execution date hereof and shall continue in effect until terminated as provided herein.

1.02 Appointment and Authorization of Agency. Client agrees to retain and appoint the Agency to represent it in carrying out its advertising program, subject to the terms and conditions of this Agreement. The Agency is authorized to enter into contracts with third parties to effectuate the purposes of this Agreement. Prior to the commencement of work by Agency, a written project-proposal(s) shall be submitted for approval by Client. The terms and conditions of such project-proposals shall become a part of this Agreement.

1.03 Agency Services. Agency agrees to act as the Client's advertising representative and to perform, upon authorization by Client, any and all of the following services to the extent necessary to meet the Client's needs.

(a) Study and analyze the Client's business and products or services and survey the market therefor.
(b) Develop an advertising program designed to meet the Client's needs and budgetary limitations.
(c) Counsel the Client on his overall merchandising program or make plans therefor.
(d) Determine and analyze the effect of the advertising used.
(e) Plan, create, write and prepare layouts and the actual copy to be used in advertisements of all types.
(f) Analyze all advertising media to determine those which are most suitable for use by the Client.
(g) Make contracts with the advertising media for space or time and with others to effectuate the advertising program and obtain the most favorable terms and rates available.
(h) Check and follow up on all contracts with the various media for proper performance in the best interests of the Client, including the appearance, accuracy, date, time, position, size, extent, site, workmanship and mechanical reproduction, as appropriate to the advertisements used.
(i) Negotiate, arrange and contract for any special talent required for all photography, models, special effects, layouts, and art work, and for all printing, including any required engravings, electrotypes, typography, and any other necessary technical material for use in the advertising program.
(j) Make timely payment to all persons or firms supplying goods or services in connection with the advertising program.
(k) Advise and bill the Client for all amounts incurred by the Agency for the Client's account and maintain complete and accurate books and records in this regard.
(l) Agency shall complete and cause to be delivered to Client, a "Call-Report" covering the information contained at all meetings, telephone conversations, discussions or any house correspondence which concerns Client advertising.

1.04 Prior Approval of Client. Agency shall not incur any obligations or provide any services for the Client's account without first obtaining the written approval from Client. In order to obtain the Client's approval, the Agency shall submit a written project-proposal(s) to the Client, containing full descriptions of the proposed advertisements and estimates of the cost of obligations or services involved, including media costs, costs of preparation of the advertisement, costs of production, and any additional costs. All estimates shall be submitted on the Agency's standard project-proposal forms with sufficient copies to meet the needs of the Client.

The Agency shall not be responsible for missed deadlines, closing dates or insertions caused by the delay of the Client in approving the advertisements to be used in connection therewith.

Production schedules shall be established and adhered to by Client and Agency, provided that neither shall incur any liability or penalty for delays caused by force majeure.

EXHIBIT 11–3—*Continued*

2

1.05 Property and Materials. All materials, sketches, copies, artwork, dummies, type, art plates, dies, photographs, illustrations, negatives, and other items supplied by Agency shall remain the exclusive property of Agency and no use shall be made, nor any ideas obtained therefrom may be used, except upon compensation to Agency to be determined by Agency. All of such items shall remain the sole and exclusive property of Agency unless otherwise agreed to in writing.

1.06 Delivery. Unless otherwise specified, the price quoted is for a single shipment without storage, F.O.B., local Client's place of business or F.O.B. printer's platform for out-of-town Clients. Proposals are based on continuous and uninterrupted delivery of complete order, unless specifications distinctly state otherwise. Charges related to delivery from Client to Agency or from Client's supplier to Agency are not included in any quotation unless specified.

ARTICLE II
COSTS AND PAYMENTS

2.01 Advertising Costs and Expenditures.

    (a) Client shall reimburse Agency for all costs incurred and expenditures made on behalf of Client for approved advertising, for which Client shall compensate the Agency as provided in Section 2.02.

    (b) Client shall pay the Agency for its direct costs of mailing, packaging, shipping, taxes and duties, telegrams and telephones incurred by the Agency in connection with its performance under this Agreement.

    (c) Client shall pay all of Agency's costs for any necessary travelling done on behalf of Client.

    (d) In the event media or any other charges increase or decrease after the Agency has submitted an estimate, the Client shall pay for such increase or be given a credit for such reduction, as the case may be. In the event the Client, after having approved any planned advertising, cancels all or any part thereof, the Client shall pay for all costs incurred therefore to date of cancellation and any unavoidable costs incurred thereafter, including any noncancellable commitments for time or space. In addition, the Agency shall receive any commissions it would have earned had the proposal been fully performed.

2.02 Agency's Compensation.

    (a) Agency shall receive a commission of fifteen percent (15%) of all gross media charges. The Agency shall charge an amount which, when added to the net cost of media allowing no commission or less than 15% commission, will yield 15% of the Agency's total media bill to the Client.

    (b) The Agency shall receive a commission of twenty percent (20%) of the charges made by third parties with whom the Agency has contracted for products or services which are to be used to implement the advertising project-proposal(s) approved by the Client.

2.03 Billing and Payment. The Agency shall bill the Client from time to time, and payment for which shall be made within ten (10) days of the invoice date. Final billing to Client shall be adjusted based upon final invoices from vendors, plus Agency's commissions. Bills and project-proposals estimating the costs involved may be preliminarily used, but final, detailed bills, supported by invoices of charges of third parties and showing all adjustments and credits, will be submitted to the Client as soon as available.

2.04 Internal Labor. All internal labor of Agency shall be charged at an hourly rate for: Creative time, concept, design, copywriting, trademark, logo-type, mock-ups, research and development, market research, media research and planning, product development, analysis & public relations.

2.05 Speculative and Experimental Work. Speculative and experimental work performed by Agency at Client's request such as sketches, research, drawings, composition, film and materials, including labor, will be charged Client at current rates and may not be utilized by Client without the prior written consent of Agency.

EXHIBIT 11–3—*Concluded*

3

ARTICLE III
TERMINATION OF AGREEMENT

3.01 Either Party may terminate this Agreement by giving the other Party written notice of at least sixty (60) days prior to the effective date of termination. Upon receipt of notice of termination, the Agency shall not commence work on any new advertisements, but it shall complete and place all advertisements previously approved by the Client. All the rights and duties of the Parties shall continue during the notice period and the Client shall be responsible to the Agency for the payment of any contract obligation incurred with third parties during this period.

3.02 In the event the Client of Agency desires to terminate all work in progress on all advertisements commenced before receipt of notice of termination, it may be so agreed upon by the Parties' mutual consent and determination of the compensation to be received by the Agency for partially completed work.

3.03 Billing Upon Termination. Upon termination of the Agreement, the Agency shall bill the Client for all amounts not previously billed and due the Agency at that time under the terms of this Agreement. Agency shall be entitled to payment for services and commissions for advertisements approved by Client prior to the effective date of termination.

ARTICLE IV
COMPLIANCE WITH LAW

4.01 Any controversy or claim arising out of or relating to this Agreement, or any project-proposal submitted pursuant to the terms of this Agreement, may be settled by arbitration in accordance with the rules of the American Arbitration Association, any judgment upon the award rendered by the arbitrator(s), may be entered in any court of competent jurisdiction. In the event of such claim, the prevailing party shall be awarded its reasonable attorney's fees and costs.

4.02 Neither Party may assign any rights or delegate any duties hereunder without the expressed prior written consent of the other.

4.03 This writing contains the entire Agreement of the Parties. No representations were made or relied upon by either Party, other than those expressly set forth herein. No agent, employee, or other representative of either Party has the power to alter any of the terms hereof, unless done in writing and signed by an authorized officer of the respective Parties hereto.

4.03 Validity, interpretation and performance of this Agreement shall be controlled by and construed under the laws of the State of California.

4.05 All notices pertaining to this Agreement shall be in writing and shall be transmitted either by personal hand-delivery or through the facilities of the United States Postal Service. The addresses contained herein for the respective Parties shall be the places where notices shall be sent, unless written notice of a change of address is given.

IN WITNESS WHEREOF, the Parties have caused this Agreement to be executed on the date first hereinabove set forth.

"AGENCY"   NORTH & FUEROGHNE INCORPORATED

                                                    BY: _____

"CLIENT"

                                                    BY: _____

EXHIBIT 11–4
Sampel Project Proposal

north &fueroghne

advertising · marketing · public relations
a professional corporation

PAGE_____OF_____
DATE_____
REQUESTED BY_____
NO._____

In accordance with your request, North & Fueroghne is pleased to submit the following project-proposal. Agency agrees to act as the Client's advertising representative and to perform any and all of the following services to the extent necessary to meet the Client's needs:

Our proposal is based upon estimates supplied by vendors. Final billing is subject to receipt of vendors' final invoices. This proposal does not include any applicable commissions, North & Fueroghne fees, expenses and costs, all of which will be contained in the final billing.

EXHIBIT 11–4—*Concluded*

PAGE_____OF_____

We shall furnish all elements and facilities necessary for the completion of the above-described work, except the following items which you shall provide:

This proposal shall remain valid for thirty (30) days from the date indicated, after which it may be withdrawn, or revised by North & Fueroghne. Any changes subsequent to approval of the proposal may affect the prices quoted and, therefore, may only be done in writing, approved by both parties. In the event of cancellation of the proposal by client after acceptance, North & Fueroghne shall be reimbursed for any expenses incurred and shall be paid any commissions it would have earned had the proposal been fully performed.

You represent and warrant that the information and materials provided North & Fueroghne and which may be included in the work performed, will not at any time infringe upon or violate any copyright, artistic, personal, dramatic or any other rights, legal or equitable of any person. You agree to indemnify, defend and hold North & Fueroghne harmless from any liability, claim or action arising out of or pertaining to the foregoing warranty. In the event of any such claim or action against North & Fueroghne, you shall defend North & Fueroghne with attorneys of your own choice, and at your own expense, and we agree to cooperate in all respects in connection with said defense.

Any disputes arising out of or pertaining to this agreement may be pursued in accordance with the rules of the American Arbitration Association, and any award made with respect to such arbitration shall be enforceable in any Court of competent jurisdiction. In the event of any such arbitration or any litigation arising out of or pertaining to this proposal, California law shall govern and the prevailing party shall be awarded its reasonable attorney's fees and costs.

All unpaid invoices in connection with the foregoing work shall bear interest at the rate of ten percent (10%) per annum until paid. All materials and/or other items produced and/or supplied by North & Fueroghne shall remain the exclusive property of North & Fueroghne and no other use or reproduction shall be made by client other than as set forth in this proposal, without first obtaining the written consent of North & Fueroghne, which consent shall include reasonable compensation to North & Fueroghne.

Very truly yours,

NORTH & FUEROGHNE
a professional corporation

BY: _____

ACCEPTED AND AGREED TO:

BY: _____   DATED _____

that time, the agency billed $9 million annually from about 25 accounts.

About that time the agency lost $6,500,000 from three accounts that left the agency. Along with that, three executives and numerous staff people resigned from the agency because, as the employees claimed, Duane Jones "had been guilty of certain behavioral lapses at his office, at business functions, and during interviews with actual and prospective customers. As a result . . . several of [Jones's] officers and directors expressed dissatisfaction with conditions—described as 'intolerable.' "

In June 1951, a private meeting occurred at a hotel in Manhattan between a number of the agency's officers, directors, and employees, led by one of the officers, Mr. Hayes. It was decided that these people would make an ultimatum to Jones: either sell them the agency or they would resign en masse. Hayes told Jones of this plan and informed him that certain clients of the agency had been presold on the idea of leaving with the employees. Jones responded, "In other words, you are standing there with a Colt .45, holding it at my forehead, and there is not much I can do except to give up?" Hayes replied, "Well, you can call it anything you want, but that is what we are going to do."

At first, Jones decided to accept the buy out of the agency, but negotiations fell through in August 1951. That same month, six officers and directors resigned from the agency. A few days later the former employees of Jones opened a new agency, Scheideler, Beck & Werner, Inc. This agency employed 71 of the 132 Duane Jones employees. Within a few weeks of its opening, S,B&W had as accounts Manhattan Soap Co., Heublein, International Salt, Wesson Oil, C. F. Mueller Co., The Borden Co., Marlin Fire Arms, McIlhenny Corp., Haskins Bros., and Continental Briar Pipe—all were former clients of Duane Jones.

When one acts as an agent or employee—the legal relationship is the same for either—a duty of loyalty, trust, and good faith is owed to the client or employer. We discussed this duty earlier. As a result of this, Duane Jones filed suit in *Duane Jones Co.* v. *Burke et al,* 281 N.Y.A.D. 622, (1953) affd 306 N.Y. 172 (1954).

The court awarded damages to Jones and said: "defendants . . . while employees of [Jones], determined upon a course of conduct which, when subsequently carried out, resulted in benefit to themselves through destruction of [Jones's] business, in violation of the fiduciary duties of good faith and fair dealing imposed on defendants . . ."

There are situations in which taking accounts away from a former employer is acceptable, however. One example of such an occurrence is found in the case of *Nationwide Advertising Service, Inc.* v. *Kolar,* 329 N.E.2d 300 (1975). Here, Nationwide sued a former employee, Martin Kolar, and his new employer Bentley, Barnes & Lynn for acquiring former accounts of Nationwide. Both agencies specialized in recruitment advertising. Not until after Kolar left Nationwide and became employed with Bentley did he solicit accounts of Nationwide. This was acceptable.

One of the issues in this case involved an implied covenant binding Kolar not to compete with his employer. But this covenant covered only confidential information gained through his employment, and then used for his benefit, and to the detriment of the employer. This was not the case here.

Granted, an agency's interest in its clients is proprietary by nature, but this is valid only when the client/agency relationship is near permanent. In the advertising business, this is a rare claim. In the recruitment advertising business, it is almost nonexistent. Also, Nationwide's client list was not confidential, and no trade secrets were used to solicit the accounts. Kolar did not solicit any accounts until after leaving the employ of Nationwide. The court held that no breach of trust or confidence occurred. Nationwide lost the case.

Restrictive Covenants

Probably the best solution to account piracy involves the use of restrictive covenants in written employment contracts. This is the only way to legally enforce damages against former employees who take accounts away.

Under an agreement containing a restrictive covenant, the employee agrees not to serve or contact any client of the former agency for a specific period of time. It is crucial that a specific period of time be stated in the agreement; otherwise it will be unenforceable. Also, the time must be reasonable, usually one to two years.

Restrictive covenants must be agreed to at the beginning of the employment. If an agency wishes to add restrictive covenants to existing employment situations, some additional consideration must be given. This can be any valuable offering: extension of employment, stock options, money, and so forth.

AGENCY LIABILITY FOR CHILDREN

This is a very important subject for advertisers and their agencies. Almost every ad agency has dealt with children in the course of producing an ad, television commercial, billboard, or brochure. Any agency that does work with children needs to understand what restrictions and requirements it must adhere to. Few photographers and fewer art directors are aware of the current child labor laws that govern employment of children.

The Problem

You're at the photo studio to photograph a client's project. Everything is going fine. The set looks good, the kids are great in their costumes, and the collie is behaving just fine. All of a sudden, the photo assistant kicks a light stand and the dog, startled, turns and bites one of the children. The child falls, knocking over a prop stand causing the entire set to crash down on top of another child. About then you wonder what else could go wrong.

Well, if the children were working without a valid work permit, you've only begun to hear your world come crashing down around you. If you, or your client, did not have the proper work permits, you could face criminal or civil prosecution, resulting in lawsuits, fines, and even jail. If the child is working without the proper permits, liability insurance could be useless. Insurance companies can deny coverage if a law was violated that led to the injury.

This was something John Landis learned the hard way. While filming the movie *Twilight Zone,* two child actors and actor Vic Morrow were killed when a helicopter crashed. The children were employed illegally for four reasons. First, they were working at 2:30 A.M. Second, they were in an extremely dangerous situation. Third, the children did not have work permits as required by California law. Fourth, no social worker was present. Had one been, the filming would probably not have been allowed. Had the laws been obeyed, the accident would not have killed the children or Morrow since they would not have been on the set at that time.

Child Labor Laws

In the early 1900s child labor laws were created in response to an increase in serious injuries of children. Most of these injuries were the result of severe conditions in mills, sweatshops, and mines where children were used as cheap labor.

Because of the enactment of child labor laws, restrictions have been placed on wages, hours of employment, and working conditions. While some of the laws are federal, the most important are state regulations. The individual states have become more involved in this area and have adopted very stringent laws to protect children. New York and California are at the head of this list.

By the way, anyone can be held liable—the photographer, the director, the ad agency, and/or the client. Each must protect itself by making sure that the proper permits are obtained and working conditions are met.

Guidelines for Working with Children

1. *Check with the state agency* that oversees child labor laws to determine the particular state's requirements. For example, in California, it is the California Division of Labor Standards.

2. *Obtain the proper permits* from the state where the photography takes place.

3. *Abide by the hours of employment* allowed by law. For example, in California, children 6 to 18 years old can only work a maximum of four hours a day and not after 6:30 P.M. A one-hour lunch break must be provided no later than 1 P.M. And, if the session is outside the studio, lunch must be provided free to the child and teacher/welfare worker.

4. *Provide the required supervision.* Again, in California, a studio teacher or welfare worker must be hired and present during any session.

5. *Check insurance coverage.* Make sure that the photographer has valid workers' compensation and liability insurance.

6. *Report any injury* that occurs to a child immediately to the insurance carrier and the state Workers' Compensation Board.

7. *Medical attention.* Make sure that the child gets immediate medical attention.

8. *Parents cannot waive liability.* Remember, a parent or guardian cannot give a release of liability by law. Even a written release will not protect you.

CONCLUSION

As we have seen throughout this chapter, the ad agency has a lot to consider in the operation of its business. The agency business is a fascinating one indeed, but it also has many risks and pitfalls. An agency must deal with many areas of law in the operation of its business. While it has certain rights of its own, it also has duties to its clients and suppliers, as well as duties to the public and to its employees. And all of those parties have rights and duties of their own.

APPENDIX A

SPECIFIC INDUSTRY INFORMATION SOURCES

In addition to the general laws we've examined up to this point, there are also heavy regulations regarding some specific product and industry areas. Because the details of these regulations are far in excess of the scope of this book, I have listed relevant sources where more information can be obtained. These include government agencies, trade associations, reference books, and law review articles.

These sources provide specific information for the advertiser. I would urge the advertiser or agency to get a copy of the appropriate guide. Familiarize yourself with the requirements of that particular area, and you'll help avoid problems.

Associations and government agencies often produce booklets and guides for their industry. Check with the appropriate association for information on the legalities of that specific trade or industry. The federal agencies are listed in the phone book under *U.S. Government*. In addition to the federal agencies listed, check with the applicable state government for specific local regulation information.

The books listed are available through the source that is listed in the entry and may be ordered through a local book store or directly from the publisher.

The law review articles are generally more technical, but they can provide a more thorough treatment of the subject. These articles are published in the college law school law review that is listed with the entry. They can be obtained at any city or county law library or college law school library. These are reference sources only and cannot be checked out or purchased. They must either be read at the library or photocopied.

First, here is a quick reference list of the federal agencies that have an impact on advertising and marketing activities and the products that each govern. These agencies often provide booklets on the regulation of these products.

Federal Trade Commission
  Light bulbs
  Binoculars
  Radios
  Sewing machines
  Amplifiers
  Appliances
  Consumer products
  Foods
  Drugs
  Cosmetics
  Medical devices
  Wool, fur, and textile products
  Cigarettes

Food and Drug Administration
  Food
  Drugs
  Nonalcoholic beverages
  Cosmetics
  Medical devices
  Biological products
  Hearing aids
  Radiation emitting devices (microwaves)

Department of Housing and Urban Development
  Real estate
  Land
  Mobile homes
  Apartments

Department of Transportation
  Motor vehicles
  Tires
  Boats

Department of the Treasury
  Imported goods
  Alcoholic beverages
  Tobacco products

Department of Agriculture
Meat products
Poultry products
Eggs and egg products
Fruits
Vegetables
Seeds

Department of Commerce
Seafood
Fire detection devices
Fire extinguishing devices
Consumer products
Fruits
Vegetables

Consumer Product Safety Commission
Consumer products
Flammable fabrics
Poisons
Hazardous materials
Bicycles
Toys
Refrigerators

Department of Energy
Dishwashers
Refrigerators and freezers
Washers and dryers
Water heaters
Air conditioners
Heating devices
Televisions
Stereos
Furnaces
Ovens and ranges and microwaves

Environmental Protection Agency
Motor vehicles
Engines
Fuels and fuel additives
Noise emitting devices
Insecticides, pesticides
Poisons
Insect and rodent traps and repellents

INFORMATION SOURCES BY PRODUCT OR INDUSTRY

Accounting

Associations
American Accounting Association, 5717 Bessie Drive, Sarasota, FL 33581
American Institute of Certified Public Accountants, 1211 Avenue of the Americas, New York, NY 10036
National Association of Accountants, 919 Third Avenue, New York, NY 10022

Law Review Articles
Haff, Robert L. "More on Advertising." *Journal of Accountancy* vol. 151 (March 1981), p. 42.

Advertising Allowances

Books
Guides for Advertising Allowances and Other Merchandising Payments and Services. Washington, D.C.: Federal Trade Commission, 1972.

Alcohol

Books
Regulation No. 5 Relating to Labeling and Advertising of Distilled Spirits. Washington, D.C.: U.S. Bureau of Internal Revenue, Alcohol Tax Unit, 1949.
Summary of State Laws and Regulations Relating to Distilled Spirits. Washington, D.C.: Distilled Spirits Council of the United States, 1980.

Automobiles

Books
Dore, Karl J. *Consumer Guarantees for Automobiles and Mobile Homes.* Washington, D.C.: Department of Justice, Law Reform Division, Consumer Protection Project, 1974.

Rothschild, Toby J. *Toby J. Rothschild on Automobile Transactions: Sales, Financing, Warranties, Repairs and Collections.* Berkeley, Calif.: California Continuing Education of the Bar, 1981.

Children

Books
Ratner, Ellis M. *FTC Staff Report on Television Advertising to Children.* Washington, D.C.: Federal Trade Commission, 1978.
Schramm, W.; J. Lyle; and E. Parker. *Television in the Lives of Our Children.* Washington, D.C.: National Science Foundation, 1961.

Law Review Articles
"FTC Regulation of T.V. Advertising to Children; They Deserve a Break Today." *University of Florida Law Review* vol. 30 (Fall 1978), p. 946.
Pauker, M. "Case for FTC Regulation of the Advertising Directed toward Children." *Brooklyn Law Review,* vol. 46 (Spring 1980), p. 513.

Consumer Credit

Books
Advertising Consumer Credit and Lease Terms: How To Comply with the Law. Washington, D.C.: The Federal Trade Commission, 1980.
Board of Governors. *Regulation Z: Truth in Lending (12 CFR 226).* Washington, D.C.: The Federal Reserve System, 1982.

Cosmetics

Law Review Articles
Orlans, M. H. "FTC Regulation of FTC Drug and Cosmetics Advertising." *Food, Drug, Cosmetics Law Journal* vol. 36 (March 1981), p. 100.

Drugs

Associations
Food and Drug Law Institute, 818 Connecticut Avenue NW, Washington, D.C. 20006

Pharmaceutical Advertising Council, 350 Hudson Street, New York, NY 10014

Books

Bond, Ronald S. *Economic Report (on) Sales, Promotion and Product Differentiation in Two Prescription Drug Markets.* Washington, D.C.: Federal Trade Commission, 1977.

Donegan, Thomas J. *Advertising for Over-the-Counter Drugs, 16 CFR 450, Public Record 215–51.* Washington, D.C.: Federal Trade Commission, 1979.

U.S. Bureau of Consumer Protection. *Advertising for Over-the-Counter Antacids.* Washington, D.C.: Federal Trade Commission, 1983.

Law Review Articles

Millstein, Lloyd G. "Drug Advertising to Consumers." *Food, Drug, Cosmetics Law Journal* vol. 39 (October 1984), p. 497.

Novitch, Mark. "Direct-to-Consumer Advertising of Prescription Drugs." *Food, Drug, Cosmetics Law Journal* vol. 39 (July 1984), p. 306.

Orlans, M. H. "FTC Regulation of FTC Drug and Cosmetics Advertising." *Food, Drug, Cosmetics Law Journal* vol. 36 (March 1981), p. 100.

Financial

Books

Advertising Consumer Credit and Lease Terms: How to Comply with the Law. Washington, D.C.: Federal Trade Commission, 1980.

Alec, Benn L. C. *Advertising Financial Products & Services: Proven Techniques and Principles for Banks, Investment Firms, Insurance Companies and Their Agencies.* Westport, Conn.: Quorum Books, 1986.

The Bank Marketing Association. *Federal Advertising Law Guide.* Chicago: The Bank Marketing Association, 1980.

National Credit Union Association. *Banks and Banking: Advertising—part 740.* Washington, D.C.: Government Printing Office, NCU 1.6/a:740.

Law Review Articles

Frankel, Tamar. "Investment Company Advertising." *Review of Securities Regulation* vol. 14 (March 5, 1981).

Food

Associations
Food and Drug Law Institute, 818 Connecticut Avenue NW, Washington, D.C. 20006

Books
Hinich, Melvin J. *Consumer Protection Legislation and the U.S. Food Industry.* New York: Pergamon Press, 1980.
Proposed Trade Regulation on Food Advertising, 16 CFR 437. Washington, D.C.: Federal Trade Commission, 1978.

General

Books
Aaker, David A. *Consumerism: Search for the Consumer Interest.* New York: Free Press, 1982.
Disclosure of Energy Cost and Consumption Information in Labeling and Advertising of Consumer Appliances. Washington, D.C.: U.S. Bureau of Consumer Protection, 1979.
Fisher, Bruce D. *The Legal Environment of Business.* 2nd ed. St. Paul, Minn.: West Publishing Co., 1986.
Kent, Felix H. *Legal and Business Aspects of the Advertising Industry.* New York: Practicing Law Institute, 1986.
———— *Legal Problems in Advertising.* New York: Mathew Bender, 1984.
Rosden, George and Peter Rosden. *The Law of Advertising,* (4 vols.) New York: Mathew Bender, 1973.
Stern, Louis W., and Thomas L. Eovaldi. *Legal Aspects of Marketing Strategy.* Englewood Cliffs, N.J.: Prentice-Hall, 1984.
Thurman, Ruth Fleet. *Direct Mail, Advertising or Solicitation? Distinction without a Difference.* Chicago: American Bar Association, 1982.

Health Care

Associations
American Academy of Psychiatry and the Law, University of Pittsburgh School of Law, Pittsburgh, PA 15260

American Hospital Association, 840 North Lake Shore Drive, Chicago, IL 60611

American Society of Hospital Attorneys, 840 North Lake Shore Drive, Chicago, IL 60611

Books

American Hospital Association Guides for Advertising by Hospitals. Chicago: American Hospital Association, 1980.

Bond, Ronald S. *Effects of Restrictions on Advertising and Commercial Practice in the Professions: The Case of Optometry.* Washington, D.C.: Federal Trade Commission, 1980.

California Legislature, Assembly, Health Committee. *Advertising by Health Professionals.* Sacramento, Calif.: Assembly Publications Office, 1977.

Federal Trade Commission. *Advertising of Ophthalmic Goods and Services.* Chicago: Commerce Clearing House, 1978.

Law Review Articles

"Advertising Restrictions on Health Care Professionals and Lawyers." *UMKC Law Review* vol. 50 (Fall 1981).

"Healthcare Advertising: What You Can and Cannot Say." *Healthspan* vol. 2, no. 1 (January 1985), p. 3.

Insurance

Associations

Life Insurance Advertisers Association, 1040 Woodcock Road, Orlando, FL 32803

Books

Alec, Benn L. C. *Advertising Financial Products & Services: Proven Techniques and Principles for Banks, Investment Firms, Insurance Companies and Their Agencies.* Westport, Conn.: Quorum Books, 1986.

Budd. *American Guidelines for Life, Accident and Health Insurance.* American Life Insurance Association, Legal Section.

Ismond, Richard L. *Insurance Advertising: Ethics & Law.* New York: Roberts Publishing Corp., 1968.

Lawyers

Associations
American Bar Association, 1155 East 60th Street, Chicago, IL 60637

Books
Anderson, Austin G. *Marketing Your Practice: A Practical Guide to Client Development.* Chicago: American Bar Association, Section of Economics of Law Practice, 1986.

Curtis, Stephen M. *Marketing for Today's Law Firm.* New York: Practicing Law Institute, 1986.

Lawyer Advertising Kit. Chicago: American Bar Association, Section of Economics of Law Practice, 1978.

Macaulay, Stewart. *Lawyer Advertising: "Yes, but . . . ".* Madison, Wis.: University of Madison Law School, 1985.

Law Review Articles
"The Advertising Guidelines: To Be, Or Not To Be?" *Texas Law Journal* vol. 43 (1980), p. 318.

Outdoor Advertising

Associations
Institute for Outdoor Advertising, 485 Lexington Avenue, New York, NY 10017

Outdoor Advertising Association of America, 1899 L Street NW #403, Washington, D.C. 20036

Books
Claus, James R., and Karen Claus. *Visual Environment. Sight Sign & By-Law.* Ontario: Collier-MacMillan, 1971.

Claus, Oliphant, and Claus. *Signs. Legal Rights and Aesthetic Considerations.* Cincinnati, Ohio: Signs of The Times Publishing, 1972.

Cunningham, Roger A. *Control of Highway Advertising Signs: Some Legal Problems.* Washington, D.C.: Highway Research Board, National Research Council, 1971.

Federal Highway Administration. *Outdoor Advertising Control & Acquisition.* Washington, D.C.: U.S. Department of Transportation, 1982–83.

Houck, John. *Outdoor Advertising History and Regulations.* South Bend, Ind: University of Notre Dame Press, 1969.

Political

Law Review Articles
Albert, James A. "The Remedies Available to Candidates Who Are Defamed by Television and Radio Commercials of Opponents." *Vermont Law Review* vol. 11 (Spring 1986), p. 33.

Real Estate

Books
California Department of Real Estate Reference Book. California Department of Real Estate.

Realtors National Marketing Institute. *Real Estate Sales Handbook.* Chicago: National Association of Realtors, 1980.

Tucker, Sterling. *Fair Housing Advertising Guidelines.* Washington, D.C.: Department of Housing and Urban Development, Federal Register vol. 45, no. 167 (1980).

Law Review Articles
Romeo, Peter J. "Advertising of Real Estate Offerings." *Review of Securities & Commodities Regulation* vol. 18 (January 23, 1985), p. 17.

Talent Labor

Associations
American Federation of Television and Radio Artists (AFTRA), 260 Madison Avenue, New York, NY 10016

American Society of Magazine Photographers (ASMP), 205 Lexington Avenue, New York, NY 10016

Directors Guild of America (DGA), 7950 Sunset Boulevard, Hollywood, CA 90046

Graphic Artists Guild, 30 East 20th Street, New York, NY 10003

Printing Industries of America (PIA), 1730 North Lynn Street, Arlington, VA 22209

Screen Actors Guild (SAG), 7750 Sunset Boulevard, Hollywood, CA 90046

Screen Extras Guild (SEG), 3629 Cahuenga Boulevard, Hollywood, CA 90068

Tobacco

Books
Fritschler, A. Lee. *Smoking and Politics: Policymaking and the Federal Bureaucracy.* Englewood Cliffs, N.J.: Prentice-Hall, 1975.

Law Review Articles
Boonin, David. "Cigarette Advertising Works—That's Why It's Protected." *Los Angeles Daily Journal,* June 5, 1987.

Molotsky, Irwin. "Push Due for Law on Cigarette Advertising." *Chicago Daily Law Bulletin,* January 23, 1987.

APPENDIX B

NBC BROADCAST STANDARDS
FOR TELEVISION

ADVERTISING STANDARDS

Clearance Procedures

While the ultimate responsibility for advertising rests with the advertiser, advertising agencies preparing commercial messages intended for broadcast on NBC facilities should consult the Broadcast Standards Department in advance of production. Such advance discussion enables the Broadcast Standards Department to provide initial guidance on questions that might arise under NBC standards.

For each commercial, advertising agencies are asked to submit shooting script or storyboard, a new product sample and label/package insert, substantiation for all material claims and authentication of all demonstrations and testimonial statements.

When the pre-production discussions have concluded, the agency produces the commercial and must submit the finished version for screening and final clearance.

NBC accepts advertising only after securing satisfactory evidence of the integrity of the advertiser, the availability of the product or service, the existence of support for the claims and the authentication of demonstrations, compliance with applicable laws and the acceptable taste of the presentation. Advertisers should deal affirmatively with the results expected from the use of the product or service, not dwell excessively on the results of failure to use the product or service.

Billboards

Billboards may be used as stipulated by NBC, provided they include no more than the identity of the program and the sponsor's name, product or service and a brief factual description of the general nature thereof. Only products, services or companies being advertised in the program may be billboarded. Any claims allowed must be supported. Billboards may not mention contests, offers, promotional teasers or cross-references to other programs.

Charitable Appeals

An advertiser may surrender commercial time to schedule an approved public service announcement or theme. Appeals within a commercial announcement will be considered on a case-by-case basis and will require submission of complete details of how the contributions will be handled. Clear sponsorship identification is required in these instances.

Comparative Advertising Guidelines

NBC will accept comparative advertising which identifies, directly or by implication, a competing product or service. As with all other advertising, each substantive claim, direct or implied, must be substantiated to NBC's satisfaction and the commercial must satisfy the following guidelines and standards for comparative advertising established by NBC:

1. Competitors shall be fairly and properly identified.

2. Advertisers shall refrain from disparaging or unfairly attacking competitors, competing products, services or other industries through the use of representations or claims, direct or implied, that are false, deceptive, misleading or have the tendency to mislead.

3. The identification must be for comparison purposes and not simply to upgrade by association.

4. The advertising should compare related or similar properties or ingredients of the product, dimension to dimension, feature to feature, or wherever possible by a side-by-side demonstration.

5. The property being compared must be significant in terms of value or usefulness of the product or service to the consumer.

6. The difference in the properties being compared must be measurable and significant.

7. Pricing comparisons may raise special problems that could mislead, rather than enlighten, viewers. For certain classifications of products, retail prices may be extremely volatile, may be fixed by the retailer rather than the product advertiser, and may not only differ from outlet to outlet but from week to week within the same outlet. Where these circumstances might apply, NBC will accept commercials containing price comparisons only on a clear showing that the comparative claims accurately, fairly and substantially reflect the actual price differentials at retail outlets throughout the broadcast area, and that these price differentials are not likely to change during the period the commercial is broadcast.

8. When a commercial claim involves market relationships, other than price, which are also subject to fluctuation (such as but not limited to sales position or exclusivity), the substantiation for the claim will be considered valid only as long as the market conditions on which the claim is based continue to prevail.

9. As with all other advertising, whenever necessary, NBC may require substantiation to be updated from time to time, and may re-examine substantiation, where the need to do so is indicated as the result of a challenge or other developments.

Challenge Procedure

Where appropriate, NBC will implement the following procedures in the event a commercial is challenged by another advertiser.

1. If an advertiser elects to challenge the advertising of another advertiser, he shall present his challenge and supporting data to NBC in a form available for transmittal to the challenged advertiser.

2. The challenged advertiser will then have an opportunity to respond directly to the challenger. NBC will maintain the confidentiality of the advertiser's original supporting data which was submitted for substantiation of the claims made in the commercial. However, NBC will ask the challenged advertiser to provide it with a copy of its response to the challenger and, where the response is submitted directly to NBC, the challenged advertiser will be requested to forward a copy of its response to the challenger.

3. Where NBC personnel do not have the expertise to make a judgment on technical issues raised by a challenge, NBC will take appropriate measures in its discretion to assist the advertiser and challenger to resolve their differences, including encouraging them to obtain a determination from an acceptable third party.

4. NBC will not withdraw a challenged advertisement from the broadcast schedule unless:

- a. It is directed to do so by the incumbent advertiser.
- b. The incumbent advertiser refuses to submit the controversy for review by some appropriate agency when deemed necessary by NBC.
- c. A decision is rendered by NBC against the incumbent advertiser.
- d. The challenged advertiser, when requested, refuses to cooperate in some other substantive area.
- e. NBC, prior to final disposition of the challenge, determines that the substantiation for the advertising has been so seriously brought into question that the advertising can no longer be considered substantiated to NBC's satisfaction.

5. NBC may take additional measures in its discretion to resolve questions raised by advertising claims.

Dramatizations and Reenactments

Dramatized or reenacted events must be clearly disclosed as such and may be utilized only when based on an actual occurrence.

Government Action Regarding a Product or Service Being Advertised

In the event government action is proposed with respect to a product or service or claims being made for it (as for example, the issuance of a complaint or proposed rules by the FTC or the FDA), Broadcast Standards will determine whether the subject questioned is part of a current schedule on NBC's facilities. If so, the substantiation and the authentication originally furnished by the advertising agency in support of the commercial message will be reevaluated in light of the matter being questioned by such proposed government action. The schedule will be maintained, if NBC is satisfied that either the advertising is acceptable under existing standards or that it presents a matter about which it would be inappropriate for NBC to make a judgment. This is done so that NBC action will not have the effect of adjudicating the question being considered by the governmental agency. A similar evaluation will be made of any proposed commercial message which involves subjects questioned by government action initiated prior to acceptance of the commercial for broadcast by NBC. If the governmental agency finally resolves the issue against the advertiser, NBC will withdraw its schedule.

Cross References in Advertising

References by advertisers within their commercial time to another program they are sponsoring are permitted provided that the references do not identify a competing facility, the day, or hour of the program. Statements urging the viewer to check television listings for such information are permissible.

Advertisers may not refer to other programs scheduled at a later hour on the same day on a competing facility.

Guarantee and Warranty Offers

Whenever the terms "guarantee," "warranty" or similar words that constitute a promise or representation in the nature of a guarantee or warranty appear in a television advertisement, certain additional information concerning material terms and conditions of such a guarantee or warranty offer must be clearly and unambiguously disclosed to the viewer.

In general, any commercial announcement in which a guarantee/warranty is mentioned should also disclose:

a. The nature and extent of the guarantee.

b. The identity of the guarantor.

c. The manner in which the guarantor intends to perform.

d. Information concerning what a purchaser wishing to claim under the guarantee need do before the guarantor will perform pursuant to its obligations under the guarantee.

e. Where applicable, whether a warranty is full or limited.

This disclosure must be made so it will not be misunderstood by the typical viewer. Simultaneous disclosure in both the audio and video often proves to be the best and most certain method of achieving full, clear and effective disclosure. However, a commercial announcement using only audio may constitute clear and conspicuous disclosure because of the clarity and completeness of the representation and the non-distracting manner of presentation. Video disclosure alone may not necessarily satisfy the above criteria.

Placement and Scheduling

NBC reserves the right to determine the scheduling, format and length of commercial breaks during and adjacent to programs carried over its facilities and the acceptability, number and placement of commercials, promotions and other announcements within such breaks, including those involving cast or celebrities.

In-program advertisements must be placed within the framework of the sponsored program. The program must be announced and clearly identified before the first commercial placement and terminated after the last commercial placement.

Research or Surveys

Reference may be made to the results of bona fide surveys or research relating to the product advertised, provided the results do not create an impression the research does not support.

Sound Level

The sound level of commercials should not appear to exceed that of the surrounding program.

Sponsor Identification

Identification of sponsorship shall be made in all commercials and programs in accordance with the requirements of the Communications Act, the rules and policies of the Federal Communications Commission and with the NBC Compliance and Practices Manual.

Time Standards for Advertising

In order to maintain the quality, audience appeal and integrity of programs presented on the NBC Television Network, NBC shall apply the following Standards to the amount, format and scheduling of non-program material.

1. Definition of Non-Program Material

Non-program material includes commercials; station breaks; promotional announcements; sponsor billboards; announcements that must be logged as commercial matter pursuant to FCC regulations and the

NBC Compliance and Practices Manual; and show credits which exceed the allocations specified on pages 8–10 of the General Entertainment Program Standards.

The following shall not be considered non-program material:
   a. Public service announcements.
   b. Paid political announcements not in excess of four minutes per hour during a limited number of broadcast hours.
   c. Credits for theatrical films, opening program titles, episode titles, starring and co-starring credits.
   d. Audio or "voice over" promotional announcements which are presented simultaneously over show credits and do not exceed 30 seconds in length.
   e. Announcements regarding the scheduling of special news programs.
   f. Scheduling information contained in programs of indeterminate length regarding an immediately upcoming program whose regular broadcast time has been affected.
   g. Certain prize-related announcements broadcast as part of a game, contest or award program or program element.
   i. Station call letter and network identification.

2. Time Limitations for Non-Program Material
   a. Prime time:
      For purposes of these Non-Program Material Time Limitation standards, Prime Time is defined as a consecutive three hour period designated by NBC between the hours of 6:00 P.M. and 11:00 P.M.

      Non-program material in Prime Time entertainment programs will not exceed 10 minutes per hour.

      Non-program material in Prime Time sports programs shall not exceed 16 minutes per hour.
   b. All other time periods:
      Non-program material in programs not scheduled during Prime Time shall not exceed 16 minutes per hour.
   c. Special promotional material:
      NBC may, in its discretion, from time to time vary the Prime Time and Other Time Periods Standards to accommodate promotional material for special programming.
   d. Children's programs:
      For purposes of these Standards, children's programming is

defined as those programs initially designed primarily for children 12 years of age and under.

Notwithstanding the Non-Program Material Time Limitations set forth in *a* and *b* above, in no event shall the "commercial matter" (any advertising message or announcement for which a charge is made or consideration received) in children's programs exceed:

(1) 9½ minutes per hour during weekend and Prime Time children's programs and

(2) 12 minutes per hour during weekday, non-Prime Time children's programs.

Fractional periods of less than one hour will be pro-rated on the basis of one hour.

3. Unit of Sale

The NBC Television Network makes sponsorship opportunities available in units of not less than 30 seconds in length for the advertising of a sponsor's product or service (except for advertisements placed in "news capsules").

4. Multiple Product Advertisements

The NBC Television Network will not accept a single commercial which advertises more than one product or service unless:

a. The participation purchased is at least 60 seconds in length and contains no more than two announcements.

b. The commercial presents the products or services of a single advertiser which have a related or common purpose and use, and such products or services are portrayed in a unified and integrated manner and setting.

c. The commercial is less than 60 seconds in length, but presents the products or services of a primary and secondary advertiser. The time devoted to the product or service of the secondary advertiser may not exceed one-sixth of the total time of the commercial.

Visual Supers

When superimposed copy is essential to qualify claims, it must be presented so it can be read easily against a plain, contrasting background, held sufficiently long and be large enough to meet NBC technical specifications (available on request).

Unacceptable Commercial Presentations, Approaches and Techniques

NBC does not accept in advertising:

1. Claims or representations, direct or implied, which are false or have the tendency to deceive, mislead or misrepresent.

2. Unqualified references to the safety of a product, if package, label or insert contains a caution or the normal use of the product presents a possible hazard.

3. Appeals to help fictitious characters in supposed distress by purchasing a product or service or sending for a premium.

4. "Bait and switch" tactics which feature goods or services not intended for sale but designed to lure the public into purchasing higher priced substitutes.

5. The use of "subliminal perception" or other techniques attempting to convey information to viewer by transmitting messages below the threshold of normal awareness.

6. Unacceptable products or services promoted through advertising devoted to an acceptable product.

7. The misuse of distress signals.

8. Disrespectful use of the flag, national emblems, anthems and monuments.

9. Direct or implied use of the office of the President of the United States or any governmental body without official approval.

10. Newsroom settings and techniques.

11. Sensational headline announcements in advertising of publications prior to the identification of sponsor.

12. Scare approaches and presentations with the capacity to induce fear.

13. Interpersonal acts of violence and antisocial behavior or other dramatic devices inconsistent with prevailing standards of taste and propriety.

14. Damaging stereotyping.

15. Unsupported or exaggerated promises of employment or earnings.

16. Presentations for professional services which do not comply with applicable law or ethical codes.

Unacceptable Commercial Classifications

1. Cigarettes.
2. Hard liquor.
3. Firearms, fireworks, ammunition and other weapons.
4. Presentations promoting a belief in the efficacy of fortune telling, astrology, phrenology, palm reading, numerology, mind reading, character reading or other occult pursuits.
5. Tip sheets and race track publications seeking to advertise for the purpose of promoting illegal betting. (See Lotteries.)
6. The sale of franchises.
7. Matrimonial, escort or dating services.
8. Contraceptives.
9. "Adult" or sex magazines.
10. X-rated movies.
11. Abortion services.
12. Ethical drugs.
13. Anti-law-enforcement devices.

Advertising Contests

Any advertiser-supplied contest furnished to NBC for proposed broadcast must be initially reviewed to insure that it is not a lottery, that the material terms are clearly stated, and that it is being conducted fairly, honestly and according to its rules.

1. Contest information is further reviewed to make certain that:
   a. The security arrangements are adequate to prevent "rigging."
   b. The terms, conditions and requirements under which contestants compete for prizes are clearly stated in the "Rules" so that there is no reasonable opportunity for any misunderstanding.
   c. The value, nature and extent of the prizes are clear.
   d. The public interest will not be adversely affected.
   e. The contest meets with federal, state and local laws.
2. Complete details and continuity must be submitted to the Broadcast Standards Department at least ten business days prior to the first public announcement of the contest.

3. All broadcast copy regarding contests must contain clear and complete information regarding:

    a. Complete contest rules or when and how they may be obtained by the public.

    b. The availability of entry forms and how to enter, including alternate means of entry where appropriate.

    c. The termination date of the contest.

    d. Any restrictions or eligibility requirements.

    e. The prize suppliers, when applicable.

    f. For chance contests, the necessary language:

        No Purchase Necessary

        Void Where Prohibited

    g. For skill contests, judging criteria must be stated.

4. A complete copy of the rules, the entry blank, a completed NBC Compliance and Practices Questionnaire, promotional material and/or any published information (e.g., newspaper advertisements) about the contest should be included with the broadcast copy.

5. All contest rules must be complete and contain:

    a. Eligibility requirements.

    b. Restrictions as to the number of entries made by an individual.

    c. The nature, extent and value of the prizes.

    d. Where, when and how entries are submitted.

    e. The basis on which prizes will be awarded.

    f. The termination date of the contest.

    g. When and how winners will be selected, including tie breaking procedures, when necessary.

    h. How winners will be notified.

    i. Time limits to claim or use prizes, if any.

    j. Restrictions as to the number of times an individual can win.

    k. Reference to "participating dealers" if not all outlets are involved.

Beer and Wine

Advertising of beer and wine is acceptable subject to federal, state and local laws and the requirements of the NBC Alcohol Products Advertising Guidelines.

Children

1. Commercial messages placed within children's programs or in station breaks between consecutive programs designed specifically for children, advertising of products designed primarily for children and advertising or other messages designed primarily for children are subject to all applicable provisions of NBC'S Children's Advertising Guidelines.

2. Within programs designed primarily for children 12 years of age or under, appropriate separator devices shall be used to clearly delineate the program material from commercial material.

3. Advertising concerning health and related matters which are more appropriately the responsibility of physicians and other adults shall not be primarily directed to children.

4. Commercial messages shall not be presented by a children's program personality, host or character, whether live or animated, within or adjacent to the programs in which such personality, host or character regularly appears.

5. Taking into account the age of the actors appearing within a commercial as well as the composition of the audience it is likely to reach, advertising approaches and techniques shall not disregard accepted safety precautions.

Door-to-Door Sales Representatives and In-Home Selling

All such advertising must be in accordance with applicable federal, state and local laws and shall be reviewed with special care. The reputation and reliability of the sponsor and the supervision exercised by the advertiser over its sales representatives, are important considerations. Each proposed commercial is evaluated on a case-by-case basis to insure its acceptability.

In general, advertising recruiting door-to-door representatives primarily for the sale of medical products and services having direct health considerations is not acceptable.

Employment Agencies

Reputable concerns are considered on a case-by-case basis and subject to exercise of care in order to avoid over-promising results.

Funeral Homes

The advertising of funeral services and mortuaries requires restrained presentation.

Health-Related Product Advertising

All advertisements for health-related products shall comply with the NBC Health Care Products Advertising Guidelines.

1. Ethical Drugs

NBC does not accept advertising for ethical drugs. Institutional advertising for pharmaceutical manufacturers, industry associations, and other responsible sponsors is considered on a case-by-case basis.

2. Proprietary Products (Over-the-Counter Medications)

The advertising of proprietary products presents important considerations to the health of consumers. The following principles and procedures govern the acceptability of such advertising on NBC facilities:

a. The advertiser must give assurance that the advertising for the proprietary product complies with all applicable governmental rules and regulations.

b. Advertising for proprietary products is accepted only after relevant data, including adequate substantiation regarding both product efficacy and any particular claims asserted, have been submitted to Broadcast Standards for examination and appraisal.

c. NBC does not accept advertising for products used in the treatment of conditions known to be chronic or irremediable or for conditions in which self-diagnosis or self-medication might present an element of danger unless:

(1) They can be self-administered without the order and supervision of a physician.

(2) They carry on their labels the cautions required by the Federal Food, Drug and Cosmetic Act of 1939.

(3) Appropriate cautionary references are included in the advertising proposed for broadcast.

d. No claims must be made or implied that the product is a panacea or alone will effect a cure.

e. Words such as "safe", "without risk", "harmless", or terms of similar meaning may not be used in an unqualified manner.

f. Advertising appeals may not be made to children for such products.

3. Statements from the Medical Profession

Physicians, dentists or nurses, or actors representing them, may not be employed directly or by implication in any commercial for proprietary products or other products involving health considerations. Advertisements of an institutional nature which are not intended to sell specific products or services to the consumer, public service announcements by non-profit organizations, as well as presentations for professional services, may be presented by physicians, dentists or nurses, subject to prior approval by Broadcast Standards.

Investments

Advertising of the services of financial institutions must be consistent with all applicable federal, state and local laws and regulations. The mention of specific securities in commercials requires the prior approval of the Law as well as Broadcast Standards Department.

Legalized Lotteries and Gambling

The lawful advertising of government organizations that conduct legalized lotteries is acceptable provided such advertising does not unduly exhort the public to bet.

The advertising of private or governmental organizations that conduct legalized betting on sporting contests is acceptable provided it does not unduly exhort the audience to bet.

Acceptable advertisements for legalized lotteries or betting shall comply with the NBC Guidelines on Gambling, Betting, Lotteries and Games of Chance.

"Personal" Products

Advertising for "personal" products, when accepted, must be presented in a restrained and tasteful manner and comply with the NBC Personal Products Advertising Guidelines.

Premiums and Offers

1. Full details and continuity including "build-up copy," and a sample of the premium or offer, must be submitted to Broadcast Standards well in advance of commitment.

2. The termination date of any offer should be announced as far in advance as possible. Such announcement will include the statement that responses postmarked not later than midnight of the business day following withdrawal of the offer shall be honored.

3. All audience responses to premiums, offers or contests made by advertisers must be sent to a stated Post Office box or to an outside address arranged for by the advertiser.

4. As to the premium merchandise offered:

   a. A premium or offer may not be harmful to person or property.

   b. The lesser of one half the total time or 20 seconds in a self-contained portion of any commercial message may deal with the premium scheduled in a children's program. Such premiums and offers will be subject to all other applicable premium and toy advertising requirements of the NBC Children's Advertising Guidelines.

   c. Descriptions or visual representations of premiums or offers may not enlarge their value or otherwise be misleading.

   d. The advertiser must provide NBC with written assurance that it will honor any request for return of money based on dissatisfaction with premiums or offers and that a sufficient supply of the premium or offer is readily available so as to avoid audience ill-will caused by delivery delay or impossibility of delivery.

5. The advertiser will hold NBC and its affiliated stations harmless from any liability which may arise in connection with any premium or offer.

6. The premium or offer may not appeal to superstition on the basis of "luck-bearing" powers or otherwise.

7. Mail order offers should indicate any additional postage/handling charges, as well as expected delivery time.

Testimonial Policy

The following seven point provision constitutes NBC policy relating to testimonials included in advertising of products, services or organizations.

1. Testimonials used, in whole or in part, must honestly reflect in spirit and content the sentiments of the individuals represented.

2. All claims and statements in a testimonial, including subjective evaluations of testifiers, must be supportable by facts and free of misleading implication. They shall contain no statement that cannot be supported if presented in the advertiser's own words.

3. Advertisers are required to disclose any connection between the advertiser and the endorser that might materially affect the weight or credibility of the endorsement.

4. In the event a consumer endorsement does not fairly reflect what a substantial proportion of other consumers are likely to experience, the advertising must clearly disclose this fact.

5. Expert endorsements are permitted only as long as the endorser continues to hold those views.

6. The laws of certain states require written consent of individuals for the use of their names. The advertiser must submit to NBC, in writing, confirmation of such consent or a blanket release assuming full responsibility for obtaining such consent for each testimonial covering its period of use on NBC facilities.

7. NBC staff employees may not give personal testimonials.

Public Service Announcements

The following guidelines are designed to assure that public service announcement time on NBC is used as effectively as possible.

1. All public service announcements proposed for network use apply to a nationwide audience.

2. The sponsoring organization must be national and devoted to public service or charitable activities. Announcements must pertain solely to public service or charitable causes and may not promote directly or indirectly the sale of commercial products or services or deal with sectarian, politically partisan or controversial subjects or issues, nor be designed to influence legislation or other government action.

3. Public service time for fund or membership solicitation is given only to demonstrably responsible organizations. In assessing the qualifications of sponsoring organizations, NBC may consult the Advertising Council, the National Information Bureau or comparable agencies for their evaluations and recommendations.

4. Public service announcements must deal affirmatively with the causes they advocate. Announcements that attack or demean other persons, organizations or causes are not acceptable.

5. The final judgment concerning acceptability and scheduling of public service messages rests solely with NBC.

6. All appeals and solicitations for charities and other non-profit organizations on NBC television facilities must have prior approval of the Broadcast Standards Department.

INDEX OF CASES

BIBLIOGRAPHY

Cone, Fairfax M. *With All Its Faults*. Boston: Little, Brown & Company, 1969.

Cooke, Alistair. *America*. New York: Alfred A. Knopf, 1973.

Della Femina, Jerry. *From Those Wonderful Folks Who Gave You Pearl Harbor*. New York: Simon & Schuster, 1970.

Fox, Stephen. *The Mirror Makers*. New York: Vintage Books, Random House, 1984.

Kotler, Philip. *Principles of Marketing*. Englewood Cliffs, N.J.: Prentice-Hall, 1980.

Nash, Jay Robert. *Hustlers and Con Men*. New York: M. Evans & Co., 1976.

Nayak, P. Ranganath, and John Ketteringham. *Breakthroughs!* New York: Rawson Associates, 1986.

Pritikin, Robert C. *Christ Was an Adman*. San Francisco: Harbor Publishing, 1980.

Rembar, Charles. *The Law of the Land*. New York: Touchstone, 1980.

Ries, Al, and Jack Trout. *Positioning: The Battle for Your Mind*. New York: McGraw-Hill, 1986.

Rosden, George, and Peter Rosden. *The Law of Advertising*. New York: Mathew Bender, 1978.

INDEX

A

Account piracy
  avoidance of, 272–73
  prevalence of, 265, 271–72
Advertising agencies; *see also*
    Client-agency relationship
  accountability of, 247
  and child labor laws, 273–75
  competing clients of, 243–45
  copyright liability of, 115, 136–
    37, 164
  defined, 239-40
  duties of, 241–54
  employees of, 260, 265, 272–73
  versus independent contractors,
    240
  liability of, 17, 115, 260, 262, 264,
    273–75
  money handling by, 245
  negligence of, 103
  purchase orders by, 249, 262–63
  self-protection by, 251
  use of celebrity look-alikes by,
    90–91
Advertising industry
  basis for regulation, 6–7
  laws affecting, 16–17; *see also*
    Federal Trade Commission
    and by area
  role in society, xi–xiii
  self-regulation of, 10–12

Advil, 185–86
Ally and Gargano, 167
Antidultion statutes
  nature of, 194
  by state, 195
Aquella, 44
Art work
  and consent laws, 111
  and copyright laws, 116–19, 123
Authors
  assignment of rights by, 125–26
  in collective works, 121
  defined for copyright, 118–19
  and work for hire, 126
Avis, 166, 181

B

Better Living, Inc., 40–41
Book of the Month Club, 46
Bozell & Jacobs, 133
Brand awareness, 154
Bristol Myers, 9

C

Campbell Soup Co., 38–39
Caveat emptor concept, 70
Cease-and-desist orders
  violation of, 14–15, 214
  use of, 16, 215